The Da Capo Guide to
Contemporary African Music

The Da Capo Guide to Contemporary African Music

by Ronnie Graham

Da Capo Press * New York

First published in the United Kingdom in 1988 by Zwan Publications
11-21 Northdown Street, London N1 9BN
Published in the United States of America in 1988 by Da Capo Press Inc
233 Spring Street, New York, New York 10013, USA

Manufactured in the United Kingdom

Library of Congress Cataloging-in-Publication Data

Graham, Ronnie.
    The Da Capo guide to contemporary African music.

    Discography: p.
    Bibliography: p.
    Includes index.
    1. Popular music—Africa—20th century—History and
criticism.   2. Folk music—Africa—20th century—History
and criticism.   3. Musicians—Africa—Biography.
I. Title
ML3502.5.G7 1988   780'.42'096   87–31073
ISBN 0 – 306 – 80325 – 9

Contents

List of Maps

Note on the Maps

The discipline of cartography is perhaps one of the most underrated and underused mediums in the dissemination and popularisation of information. In terms of visual representation of knowledge, a good map can be worth a thousand words. We have therefore placed special emphasis on the preparation of over twenty maps which we hope will help readers familiarise themselves with the ethnic and linguistic diversity of Africa. Each map seeks to identify and locate the principal ethnic groups in a selection of countries, although the main criterion in devising the maps has been to locate specific groups mentioned in the text. However, what must be made clear is that these maps direct the reader to areas of origin only. The modern ethnolinguistic map of Africa would today be considerably more complex given the impact of both migration and urbanisation. Secondly, it should be made clear that while the maps adopt the national boundaries inherited from colonialism and accepted by today's nation states, they often mean little in terms of cultural, linguistic or musical configurations. For example, the Ewe extend through Ghana, Togo and Benin; the Yoruba live in both Benin and Nigeria; the Hausa and the Mandingo extend across most of the Sahel region; while the Lingala and Swahili languages are spoken in many countries across East and Central Africa.

None the less, we feel that the inclusion of so many maps will help readers less familiar with the cultural diversity of Africa to identify the main areas of musical development and thus enhance their capacity to discern one specific style from another.

Note on Spelling

The material presented in this guide has been drawn from original material appearing in an immense variety of African languages and at least five European languages – English, French, Spanish, Portuguese and Dutch. This has raised a number of problems with regard to the standardisation of spelling. In English, for example, we find Miriam Makeba – whereas the French spell her first name Myriam. Whenever possible, we have tried to present information in its English usage, but where information has been taken directly from an original source, we have felt it better to present the original spelling.

Acknowledgements

It has taken over three years to prepare this guide to Contemporary African Music. The search for information has been long and arduous given the paucity of published material on the development of music in post-war Africa. In this respect it would have been impossible to compile this discography without the expert knowledge and help of dozens of enthusiasts and aficionados. It is therefore a great pleasure to acknowledge the specific contributions of the following people.

Don Bayramian, Charles Easmon and Robert Urbanus of Stern's African Records; Iain Scott of Triple Earth Records; Jumbo Van Renen of Earthworks; Ben Mandelson of Globestyle and John Storm Roberts of Original Music. Others whose help was freely given in include Lois Darlington, Sue Steward, Lucy Duran, Tineke Van Broedeke, Renc Williams, Kwabena Oduro-Kwarteng, Mr Soares, Kevin Eden, Charlie Gillett, Fleming Harrev, John Collins, Jon Harlow, Ian Watts, Jak Kilby, Gunter Gretz, Wolfgang Bender, Roger Thomas, Nick Van Hear, Bert Spliff, Mr Oranga, Kris Bediako, Chris Stapleton, Kofi Grey and Kwabena Fosu-Mensah.

Working in Stern's afforded me the opportunity to discuss recent musical developments with many of Africa's most outstanding musicians and I would like to thank the following for the time they so freely gave to answer my questions. From Zaire: Tabu Ley, Kanda Bongo Man, Mose Se Sengo (aka Fan Fan), Nsimba Foquis and Nyboma. From Ghana: E.T. Mensah, A.B. Crentsil, Pat Thomas, 'Big Joe' Asiedu, Kofi Adu, Herman Asafo-Agyei, Malcolm Mohammed Ben, Alfred Bannerman, Opata, M. Rossy, J. Kofi Brown, Josephine Zagbeli-Thomas, Sam Ashley and Debbie Mensah. From Nigeria: Segun Adewale, Ebenezer Obey, Leader, Wasiu Ayinde Barrister, Gaspar Lawal, Prof. Akin Euba, Sonny Okosun, Juwon and Ibilola. From Senegal: Toure Kunda, Youssou N'Dour and Musa Suso Foday. From Southern Africa: Fred Zindi, Frank Williams and Russell Herman.

Finally, there are several individuals without whose help this volume would not have reached the printer. The chapter on South Africa was entirely written by Nick Carnac and Trevor Herman, the section on Côte d'Ivoire could not have been written without the help of Mr Njore, while the maps were entirely designed and produced by Paulyn De Fresnes of Visual Image. But above all I would like to thank Graeme Ewens who willingly shouldered the burden of completing the text and bringing the book to the printer's stage when I was obliged to move to Central America early in 1987. His deep knowledge of contemporary African music allied with his editorial experience made his support in this venture all the more significant.

Thanks of a more personal nature go to my wife, Mivvi, who endured my irregular working hours with a stoicism and humour which helped ensure the completion of this project.

This volume is dedicated to music lovers around the world, particularly the customers of Stern's, whose enthusiasm made light work of the task of promoting contemporary African culture.

Ronnie Graham
Belmopan,
Belize, 1987

Key to prefix codes of main labels specialising in African releases

AB	A&B Records
AF	Afrovision (Manu Dibango)
AFRI	Discafrique
AK	Akoben (Dade Krama)
AP	IAD productions (Brazzaville)
ASR	Asona
CEL	Celluloid
CHOC	Choc Choc Choc (Franco)
DEBS	Debs Int.
DWAPS	Decca West Africa
ELP	Earthworks
EM	E.M.I
ESP	Disques Esperance
EMW	Earthworks
ERT	Earthworks /Rough Trade
ETH	Ethnic
GEN	Genidia (Tabu Ley)
HMV	His Masters Voice
HT	Heritage
HQ	Harlequin
ILPS	Island
KAM	KAM
MA	Mayala
OM	Original Music
ORB	Globestyle
OTI	Oti
OVLP	Oval
PAM	PAM
POP	Edipop (Franco)
POLP	Polydor Nigeria
PZL	ProZal (Zaiko Langa Langa)
RAS	Rogers All Stars
REM	Rhythmes et Musique
RETRO	RetroAfric

ROU	Rounder
SAF	Safari Ambience
SALPS	Sunny Alade
SERLP	Serengeti
SHAN	Shanachie
SON	Sonodisc
STERNS	Sterns African Record Centre, London
SYL	Syllart
TAM	Tamwo
TAN	Tangent
TERRA	Triple Earth
TSHI	Tshi Tshi
V	Virgin
VISA	Visa 80 (Franco)
WAL	Decca West Africa
WAZ	Wazuri
WCB	World Circuit
WOW	War on Want
360 000	African (Sonodisc)
362 000	African (Sonodisc)

Note on the Discography

Wherever possible we have attempted to present basic information on each record appearing in the discography. This has taken the standard form of noting the date or release, the company's catalogue number, the name of the artiste and the title of the record. However, on several occasions, and for a variety of reasons, it has not always been possible to locate such data. Readers are therefore urged to excuse those inconsistencies or omissions they come across in the present volume, and to contribute any additional data to the second edition. In several respects this volume remains a work in progress, a guide rather than an encyclopedia; nevertheless, we very much hope that readers will find it valuable in locating and appreciating the recorded music of Africa.

Introduction

As far as we know, this Guide to Contemporary African Music is the first serious attempt to catalogue and describe the enormous amount of music recorded in Africa since the end of the Second World War. The aim is to document the *commercially available LP recordings* of Africa's leading musicians in an effort to widen the scope of appreciation and deepen our historical understanding of the modern music of Africa. It is, therefore, basically a discography, to which have been added elements of biography, history and economic analysis. The primary purpose of the Guide is unambiguously commercial; to develop a growing international market for African music from which musicians can benefit through increased sales and thus continue to reproduce the sounds which guarantee their professional livelihood. This approach is not intended to undervalue the purely aesthetic appreciation of African music; it simply acknowledges that in Africa piracy, bootlegging and the non-payment of royalties are facts of life and that without proper documentation and protection, the future of rural and urban popular music is at risk.

The scope of this discography has been delineated by three basic criteria comprising a geographical, an historical and a commercial dimension.

Geographical. The area of coverage has been limited to sub-Saharan, Black Africa. We have not attempted to catalogue the recorded musical output of the Maghreb for the simple reason that while its musical contacts with Black Africa are both historic and wide-reaching, the music of North Africa owes more to the Middle Eastern musical tradition than it does to the traditions of sub-Saharan Africa. We have divided sub-Saharan Africa into regional groupings; West Africa; Central Africa; East Africa and Southern Africa. On occasion these divisions may appear quite arbitrary, but for the purposes of classification we believe that these basic groupings encompass musical styles of fundamental cultural, ethnic and linguistic unity. Each section is then subdivided into separate chapters covering the major musical epicentres like Ghana, Nigeria, Zaire, Kenya and South Africa and a cluster of smaller, less musically influential countries.

Historical. The recording and reproduction of African music really started towards the end of the 1920s when a number of European trading companies recognised the potential profits to be made from local releases. For the next three decades, the fragile shellac 78 rpm dominated the market before the introduction of the vinyl 45 rpm and later, the 33 rpm 'long-player' towards the end of the 1950s. The long-player remained the favoured medium until the introduction of the C-60 cassette during the 1970s seriously threatened the market for records. The ease with which music could be reproduced on cassette and the proliferation of battery cassette players throughout Africa (they were comparatively cheap and were not dependent on the provision of electricity), not only undermined the earnings of professional musicians but flooded the market with cheap copies of Western soul, disco, rock and reggae records. The full implications of this development are still to be analysed but it is becoming increasingly obvious that the heyday of the LP is coming to an end. In Africa, the cassette is dominant, while in the more technologically developed West the introduction of compact disc and video threatens the future of the long-playing record.

The bulk of the references will inevitably concern the recordings of the last decade (1976–86). None the less, this Guide also hopes to provide a deeper historical analysis, tracing the evolution of recorded music in Africa, from its origin in the 1920s through the flowering of the 1950s and 1960s to the current situation of growing international appreciation.

Commercial. The total recorded musical output of Africa is probably incalculable and therefore no attempt has been made to provide complete listings. The study of music in Africa is similarly in its infancy and it is therefore equally difficult to provide an objective assessment of its evolution during the twentieth century. However, despite these constraints (or perhaps because of them), we have felt it necessary to try to bring together in one volume a review of contemporary musical styles; an assessment of what has disappeared from the public domain, and a preview of what the future might hold. Mention will therefore be made of items no longer commercially available and of artistes no longer performing or recording; allusion will be made to styles which are no longer played and to companies which no longer exist. No attempt has been made to document the issue of 78 rpms, 45 rpms or EPs. Taken together these would exceed 100,000 items. Instead, we have tried to present a representative listing of 33 rpm albums, concentrating on recordings which are, or have been, available on the international market.

Bearing these three criteria in mind, I would also like to establish a number of provisos which further delineate the scope of this volume.

First, the impossibility of compiling complete discographies even for Africa's major recording stars. To take one example, we can consider the recording career of Luambo Franco – surely the most popular and prolific musician in Africa. He started recording in 1953, establishing OK Jazz in 1956. Since then, the band has recorded in excess of 200 45 rpms, several dozen EPs and over 100 33 rpms. Graeme Ewens, in a recent publication, attempted a discography of Franco only to find that the band has recorded for more than 20 companies and that recordings released in Europe are often duplicated by African releases. It is doubtful whether Franco himself has an accurate record of what has been released, for whom and when. Given these complications, this volume attempts no more than a representation of perhaps the major artistes and the classic recordings which can still be found in good record stores. Even this preliminary discography would have been impossible, in both the financial and cultural sense, without the support of my friends at Stern's African Music Centre – to my knowledge the largest and most dynamic base for African music and musicians outside Africa. Carrying a catalogue of over 1,000 titles and with the knowledge and enthusiasm to match, Stern's remains a 'mecca' for lovers of African music – African and non-African alike.

Secondly, there are clear and obvious regional and national weaknesses within this volume. This, I feel, is unavoidable at this stage of analysis and documentation. On the one hand we have the excellent studies of traditional music produced by Nketia, Bebey and Kebede to complement the less satisfactory post-war surveys of Collins, Roberts and Bergman. We can also refer to the excellent work done by a number of specialists on particular countries and musical styles. Reference will therefore be made to the work of Collins on Ghana, of Euba on Nigeria, of Coplan and Anderson on South Africa, Zindi on Zimbabwe, Low on Kenya, Kebede on Ethiopia, and Kazadi on Zaire. However, while emphasis has so far been placed on the major epicentres of modern African music (and rightly so), there are still several important countries whose musical development has not yet received the kind of scholarly attention which their richness and popularity so obviously deserve. It is our hope that the imperfections of this volume will help stimulate others to conduct more thorough surveys of these hitherto neglected areas.

Finally, by describing the most popular styles and musicians, we are aware that we are only scratching the surface of a vast panorama of music, much of which remains unheard in the West. We have attempted where possible to provide as comprehensive discographies as possible for those widely regarded as the most popular and influential. Consequently, more attention has been paid to legendary stars like E. T. Mensah and Nana Ampadu, to Fela Kuti and Sunny Ade, to Manu Dibango and Francis Bebey, to Franco and Tabu Ley, to Thomas Mapfumo, Youssou N'Dour, Makeba and Masekela than to the thousands of African musicians whose art has seldom spread beyond a particular region or country. Sadly, even less can be said about the thousands of musicians who are denied the opportunity to record their music. Bearing these limitations in mind, I would like to urge readers to contribute to further editions of this Guide by sending details of albums by major stars which have been omitted from the current listing. Inevitably many readers will possess albums not included in this volume; however, I would regard it as a more serious omission to have entirely neglected musicians whom readers consider to be worthy of inclusion. Again, all such information will be warmly welcomed for inclusion in future editions.

There are bound to be those who disagree with this approach to compiling a discography in the sense that there are well-established techniques for annotating and cataloguing music. Yet, it was felt to be worthwhile to bring as many records as possible together in one volume, at a price within the means of most record collectors. There will be those who feel that undue attention has been paid to some musicians while others they consider more influential will appear to have received scant attention. However, by constantly bearing in mind the principal criterion for inclusion, i.e. availability, perhaps the selection will not appear to be so arbitrary.

The production and reproduction of music in Africa is part of a vital process of creation and recreation 'growing endlessly from within the pulse of a people's life'. If this volume succeeds in only partly illuminating this vital process of creation and recreation then author and editors alike will feel that their work has not been entirely in vain.

Part I
The Music of Africa

AFRICA POLITICAL

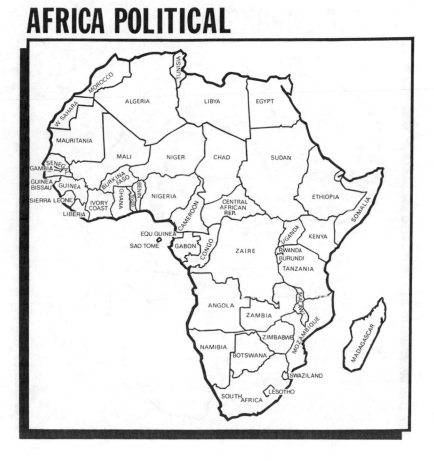

AFRICA LINGUISTIC

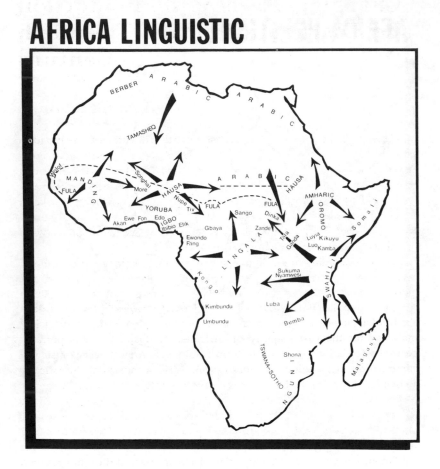

1
Changing Patterns of Production and Distribution in the Twentieth Century

Music in Africa

In Africa, music is perhaps the main manifestation of culture in its broadest sense. It is seldom performed on its own, as a pure art, and is invariably accompanied by dance, song, poetry, mime, masquerade or drama. It can be either communal or personal, recreational or ritual and was traditionally performed on an enormous variety of instruments which, for the sake of convenience, are usually classified in the following families; chordophones (stringed instruments), idiophones (shaken instruments), aerophones (wind instruments) and membraphones (drums).

Given the centrality of music to many aspects of everyday African life, it becomes almost impossible to conceive of a division between 'classical' and 'popular' music in Africa as obtains in the west. In this sense, all music in Africa is popular music and we should not forget that not only does 'traditional' music continue to flourish but indeed remains the musical mainstay for the vast majority of Africans. At this stage, it is perhaps necessary to clarify our use of the term 'traditional'. Almost every music is a combination of tradition and innovation. African music has historically enjoyed a high level of innovation, although many western listeners, concentrating on tradition rather than innovation, consider African music to be repetitive. However, in Africa, repetition is used as the basis for innovation in relationship to traditional patterns or those aspects of music which do not change significantly over a given period of time. To reinforce this important point, John Collins, the Ghanaian-based writer, has rejected the traditional–modern dichotomy entirely in favour of the concept of the urban–bush continuum wherein styles of music are situated somewhere along the continuum depending on the degree to which they approximate stereotypes of 'traditional' or 'modern' music. This is a much more dynamic approach to the classification of music and can indeed be extended further to encompass a metropolitan–periphery continuum reflecting the truly international dimensions of popular African music.

In this respect, it is worth observing that ethnomusicologists are in the main much more comfortable with tradition than with innovation and are often biased against music with any overt western influence. However, we shall argue that all music is transient and that various forms and styles exist only for a short period before they are replaced by new forms. The African music which has been preserved on disc is therefore an invaluable record of the evolution of popular culture – a musical snapshot from a particular era. While we must thank the ethnomusicologists for their efforts to record and describe the music of Africa, it is now time to take the analysis one stage further and to describe the changing patterns of production and distribution of music in twentieth-century Africa. Historians are equally guilty of neglecting popular music in Africa. For many of them, the very term 'music' has often found itself possessed of strangely forbidding and even frivolous connotations. When the attribute 'African' is attached to 'music', the aversion is almost complete. African music is at best considered to be of secondary importance in our comprehension of social change in Africa. Yet nothing could be further from the truth. Music has been one of the continent's strongest characteristics, influencing the social and cultural development of societies far beyond the shores of Africa. We only have to consider the debt which western popular culture owes to Africa to apppreciate this point. Even more significant has been the role of the individual musician in the creation of a popular mass culture.

From the beginning of the twentieth century, music has acted as a catalyst of social change, along the way providing hundreds of shrewd and informed critiques of the political and economic forces which have shaped the continent. Musicians commented on colonialism, the flourish of the nationalist challenge and the problems arising in post-colonial Africa. The changing position of women, the introduction of money, the value of education, the role of the military and the conflict in Southern Africa are only a few of the topics which have been discussed in hundreds of songs. Occasionally certain specific songs have played a key role in forming public opinion, most notably Fela's pointed attack on military regimes in 'Zombie'; Sonny Okosun's plea for change in 'Fire in Soweto'; Franco's satirical attacks on Mobuto; Mapfumo's liberation songs in Zimbabwe and Makeba's continued insistence on the need for African unity. Music in Africa is seldom as simplistic as 'the boy meets girl, erotic, romantic stuff of western pop'.

Today, the role of the African musician is not too far removed from the traditional role of entertainer, newscaster and therapeutic healer. Music acts as the cement which holds society together – a hidden form of consciousness which is at once both more pervasive and more important than the overt forms of resistance to the exigencies of everyday life. In short, music constitutes the bed-rock, the grass roots of popular consciousness.

During the twentieth century, African music has moved rapidly from its original form and function, through the application of industrial processing to encompass hundreds of external influences, in turn itself influencing the musical evolution of societies far beyond the continent. The commercialisation of African music, while obliterating several styles entirely, has however left us with a treasure-trove of over 50 years of recorded sound.

In this introductory chapter, we shall only trace the dynamics which underlie these broad changes in African music. As music is not always amenable to either chronological or linear analysis, it can at best be only an outline – an agenda for further research.

First, we will examine the development of the international music industry in an effort to establish the place of African music within a wider context. The following section concentrates on the development of the music industry in Africa, while the final section presents four case studies to illuminate the differences and the similarities between four major centres of musical development.

The Development of the International Music Industry

Music has existed in every society throughout history, yet it is only during the twentieth century that the world has seen the industrial processing of music and the deliberate creation of a gap between music makers and recipients.

From its origins in the late nineteenth century, the music industry possessed all the characteristics of the typical capitalist firm; producing, reproducing and finally mass producing cultural products for the market. Mediated by the frequent introduction of new recording techniques, music, in time, became a commodity like any other, with a new division of labour enabling individual record companies to mass produce for the benefit of individual consumers. As part of the 'Second Industrial Revolution', based on the application of electricity to culture as well as to industrial manufacturing, the transformation of music first involved the mass production of hardware – musical instruments in the 1840s, gramophones in the 1880s, followed by radio in the 1920s, television in the 1940s and cassette recorders in the 1970s. Each of these innovations was accompanied by the appropriate software – sheet music, shellac discs, long-playing vinyl records and most recently the audio and video cassette.

Shortly after the introduction of the gramophone, new companies emerged to profit from this development in the means of artistic production. A new division of labour was established, in the process creating new links and barriers between music makers and audiences in the form of company managers, producers, publishers, manufacturers and accountants, not to mention a host of minor functionaries such as A & R men, PR men and so on. These intermediaries, with their access to substantial amounts of capital and constantly improving recording techniques, were able to subordinate musicians and audiences alike to the dictates of capital accumulation.

By the beginning of the twentieth century all the leading industrialised nations possessed their own music sector, comprising instrument production, recording facilities, pressing plants, retail and wholesale outlets. In a complex pattern of social, cultural and technological factors, the 'music industry' developed, encompassing everything from the skilled artisan to the 'tune factory' where music was subjected to the same kind of assembly-line process obtaining in other industrial enterprises. Wallis and Halm, in *Big Sounds From Small People,* have identified the cultural consequences implicit in the organisation of music for profit. To begin with, the mode of performance changed from folk culture to organised stage shows. Secondly, there was a significant loss of spontaneity and a decrease in the number of stylistic variations as concert performances came to be structured around audience, organiser and sponsor. Thirdly, as a national administrative apparatus emerged, 'Maisons de Culture' came to replace more traditional (and informal) venues. Finally, the music itself became more streamlined in both form and content, more or less devoid of any organic link with the society from which it arose. Tradition was rationalised into a few standard forms under the control of multinational companies who then assumed the role of interpreters of a nation's cultural heritage. As the companies grew, so too did their capacity to manipulate taste and exploit musicians.

Early pioneers in the UK included several companies which are today household names. First off the mark was HMV which, with its American affiliate Victor, dominated the early market. Decca, another famous brand name followed in 1929 with new, state-of-the-art studios in Chelsea. A competitive price allied with an imaginative selection of music kept the company at the forefront of music reproduction until its eventual demise in 1980. But already the process of amalgamation and take-over was underway and in 1931, EMI was formed as a consortium of HMV, Columbia, Parlophone and all their respective subsidiaries. To further complicate affairs, Parlophone was itself a subsidiary of the German Lindstrom group who also owned the prestigious Odeon label. Other leading British labels of the early years included Rex, Brunswick and Vocalion.

Meanwhile, across the Atlantic, the US had also made substantial headway in its efforts to establish a domestic music industry. Columbia, Brunswick, MGM, RSO and Victor were responsible for early growth and as the use of electricity spread, soon almost every home acquired a radio. As markets grew, the companies not only integrated and amalgamated but also diversified until a tight oligopoly, comprising a few major companies, which owned and controlled hundreds of smaller labels. In Europe, a similar process of growth and consolidation was underway with such famous names as Pathe-Marconi, Philips, Barclay and Fontana dominating the early years.

It would not be difficult to overstate the extent to which these various companies not only dominated national markets (and by implication music and musicians alike) but also became involved in labyrinthine licensing, production and distribution deals. In the UK for example, during the peak years of the radio/gramophone era, the industry was already under the control of only two companies. In the pursuit of profit, EMI and Decca established agreements covering the division of markets while adhering to a common pricing structure. They were not, as a 1939 Monopolies enquiry revealed, financially linked, but together their power over the market, over musicians and over the public was more or less absolute.

By the 1930s, with international financial interests in both radio and records, the world's major music companies had largely succeeded in rationalising the industry and dividing the world market into distinct spheres of interest and control. By this time, the music majors had assumed a corporate identity, far removed from folk culture and with the ability to manipulate taste and exploit musicians on a truly global scale.

RCA, GEC, ITT and Westinghouse controlled the entire American market, both north and south; Decca and EMI controlled not only the British market but that of the entire British Empire; while in France, a single company, Pathe-Marconi, enjoyed unrestricted access to French and French colonial markets. Finally, although based in the Netherlands, Philips dominated the markets of north and central Europe. Through the combined activities of these companies, more and more music was brought to the market place.

In the years following the Second World War a series of technological and structural changes further reinforced the power of the music majors as they expanded into new media and cultural sectors. The companies not only became larger but fewer in number, with their leading subsidiaries establishing themselves by the very procedure that would eventually lead to their own takeover. One by one, as potential competitors emerged in the form of small independent companies with perhaps more imagination and more commitment to the reproduction of original music, these independents were swallowed up and incorporated into the music majors.

As the largest market and the pre-eminent world power, the USA was not blind to its strength in the field of communications. In time, this strength came to be consciously utilised to promote the images, values and lifestyle of the US against those of other cultures.

By the 1980s, with record sales topping $4 billion, 60 per cent of the industry was in the hands of only five companies, three of them based in the USA – CBS, WEA and RCA – supported by EMI in the UK and the giant Polygram, domiciled in the Netherlands. Occasionally, new companies – such as Virgin, Island and Celluloid – emerged to challenge the dominance of the big five, but the international planning, marketing and access to capital of the majors gave them unrivalled power to stimulate demand, in terms of both quality and quantity, on a truly global scale. As these companies consolidated their hold over the production and distribution of music, growing ever larger in the process, so too did the music itself become more streamlined, bland and boring. Having tried and failed to incorporate African music into their international repertoire, for reasons which this guide will explain, the music majors now face the danger of being overtaken by the sounds of a continent which will surely come to dominate the popular dance music of the future.

The Music Industry in Africa

In this section, we would like to pay more attention to the way in which music in Africa has moved from its traditional base, through the application of industrial processing, to a new stage of commercialisation which increasingly emphasises quantity of sales and not quality of performance. The emphasis, therefore, is on the organisation of production and distribution, in the purely economic sense, rather than on the development of various forms and styles. Here we wish to establish, perhaps for the first time, a chronology of the development of African music in the twentieth century.

Over the last 80 years, it is possible to identify four clear stages in the organisation and reorganisation of African music. Several trends emerge from this analysis which inform not only the periodisation which follows but the general discourse of the entire text. In this respect we would argue that the music of Africa has not only sacrificed variety and spontaneity on the altar of commercial success but that in each period, the economic well-being of the industry in Africa, and the options open to it, have been adversely affected by the wider relationship between Africa and the western world. Of course, these comments are not intended to denigrate the magnificent music of Africa now penetrating western consciousness. On the contrary, they are intended to draw attention to the incontrovertible fact that the continent of Africa has been so exploited over the last 500 years that it would be hypocritical to suggest that music has somehow been exempted from the forces which have shaped the overall social, political and economic development of the continent.

It is therefore necessary to restate the general western perception of African music, if only to remind readers that their interest in African music is far from generalised and that popular conceptions of African music have in fact moved very little over the last eight decades; for the majority of Europeans, African music remains 'jungle' music, repetitive, boring and primitive. Christian missionaries did their best to stamp it out and the same uninformed and often racist views sadly still prevail today. In the same way, we have seen how western capital, in the form of music multinationals, has attempted to coopt or at least to profit from the current wave of popularity enjoyed by Africa's electric guitar bands. To a lesser extent, we have seen how several western pop musicians have attempted to incorporate African rhythms and styles into their career development. While many observers consider these phenomena to be positive developments in the promotion of African music, we would beg to differ and instead argue that the efforts of Paul McCartney, Brian Eno, David Byrne, Peter Gabriel and Paul Simon are largely meaningless (and often selfish) in terms of the overall development of African music. We only have to consider the fact that over 90 per cent of Africans remain in close articulation to pre-capitalist economic and social formations and it is they who provide the great strength and vitality of contemporary African popular music. For the majority of Africans, music remains live and closely tied to their daily lives. The fact that this existence is now under threat from war, famine, invasion and western cultural imperialism in no way diminishes the continuing contribution which Africa makes to the enrichment of our daily lives.

Before we attempt to isolate four periods in the development of contemporary African music, it is perhaps worth while reminding readers of the prescient words of Hugh Tracey, the most accomplished and committed of all Europeans involved in the African music industry: 'Before we can trace the directions in which indigenous music is travelling, it is necessary to ascertain from where it appears to have come.'

Before the European conquest of Africa, African music remained directly tied to the everyday life of the various African societies. Music was used in both the ritual and the recreational sense. Yet this is not to suggest, as the first Europeans in Africa did, that these societies were static, stagnant and without history. We now understand that every music is in itself a combination of tradition and innovation and that far from being an exception to this rule, Africa possessed a very high level of innovation within traditional structures.

In the first place, there was innovation within particular styles and patterns; secondly, there was a high degree of cultural diffusion throughout the continent, based on both permanent migrations (Fulani, Bantu, etc.) and seasonal migrations (fishermen, traders, etc.). Through these mechanisms, instruments and styles were carried long distances. Finally, and corresponding to the steady opening up of Africa to foreign influences, from the Chinese in the ninth century and the Indians in the eleventh, to the arrival of the Arabs and the Europeans in the twelfth and sixteenth centuries respectively, Africa experienced a variety of external influences, all of which played a part in the process of innovation within African music.

The Portuguese are reported to have introduced the Spanish guitar to Africa in the sixteenth century, while the first western written records of African music originate from the same period. During the seventeenth and eighteenth centuries, little attention was paid in the west to African music, although the sources remain rich in material (the reader is referred in particular to the published works of Nketia). By the nineteenth century, West Indian troops were being stationed in West Africa while black Brazilians helped the Portuguese to reconquer Angola. Finally, thousands of Africans returned to Africa as freed slaves, carrying with them a hotchpotch of new and old world culture. Already 'cross-over' and 'feedback' was making its presence felt in the evolution of particular African styles.

Meanwhile, down the East Coast and across the Sahara, Arab music was making a similar impact. The first incursion occurred in the twelfth century, with a further burst of influence during the jihads of the fifteenth century. However, it was during the nineteenth century that Arab (and Muslim) influence made its presence fully felt in large areas of the Sahel and the East Coast. What is important to remember is that Arab influence in Africa was, like the western influence, mediated through the doubly destructive forces of slavery and religion.

Then, towards the end of the nineteenth century, the technology of producing music underwent a profound change in Europe whereby it was possible, for the first time, to reproduce music. It is the establishment of this new relationship between industry and culture that will be the focus of the rest of this section.

The Early Colonial Period, 1900-30

By the beginning of the twentieth century, the west was well placed to exploit and influence the evolution of African political, economic and social life. The bulk of the continent had come under European control towards the end of the nineteenth century and in the wake of military conquest and the search for markets came the colonial social anthropologists, more curious about the societies now under European domination. Motivated by the desire to preserve traditional (and therefore 'authentic') culture, these early expeditions attempted to record as much original music as possible, travelling into remote regions of Africa with their bulky, fragile equipment, sometimes weighing up to half a ton. The recording technique consisted of holding a single microphone in the middle of a group of musicians; the music was then transcribed on to wax cylinders. The earliest known collection is that of Carl Meinhof who was recording in German East Africa (Tanzania) as early as 1902. In 1905, Pater F. Witte made several more recordings in Togo and in 1908 N. W. Thomas made the earliest surviving recordings from Sierra Leone and Nigeria. Other pre-war collectors included Sir Harry Johnson in Buganda (a province of Uganda) and Alice Werner in Kenya and Tanzania. Apart from these collections, few recordings from the first three decades of this century have survived.

Meanwhile, other anthropologists were concerning themselves with the role of music in African society, producing invaluable data on instruments, dances, styles and the emotional and aesthetic content of music. These various lines of enquiry finally culminated in Hornbostel's majestic study of music in Africa, published in 1934.

The early 1930s marked a significant turning point in the development of a music industry in Africa. The wax cylinders of the anthropologists had never been intended for commercial use, being purely academic in purpose. However, with the invention of the cut acetate-coated 78 rpm disc and its introduction to Africa, western record companies were able to produce music for the market. But this breakthrough, while signalling the beginning of a new era, did not quite spell the end of the old one, for it was during the early 1930s that Hugh Tracey started his career as a field recordist. Over the next 40 years, Tracey made thousands of recordings in over 15 East, Central and Southern African countries. In a sense he spanned the transition from purely academic to commercial recordings by not only establishing the International Library of African Music but by supplying Gallo Records with much of their best material. None the less, the era of the field recording was drawing to a close as the wind-up gramophone and the shellac 78 rpm began to make their commercial presence felt.

The Zenith of Colonial Rule, 1930-50

During these two decades, the various colonial powers maximised their exploitation of Africa, investing heavily in massive infrastructural projects to support the major extractive industries. At the same time, urbanisation and elite formation proceeded apace with dramatic consequences for the performance, production and distribution of music. Perhaps the most significant development was the introduction of radio which, while initially a wartime propaganda measure, in time came to play a major role in the diffusion of both indigenous and international music. By the end of this period, the majority of Africans would have had access to a radio whether privately owned in the home or strategically placed in the centre of a village.

Little change was seen in the actual performance of music. The instrumentation remained largely the same, although many more night clubs and dance halls had opened up during the war, providing more employment and better conditions for musicians. On the production side, these years saw enormous advances in the techniques of recording and the quantity of records produced. Yet the Africans themselves were largely excluded from the profits to be made in the new music industry. Lacking access to capital, African businessmen failed to capitalise on the opportunities opening up to the major European record companies who, through their African subsidiaries, monopolised the market for 78 rpms. These companies recorded a great deal of local music, both traditional and urban, which was then sent to Europe for pressing into discs. The final products were then exported back to Africa in a lucrative double trade which guaranteed handsome profits for the companies astute enough to appreciate the potential of the market. Of course the market was restricted to 78 rpms by the almost total absence of electricity in Africa and the era of the 78 rpm was consequently prolonged in Africa until national Independence in the 1960s saw increased investment in the generation of electricity.

More generally, the years between 1930 and 1950 can be characterised as years of intense exploitation of African music and African musicians by expatriate companies. Royalties were seldom paid and the companies preferred to operate on the basis of single session fees. The protection afforded musicians by copyright and publishing laws was almost entirely lacking. This exploitation reached its most intense level in South Africa.

Music in Independent Africa, 1950-75

In terms of performance, these years witnessed the almost universal introduction of amplification and electric instruments, substantially changing the sound if not the structure of African music. In this respect, this volume defines 'contemporary' African music as basically the electrified popular music which first appeared in the mid-1950s. As far as production was concerned, these years witnessed several contradictory tendencies. In some countries, encouraged by nationalist legislation, local entrepreneurs were able to seize the initiative and even replace the European companies. Thus in countries like Ghana, Nigeria and Zaire, the music industry was steadily brought under national control – albeit in private hands. Other countries, most notably Tanzania and Guinea, opted for socialism and in time brought the music sector under direct state control, paying musicians and owning the recording facilities. However, in other countries, like Kenya, South Africa and Côte d'Ivoire, the music multinationals were able to strengthen their grip, hindering the growth of a local industry and limiting the development of an authentic national sound. More money could be made importing western music; local music suffered accordingly. Finally, there were several countries where civil war or natural disaster completely destroyed the fragile infrastructure which had been established during colonialism. Thus in Chad and Uganda, and even for a time in Ghana, the industry collapsed entirely as studios broke down, the supply of vinyl dried up and instruments proved beyond the means of most musicians.

In terms of technology, this period witnessed the gradual phasing out of the 78 rpms and the introduction of the 45 rpm, 33 rpm and the extended play – all of which found growing markets in the rapidly developing urban centres. These years can be considered something of a golden period in the development of the music industry in Africa. Many countries asserted their control over national culture and a new awareness of the importance of music appeared. Musicians began to form unions to protect their interests, and the outside world began to pay more attention to the music of black Africa. While for thousands of musicians the dream of owning electric instruments and recording in a studio remained just that, there were also those who were able to amass substantial fortunes from their musical gifts. For many, the future looked bright.

African Music in Crisis, 1975–85

Over the last decade, two distinct developments have altered the structure of the music industry in Africa. The first concerns the general deterioration in the economic position of Africa within the world economy. The rise in the price of oil severely damaged prospects for economic growth in the majority of African countries, while even African oil producers like Nigeria largely failed to capitalise on their new-found wealth. In many countries war, famine, drought and foreign intervention compounded the growing economic problems. As foreign debt grew, the IMF and the World Bank imposed draconian austerity measures on country after country. Of course music continued to flourish in the countryside but for many urban musicians a decline in income and opportunity occasioned a move out of Africa to the metropolitan capitals of Europe.

However, it was the second development, the widespread introduction of cassette technology, which seriously threatened the existence not only of the established record companies but also the livelihood of individual musicians. Bootlegging and record piracy on a massive scale deprived musicians of royalties while record companies proved unable to deal with the situation and similarly were deprived of income – an important consideration when it comes to maintaining existing facilities and keeping up with the latest technological developments. The only way musicians could cope with the problem was to keep one step ahead of the pirates by releasing as many as five or six albums per year.

On the other hand, cassette technology is very much a 'people-orientated' technology, obviating the need for expensive decks and amplifiers and bringing music into almost every home. Cassettes now dominate the African market and there is evidence that companies and musicians alike are adapting to the situation by releasing their product directly on cassette. While western companies still prefer the vinyl disc, there are signs that the era of the LP has come to an end in Africa, making the mid-1980s an appropriate time to conclude this survey of the development of the music industry in Africa.

Selected Case Studies

London

It may seem strange to include London in our selection of case studies of the growth and development of modern African music; the choice would appear to go against our earlier insistence on the need to consider Africa herself to be the focus of this study. Yet while acknowledging the dangers of an overtly Eurocentric approach, it should be made clear that to a large extent it has been western record companies which have been responsible for the growing western interest in African music. In this respect, we need to ask why African record companies have not been able successfully to promote African music in the west in the way that Jamaican companies have been able to influence the evolution of reggae music in the west. Musicians themselves appear to play little part in the process of promoting and selling African music abroad. Their main concern, and rightly so, has always been the creation and performance of music; it would be asking too much to expect them also to be successful businessmen controlling the destiny of the music they create.

Yet to a great extent, the record of European companies (for the most part independents) becoming involved in the promotion of African music has generally been good. Possessed of the imagination and flexibility so lacking in the major companies, many of these independents have been able to make significant contributions to the promotion of African music while, in the main, correctly interpreting trends originating in Africa and throwing their meagre resources behind these innovations. While the success and popularity of these independent labels is incontrovertible, the danger still remains that without a direct African input into the commercial aspects of African music these labels will in time either sacrifice imagination for conformity or abandon their self-imposed responsibility to nurture and encourage younger and hitherto unknown musicians. If this were to happen, then many of these companies would cease to assist in the further development of African music and instead become obstacles to be overcome in much the same fashion that African musicians in Europe currently confront the sterility of the major record companies.

However, on the evidence of the last five years, this danger remains a long way off. It is on this understanding that we believe that the story of the London-based independents is not only relevant but central to the current analysis of contemporary African music.

The existence and popularity of African music in London is neither a new nor a particularly surprising phenomena. Indeed the opposite formulation, why it has taken so long to become established in the British musical psyche, could perhaps provide a more productive line of enquiry given both the historical presence of Africans in London and their contribution to modern popular music.

As early as the 1930s, there is evidence of African musicians not only participating in non-African musical events, particularly through the churches, but also performing specifically African music for specifically African audiences such as the West African Students' Union. This physical and musical presence was confirmed during the Second World War when many Africans arrived in the UK as servicemen and merchant seamen, ofton forming transient associations with other Africans and West Indians to entertain African and mixed audiences alike. The most durable and popular of these bands proved to be the West African Swing Stars led by the Nigerian Ambrose Campbell. By the 1950s, many talented musicians had returned to their native countries, encouraged by the development of progressive nationalist movements and the new spirit of freedom blowing through Africa with the demise of the European colonial empires. During the 1960s several individual musicians, most notably Ginger Johnson, Remi Kabaka and Rebop, settled in the UK to add a new rhythmic dimension to the European pop scene, performing with such bands as the Rolling Stones and Cream, but apart from these individual contributions and the occasional tour of a leading African band, the specifically African input was minimal.

The 1970s, however, witnessed a resurgence in the popularity of African music in Europe with Osibisa and Assegai leading the way. Leading European musicians, including Ginger Baker and Paul McCartney, travelled to Nigeria to learn more about the indigenous music of Africa. At the same time, several of Africa's leading musicians, including Hugh Masekela, Manu Dibango and Fela Kuti, began to make their presence felt in Europe amongst more progressive musicians and more discerning audiences. By the 1980s, given the bankruptcy of western pop music and the growing influence of Africa's top performers, the time was right for a more widespread appreciation of the unique contribution Africa could make to the more general evolution of popular dance music. At the same time, and without doubt part of the same process, Africa itself was undergoing the traumatic experience of economic collapse, civil strife, famine, foreign intervention and cultural collapse. The problems were of course more extreme in some countries than in others but there is little doubt that during the late 1970s and early 1980s many African musicians migrated to Europe both to escape problems at home and to contribute to the African musical renaissance currently underway in Europe's major capitals.

The sheer presence of so many gifted musicians in London made it almost inevitable that new bands would form, rehearse, perform and look for a record label to underwrite their potential. In other words, the creative input existed and all that was required was the capacity of the British public to absorb what was literally on their doorstep. As Nigerians, Ghanaians, South Africans, Kenyans and Sierra Leonese arrived in London (matched, it must be said by the arrival in Paris of Senegalese, Ivorians, Cameroonians and Zairois), so too was the imagination of Europeans fired to help develop the new and astonishing sounds of contemporary Africa.

At first, the potential of African music was seen simply as yet another raw material ready for exploitation. The majors all tried their hand at recording and selling African music. Yet while African music had made extraordinary headway in popularity, the market as it was could still not justify, in purely economic terms, the money required to promote a particular sound, style or artiste. As a result, several major companies tried and failed to make money from African music. Island Records did reasonably well with their two sampler compilations from francophone Africa, but saw Sunny Ade's early commercial promise fade away; Celluloid almost broke through with Manu Dibango, but the Virgin experiment with Ebenezer Obey proved to be an embarrassment for all involved.

In their wake, several other companies, perhaps stimulated more by their general understanding that something new was coming out of Africa than by any real interest in the continent, continued to pick up and promote individual sounds and styles in the hope that eventually one of them would prove palatable to the British public. This 'pick and miss' approach proved to be not only totally misguided but also totally self-interested. Relative failure followed relative failure as Youssou N'dour, Ladysmith Black Mambazo (thanks to Paul Simon) and Fela were all picked up by western companies in the hope that one of them would become a true international superstar, thus making millions for the company astute enough to have 'selected' the artiste involved.

While there is no doubt that the intermittent exposure of these musicians to the western public has helped in the general evolution of African music (often, in the process, making already wealthy musicians even richer), there can be little doubt that, in the majority of cases, commercial gain has proved to be the principal motivation.

Against this tendency, which still exists and may well enrich certain companies and individuals, the early 1980s also witnessed the emergence of a number of 'independent' companies for whom profit was not necessarily the primary consideration. Enthusiasm, imagination, a background in Africa and, most of all, access to 'progressive capital' stimulated a variety of individuals to form independent record labels with the wherewithal to help develop African popular music.

First off the mark was Earthworks, a small dynamic company formed by the husband and wife team Mary and Jumbo Van Renen. Jumbo had worked for years with Virgin Records and having become disillusioned by the company's lack of imagination when it came to Africa, decided to use his knowledge and experience to form a new outfit, committed to the promotion of African music. By licensing material from older, more established African specialists such as Serengeti, Jumbo succeeded in pushing the music of Southern Africa, including Thomas Mapfumo, Ladysmith Black Mambazo and the Mahotella Queens to more discerning western audiences.

Then, in 1983, came a major breakthrough when Robert Urbanus, Charles Easmon and Don Bay (hailing respectively from Holland, Ghana and Armenia) took over the Stern's trade name from an elderly entrepreneur in central London. The original Mr Stern had started business in the 1950s as a general tradesman dealing in electrical goods and middle eastern music. However, his proximity to the University of London and the number of African students attending courses in London encouraged him to start importing a few African records. He continued to expand this particular interest, becoming known as the only source of recorded African music in London. From the early 1950s to the early 1980s, Stern's established a reputation in London, Africa and beyond as the only reliable if somewhat disorganised source of African music outside Africa. Consequently, when Mr Stern retired and tried to sell off his business, Robert, Charles and Don stepped forward to inherit not only the African side of the business but also a substantial mail order business and a trade name which had served well for over three decades.

The new Stern's was able to combine all the necessary ingredients for success – knowledge, commitment, imagination and money – in a way that no independent had mastered before. They quickly expanded the retail catalogue before moving into wholesale marketing and recording. New artistes, including Hi-Life International and Somo Somo, provided the basis for the Stern's catalogue and with some imaginative promotions and an informed approach to the media, the company soon became a Mecca for musicians and music-lovers alike. Within four years they had released 16 albums and contributed greatly to the promotion of African music.

While lacking the capital available to the 'music majors', Stern's has become a byword for African music in Europe. Indeed, while Stern's moved from strength to strength, widening the appreciation of all forms and styles originating in Africa, their very success encouraged others to establish new companies dedicated to the further promotion of African music. By the end of 1986, London could boast a multitude of independent record companies specialising in African music. Triple Earth, specialising in traditional music, emerged in 1984; Globestyle, specialists in world music, followed in 1985, with Oval Records and Discafrique appearing during the same period. Finally, the London market became ever more specialised with the formation of RetroAfric (committed to the re-release of classic African music) and Asaase Productions – a highlife company formed by guitarist Kwabena Oduro-Kwarteng.

Nigeria

Nigeria, with an estimated population of over 90 million, is Black Africa's most populous country. As such, it is not surprising that Nigeria also possesses the largest and most sophisticated music industry in Africa outside the white-minority-ruled South Africa. The industry in Nigeria remains entirely in private hands, reflecting both the more generalised development of Nigerian industry and the historically close connections between musicians and patrons in the country. Music has deep roots in all parts of Nigerian society and has always been considered an enticing area of investment for entrepreneurs keen to enhance their social status while making more than a bit of money on the side. Consequently, many businessmen have graduated from employing praise singers to owning equipment, nightclubs and even musicians.

However, while a great deal of music has been financed and promoted by individual music patrons, it remains the case that the great bulk of Nigerian recordings are under the control of large, often expatriate commercial companies such as EMI and Polygram. We only have to consider the number of leading musicians contracted to the music majors to appreciate the scale of non-Nigerian involvement in the Nigerian music scene. Ade, Osadebe, Ukwu, Kuti, Okosun, Obey, Orientals, Olaiya and Uwaifo have all at some stage in their careers come under the financial management of non-Nigerian companies.

Yet this aspect of the development of music in Nigeria cannot be considered to be a recent phenomenon. Since the early 1930s expatriate companies have recognised the attractions of operating in what is Africa's largest domestic market. Early labels which promoted Nigerian artistes in the 1930s included Zonophone, Olutone, Odeon and Decca West Africa (NWA), with the majority of records actually being manufactured in the UK by the export division of EMI. Until the 1950s, the market was dominated by 78 rpm discs until they were steadily replaced by 45 rpms and the EP, which, with four songs, enjoyed huge popularity in the country. During the 1940s and 1950s the early companies were joined by HMV, Parlophone and Pathe-Marconi which collaborated with EMI/Decca in the introduction of music from francophone Africa in an early example of multinational market sharing. However, by the 1960s, with the introduction of the long-playing disc and more sophisticated recording and pressing equipment, many of the smaller labels disappeared, to be replaced by larger companies like EMI and Polydor.

Independence came to Nigeria in 1960, and while this implied a certain indigenisation of the economy, the music sector remained to a great extent under foreign control. By this time, Nigeria was the largest music market in Black Africa, with an enormous output and a market dominated by the 45 rpm. However, by 1970, Nigeria had settled down to basically an LP market comprising both local and imported products. The oil boom of the 1970s permitted rapid growth in virtually every sector of the economy; music was no exception.

By 1974, for example, Nigeria was supporting a record market of 10 million albums, although imported discs accounted for 7 million. The country could boast 3 major record companies, 12 recording studios, 2 major indigenous labels, 2 pressing plants and over 50 small local labels producing a variety of music reflecting the cosmopolitan nature of Nigerian society. Several of the new indigenous labels, financed by ambitious entrepreneurs, succeeded in attracting the attention of the international market with both regional and continental success. An increasing amount of non-Nigerian African music also found its way into the Nigerian market. Leading Nigerian-owned companies included Rogers All Stars (RAS), Tabansi, Leader and Mut-Moksons.

None the less, while Nigeria has made great progress in bringing the music sector under national control, albeit in private hands, the introduction of the cassette posed a serious threat. The oil boom permitted almost every household in the country to own a cassette player, which in turn opened the way for music piracy and bootlegging on a massive scale. Indeed, so prevalent was the easy-money mentality that leading musicians such as Ebenezer Obey were obliged to rehearse new material in the recording studio lest an unscrupulous observer sold the song in advance. At the moment, musicians and companies are making great efforts to try to control the piracy of material, but in such a huge country their task appears almost impossible beyond the existence of a strong musicians union with serious government support. In the meantime, Nigeria continues to be flooded with cheap and low quality cassettes of bootlegged material – both local and imported. The long-term implications of cassette technology on the Nigerian market are still to be calculated but the danger clearly exists that original compositions and creativity will continue to suffer at the hands of the 'get-rich-quick' middlemen.

But Nigeria remains a country with enormous potential to develop an internationally acceptable music industry. Fela is at his peak, Sonny Okosun has made inroads into the US market, while Sunny Ade made a short and sharp appearance on the international stage. Hundreds of other equally talented musicians are waiting in the wings and in time, the sheer power and variety of Nigerian music will make its presence felt.

Zaire

The Belgian Congo was perhaps the most highly exploited of all the areas of Africa which came under European colonial domination. The barbaric and destructive policies of King Leopold of the Belgians, who ruled the territory as a personal feudal fief, left many marks on the huge central African country. Yet despite the fact that the Belgian Congo remained one of the most underdeveloped countries in Africa, many of the factors which created this underdevelopment also contributed to the growth of one of the most powerful musical styles in the continent.

The modern 'Congo' sound first emerged in the mining and urban centres which were themselves the direct product of colonial exploitation. These 'detribalised' centres, created by pure economic greed, with the subsequent emergence of a new language – Lingala – had by the 1930s given rise to a new style of music combining indigenous rhythms with other African influences brought in by migrant workers from Ghana, Cameroon and Nigeria.

The first recording studio was opened in 1939 (Editions Olympia) but it was the Second World War which saw the final touches added to the nascent Congo sound as first, a powerful radio station was opened (Radio Congo Belge) and then Cuban rumba records began to be played. The full story of this important cross-cultural diffusion has yet to be told in full but, wherever Cuban records appeared from, they struck an immediate and responsive chord both with Zairean musicians and the public, and within a decade the rumba rhythm had become synonymous with the Congo sound. However, while the music developed apace, we should not ignore other more important changes taking place in the Belgian Congo. The Second World War, and the occupation of Belgium by Hitler's armies, severely weakened the Belgian hold on its colonial empire; the US and the UK stepped in to continue the exploitation of the colony. Fabulous mineral resources were discovered which in time would come to replace rubber as the colony's economic mainstay; in purely political terms, the Congo became more and more part of the US post-war empire. Like all the European colonial powers, Belgium was fatally weakened by the war and while nationalism made a brief but impressive appearance in Zaire (as it was now known), the reality was to be an increasing US dominance of the Zairean political economy.

Like the majority of Zairois, the musicians would in time have to come to terms with living and working in an American neo-colony run by one of the most brutal of all African dictators – Field Marshall Mobutu Sese Seko. The contradictions inherent in such a situation cannot be better illustrated than by noting that within the space of five years, Franco had not only been imprisoned by Mobutu but had dedicated an entire album to his re-election. Such are the ways of dictatorship.

By the mid-1950s electric instruments and amplification had arrived in the Belgian Congo (with the first set reputedly being given to Le Grand Kalle by a Greek businessman). The introduction of electric equipment did not exactly transform the 'Congo' sound but there can be no doubt that the musical options open to guitarists in particular helped establish the continental dominance which Zaire has enjoyed over the last four decades. By 1955 four new studios had been opened in Kinshasa (Leopoldville); Editions Ngoma in 1948 with Wendo Kolosoy, Malapet and Essous as the major stars; Editions Opika in 1950; Editions Esengo in 1951 featuring African Jazz and finally Editions Loningisa, owned by Papadimitriou and utilising the talents of Jhimmy, Mwanga, Bowane and eventually Franco. By 1955 these studios had released in excess of 4,000 shellac 78 rpms – three-minute recordings which, if popular, enjoyed huge sales amongst the Zairois for up to three months.

It was indeed a vibrant music scene, entirely in private hands, but at least the music flourished and the audiences in Kinshasa were thrilled by sounds never before heard on the African continent. As the music flourished so new and ever more exciting bands emerged – African Jazz in 1953, OK Jazz in 1956 and Les Bantous de la Capitale in 1959, over the river in Brazzaville.

By 1965 the number of recording studios had doubled and within a decade many of the biggest orchestras owned their own recording facilities. Several, including Franco, Tabu Ley and Verckys, became key shareholders in the development of the Zairean sound as they established control over instruments, musicians, nightclubs, hotels and recording facilities and record distribution. However, while a few of the best bands made it to the top, literally hundreds of others continued to pump out authentic Kinshasa sounds to enthusiastic audiences throughout Zaire, Congo, Uganda, Kenya, Tanzania and Zambia, as Zairean musicians carried their infectious dance rhythms throughout East and Central Africa.

The Zairean music industry remains one of the few sectors of the modern Zairean economy to resist the destructive effects of the historic and current crisis of capitalism in Africa.

South Africa

The music industry in South Africa is not only the oldest but also the most highly developed in the continent of Africa. However, the circumstances under which the industry developed are unique in Africa and in no other country can we demonstrate so vividly the wider connections between music and society. In the first place, western influences have historically played a much more important role in the evolution of a distinctive South African sound than they appear to have played in other countries. American jazz and swing appear to have been particularly prominent external influences. Secondly, in terms of the development of an industry, black musicians in South Africa have a greater collective experience of exploitation at the hands of what is still basically a white controlled industry. The exploitation of their talent and the subordination of their music to white-run multinational companies has had serious repercussions on the evolution of the South African sound. Exploitation and exile, censorship and state control are just a few of the many obstacles confronted by some of the most creative musicians in Africa. Of course, the problems faced by musicians simply reflect the wider contradictions of the apartheid system and we should at all times be aware of the circumstances under which music is both produced and reproduced in the minority-ruled republic.

It is generally accepted that the guitar arrived in Southern Africa towards the beginning of the seventeenth century; whether it was introduced by the Portuguese or the East Coast Arabs is disputed. The arrival of Malayan indentured labour during the nineteenth century facilitated the introduction of the banjo and the violin while towards the beginning of the twentieth century, English settlers introduced the concertina. The introduction of these new instruments had a profound effect on the musical horizons of rapidly urbanising South Africans, given that the great strength of their indigenous musical traditions lay in the area of vocal harmonies and polyphony.

By the early twentieth century, the full complement of modern instrumentation was almost complete, with a prototype urban music – marabi – being regularly and enthusiastically performed in the shebeens of Johannesburg. Featuring guitars, concertinas, pianos and home-made percussion, marabi became the standard recreational music of the new urban centres. The South African vocal tradition continued to provide a tamer kind of entertainment for the more genteel classes, while out of the same vocal tradition began to emerge the early South African protest songs. However, it was to be the almost simultaneous arrival of the radio, gramophone and American jazz which did most to transform the nascent South African sound and create an identifiable urban sound over the next three decades.

The first records appeared in South Africa in 1914 when the Mackay Brothers started to sell imported British gramophone records from the back of their ox-cart as agents for HMV. A few years later they were joined by Polliacks, who acted as agent for Columbia, and by the 1920s the first gramophones were finding their way into black urban homes. However, from the very beginning the music industry was either in the hands of local whites or under the control of foreign companies.

By the mid-1920s, the search for new markets was underway and although the Afrikaner interpretation of history precluded any serious attempt to assess black urban music, a few urban vocal groups succeeded in getting their music recorded. Otherwise, despite the potential of the black market, black music was more or less ignored as missionaries, educationalists and white supremacists pushed the values, lifestyle and ethos of white society. Under these circumstances, the black culture in the urban environment was destroyed more completely than perhaps anywhere else in Africa.

Then, in 1932, Eric Gallo, the most prominent figure in the early days of the South African industry, opened the first proper recording studio in Johannesburg. Prior to the opening of the Gallo studio, all South African musicians, including several prominent black vocalists like Ruben Caluza, had been forced to travel to Europe to have their music properly recorded. Gallo Records proved to be of great benefit to black musicians prior to the inauguration of apartheid in 1948. Gallo not only cooperated with the doyen of African recording engineers, Hugh Tracey, but established Gallo Bantu Records, a subsidiary specialising in the production of hundreds of ethnic records sung in various local languages – Sotho, Zulu, Xhosa, Mpondo, Tswana, Shona and Swazi. Various styles were represented on these recordings including jive, sacred, concertina and traditional. There are those who will question this assessment of the role of Gallo Records, correctly pointing out that this very division of the black population into 'tribal' groups reinforced the nascent apartheid philosophy. None the less, we believe that Gallo left behind a treasure trove of music which future generations of South Africans will look to when they start to reconstruct the black cultural history of the dark days of apartheid.

During the mid-1930s, Gallo's supremacy was challenged when Zonophone opened a second recording studio. Specialising in tribal music, folk music, choral music and the songs of the mineworkers, Zonophone were also responsible for the earliest recordings of mbaqanga. By the time of the Second World War, EMI, Teal, Trutone and GRC had all established footholds in the South African market. Yet the spectre of apartheid was already casting a threatening shadow over the continued cultural development of the black population and by the 1950s, while white musicians were able to press in excess of 50,000, black musicians were seldom able to press more than 10,000 copies. Yet despite the naked exploitation of musicians, the censorship of lyrics and the total control of the white record companies, the 1950s and 1960s saw a great flowering of black music in South Africa with the popularisation of kwela, the continuing success of mbaqanga and the revitalised 'mbube' vocal tradition. A new jazz sound also emerged from the big band swing music of the 1930s featuring such luminaries as Abdullah Ibrahim (Dollar Brand), the young Hugh Masekela, Kippie Moeketsie, Jonas Gwangwa and Bra Solle.

By the 1980s, despite the imposition of the State of Emergency and the introduction of totalitarianism, the musical scene in South Africa had seldom been so vibrant or so popular on the international scene, as people everywhere identified with the cultural expression of the struggle against apartheid. The resolution of the crisis in South Africa and the emergence of black majority rule will surely pave the way for the real coming of age of South African black music.

Part II
Anglophone West Africa

NIGERIA

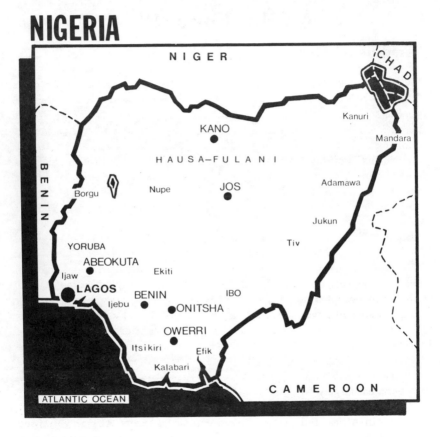

NIGER

CHAD

Kanuri

Mandara

KANO
●

H A U S A — F U L A N I

BENIN

Borgu

Nupe

JOS
●

Adamawa

Jukun

Tiv

YORUBA

ABEOKUTA
●

Ekiti

Ijaw

●LAGOS

BENIN
●

Ijebu

IBO

●ONITSHA

OWERRI
●

Itsikiri

Efik

Kalabari

CAMEROON

ATLANTIC OCEAN

2

Nigeria

Traditional Music

With over 400 distinct ethnic groups, Nigeria presents perhaps the most complex cultural scene in all of Africa. Today Nigeria contains somewhere in excess of 90 million people and has rightly been referred to as 'The Giant of Africa'. Nigeria possesses a fairly well developed music industry with dozens of studios, several pressing plants and thousands of talented musicians, working in both the modern and the traditional sectors. The development of music in Nigeria has also been well documented by academics and musicians alike and accordingly, there is no shortage of information about the emergence of a modern music scene. More detailed analyses of the three main urban pop styles – juju, fuji and highlife – will be found later in this chapter; this brief introduction is only intended to outline some of the major traditional styles.

Nigeria can for convenience be divided into three principal regions, namely the west, occupied by the Yoruba, the east, occupied by the Ibo and the north, occupied by the Hausa-Fulani. Historically each region enjoyed a distinct style of government prior to the imposition of colonialism in 1914. However the advent of colonial rule and the introduction of the policies of divide and rule created very real tensions amongst the major ethnic groups which exploded into three years of civil war in 1967. Since then, despite the oil boom which made Nigeria one of Africa's most prosperous countries, Nigeria has largely failed to create a stable political order.

In terms of culture and music, Nigeria still enjoys a diversity and vitality unique in Africa. Indeed, in marked contrast to many African countries, Nigeria seems consciously to have fostered the preservation of traditional cultures which remain as potent and popular as modern urban varieties of music. In the Hausa dominated north, the most popular ensembles comprise percussion of various types, male and female vocals and various trumpets and horns. Yoruba music is dominated by drums, while in the east, Ibo traditional music features percussion, vocals and flutes, xylophones and lyres. A great deal of traditional music is currently available on disc and those listed below represent only those most likely to be available outside Nigeria.

OCR 85	Musiques du Nigeria Central (Idoma, Jukun, Eggon, Lindiri music etc from the central Plateau region)
KR 20	Alhaji Ahmadu Doka: Hausa Music
KR 21	Alhaji Haruna Uji: Hausa Music
KR 22	Akpanchala Idoma Music
KR 23	Idirisu Egbebi: Igala Music
ALPS 1028	Nkwerre Aborigines Union (Ibo female Choir/Percussion)
POLP 121	Alhaji Mamman Shata: Hausa Traditional Music on goje.

Rarely available, but certainly worth re-release are the Decca 'Native Music' discs originally released during the 1960s and running into several dozen titles

WAPS 170	Chief Adebisi Omolowo: Yoruba Native Music
WAPS 171	Hajia Uwalia Mai Amada: Hausa Native Music
WAPS 178	Esan Pioneers Band: Esan Native Music
WAPS 194	Saliu Okobo: Igala Native Music

The Roots of Juju

The origins of Yoruba juju music, a twentieth-century guitar style from western Nigeria, remain the subject of much research and discussion. At least half a dozen researchers have looked into the subject and seem to agree about very little. All I hope to do in this section is allude to the various interpretations and attempt a synthesis of what is generally agreed.

All writers agree that juju is a progressive musical style which originated in Lagos and which has, over a period of 50 years, evolved and developed from an unsophisticated, urban roots music into a hi-tech, international style. Exactly when and how these changes took place remains a source of much controversy. Writing in 1972, John Storm Roberts argued that juju had undergone a slow evolution, but by 1944-5 a recognisable juju sound had been introduced by Tunde Nightingale. I.K. Dairo brought the style to its modern form during the 1950s and even today he is still regarded by many Yorubas as the father of juju. As Roberts says 'He made a rich music out of a comparatively thin one.' Dairo was also responsible for introducing the accordion to juju music as well as the double bass, and later the electric hass, to replace various drums. He also benefited from being one of the first to have access to electric instruments and amplification. If Dairo thus marked one stage in the development of juju music, Ebenezer Obey equally moved the music on a stage by introducing western drumkits and congolese elements.

By 1981, Collins and Richards had traced the origins of juju back into the late nineteenth century. The precise origin remained obscure but the term itself seemed to apply to a small hexagonal tambourine with bottle-top jingles with possible roots in the Lagos Brazilian community. The spread of Christianity and the growth of indigenous 'Aladura' churches also helped spread this proto-juju sound. Simple percussion instruments were available in the churches while, in marked contrast to its later sophistication and elite connotations, this early style was most definitely from the more unsophisticated end of the social spectrum. They also note the later introduction of the talking drum which by the 1960s was considered central to the juju sound.

In 1984 Brodeke argued that juju, while originating in Lagos, dated from the 1920s and had developed from the native blues style performed on box guitar and small percussion instruments. It was neither a development from highlife nor palm-wine music. By the 1930s Babatunde King had added elements from 'ashiko' music and was the first to dub the resulting sound juju.

Finally, on the sleeve notes of the excellent compilation *Juju Roots 1930s-1950s*, Chris Waterman traced the emergence of juju to 1932 as a specifically Lagosian variant of the palm-wine style of music. Lagos had long been an important centre of cross-cultural diffusion. Not only were there important Sierra Leonian and Brazilian communities but there were dozens of Yoruba groups as well as itinerant West African traders and seamen, including Krus, Fantes and Efiks. By the 1920s, guitars and gramophones were in circulation and imported recordings of other styles were being heard in private homes and beer-bars. The most popular external influences appear to have been country music, Cuban, Hawaiian and British ballroom. In this hotbed of styles and influences, musical ideas spread rapidly. By the 1930s, a form recognisable as juju had not only emerged but was considered a stable and specific style. Waterman emphasises the central role played by Irewolede Denge – the 'grandfather of juju'. He was a palm-wine guitarist who recorded the first Yoruba urban music for Zonophone in 1929. He was followed by Tunde King when, in 1932, he recorded the first records for Parlophone which actually stated 'juju' on the label. The music had thus emerged by the 1930s and for the rest of the decade remained similar in sound and instrumentation. Juju took a gigantic step forward after the Second World War with the introduction of amplification and the talking drum. In a sense the music was both modernised and Africanised at the same time. Other major 'juju' stars of these years of 78 rpms included Ayinde Bakara, the Jolly Orchestra, Ojoge Daniel from Ibadan and the Lagos street musician Kokoro (Benjamin Aderouama). By the 1960s, the stage was dominated by I.K. Dairo and Ebenezer Obey but so popular had the style become as the main recreational music of the Yoruba that dozens of other outfits commanded sizeable audiences. These included Sunny Agaga and his Lucky Stars, Olufemi Ajasa and his New Nigerian Brothers, Uncle Joe Ajayi and his Onward Orchestra, Ola Jombo and his Smart Band, Jimmy West and his Juju Band, Dele Akindele and his Dandies and K.K. Kolade and his Melody Stars.

But perhaps juju music received its greatest boost during and after the Nigerian Civil War (1967-70), when many highlife musicians fled to the east and highlife as a whole took a nosedive in the west. Few highlife musicians remained in Lagos and juju largely took over. New stars emerged, including Obey and Sunny Ade, but dozens of lesser luminaries also played their part in the spread and development of juju music. These would include Kayode Fasola and the Music Makers, Prince Adekunle and his Supersonic Sounds, Francis Akintade and the Great Brothers, Idowu Animashawun, Suberu Oni and his Why Worry Orchestra and Tunde Nightingale, who maintained his appeal throughout three decades.

While there still remains considerable disagreement about the musical development of juju and it pre-war origins, most writers are agreed on the rough outlines and on the social context of the music. Juju is a progressive music, always moving forward in terms of performance and instrumentation. Musicians are under considerable pressure to come forward with new 'systems'. Lyrically, the subject matter seems to be confined to several broad themes including religion, money, jealousy, patronage (and occasionally ridicule). Today several juju stars are millionaires, although many, of course, continue to eke out a living on the margins of society. The ambiance of juju is definitely up-market and sophisticated with a common thread running through both the music and the lyrics – that of the self-made man, the rich Lagosian entrepreneur.

Yoruba Traditional Music

ETH 4294	Yoruba Elewe: Bata Drums
ETH 4441	Drums of the Yoruba
KR 29	Roots of Juju Vol. 2
ROU 5517	Juju Roots 1930s-1950s

Dairo, I.K. (b. Isaiah Kehinde Dairo, Offa, Nigeria, 1930). Best known as singer, composer, accordion player and band leader, I.K. Dairo is widely recognised as the 'Father of Juju Music'. I.K. has led a chequered career from manual labouring to the award of an MBE (1957) – the first African musician to be so honoured. He was educated at the Church Missionary

School in Offa before moving to his father's town, Ijebu-Ijesha in 1957. Unable to complete his education, I.K. started work as an apprentice barber, learning to play and make drums in his spare time. In 1942 he started his own band although it soon collapsed when economic pressures of war-time Nigeria forced him back into full-time employment. For the next four years he travelled widely in Nigeria, working variously as a cloth seller, road worker, farm labourer and carpenter. Eventually he settled in Ibadan, where he performed with one of the great early exponents of juju – Ojoge Daniel. For the next ten years he served his musical apprenticeship, refining the juju style and developing his own ideas. In 1957 he formed the ten-strong Morning Star Orchestra, changing the name to the better-known Blue Spots in 1961. It was during this period that I.K. Dairo started his recording career with Decca, releasing an astonishing number of 45 rpms and EPs over the next 25 years. The early sounds of the band are captured on the album *The Juju Music of I.K. Dairo*. By this time I.K. Dairo was established as the top juju artiste in western Nigeria, although the music as a whole tended still to remain in the shadow of highlife. In 1956, I.K. Dairo travelled to Dakar in Senegal to represent Nigeria at the first Negro Arts Festival. By the end of the Nigerian Civil War, juju had largely replaced highlife as the main recreational music of the Yoruba. Albums from this period include *Taxi Driver, Ashiko Music* and *Iyo Mi Iyo*. Singing mainly in Yoruba, but occasionally in Hausa, English, Urohobo and Itsikerri, I.K. modernised juju music introducing both the accordion and the talking drum to the genre. A devout Christian and a leading member of the Aladura Church Movement, I.K. Dairo's popularity extends beyond Nigeria into neighbouring countries. He has visited the UK on several occasions. Despite the challenge of Obey and Ade, I.K. Dairo retained his broad appeal throughout the 1970s with a string of hit albums including *Kekere* and *Talaka Nke Ebi*. In 1980 he featured in the highly acclaimed TV documentary 'Beats of the Heart'. Today, I.K. Dairo remains an active force both in the music scene and in his church. Recent releases include *Iyo O Yemi* and *Mino Mimo L'Olorun*.

1960s	WAPS 23	Stars of West Africa Vol.2
	WAPS 26	Taxi Driver
	SOP 15	Emi Oni Gbe Sajo
1970s	WAPS 33	Ashiko Music
	WAPS 34	Ashiko Music Vol. 2
	WAPS 47	Eni Mi Ko Se Nla
	WAPS 57	Ijo Omo Moji Fowuro Jo
	WAPS 75	Iye Iye Iye
	WAPS 116	Iyami Iya
	WAPS 134	O Yenia Igbnedion. Dairo
	WAL 1206	Juju Music of I.K. Dairo

1980s	WAPS 2050	Kekere Nke O
	WAPS 2067	I.K. Dairo MBE and His Blue Spots
	WAPS 2088	E Bami Yo Sese
	WAPS 2096	Iyo Mi Iyo
	WAPS 2172	Easy Motion

Eppi Fanio

1975	NEMI 0135	Farofa
	NEMI 0256	Farofa Dancer
1985	BLP 001	Farofa Joy Movement

Obey, Ebenezer (b. Idogo, Western Region, Nigeria, 1942). With over 50 albums to his credit and innumerable singles and EPs, Obey is without doubt one of the most popular and influential band leaders in Nigeria today. Strongly influenced by I.K. Dairo, the father of modern juju, Obey started his career in 1954 with the Royal Mambo Orchestra. He moved on to the Guinea Mambo Orchestra in 1958, also playing for short spells with Fatai Rolling Dollar and the Federal Rhythm Brothers before establishing his own band, the International Brothers, in 1964. Shortly afterwards, he released his first single 'Ewa Wowun Ojumi Ri', bursting on the juju scene with his unique blend of talking drums, guitars, vocals and percussion. By the late 1960s, Obey and his band were releasing LPs at the rate of four a year. Early successes included *In London, Board Members, Christmas Special* and *The Horse, The Man and His Son*. In 1970 he renamed the band the InterReformers and proceeded to consolidate his reputation with dozens of new recordings including *Murtala Mohammed* and *Adam And Eve*. By this time he had christened his music the Miliki System, opening his own Miliki nightclub in Lagos as a permanent base for his band. As a devout Christian, Obey's lyrics reflect his concern for Christian morality and honesty with many other songs maintaining the praise singing tradition of Yoruba music. Meanwhile, inspirational albums continued to flow from the InterReformers with each new release chalking up advance sales in excess of 100,000. By the 1980s, his national reputation was secure and, like Ade, Obey began to consider the international market. In 1980 he licensed a number of albums to the OTI label in London, including *Current Affairs, Eyi Yato* and *What God Has Joined Together*. He also began to consolidate past glories with a series of greatest hits albums. In 1983 he signed with Virgin Records as the company sought to cash in on the popularity of Ade's style of juju. With Virgin, he released *Je Ka Jo*. In 1984 he tried again with *Solution* on the London-based Stern's label. Meanwhile, in contrast to Sunny Ade, Obey was able to maintain his domestic market and by 1985 was considered to be at the peak of his powers. He had toured the UK in 1969 but it was in the mid-1980s that Obey, with the 18-strong InterReformers, established a truly international reputation with successful tours of the USA.

1969	WAPS 28	In London
1970	WAPS 30	On the Town
	WAPS 38	Board Members
1972	WAPS 48	Aiye Wa A Toro
	WAPS 58	In London Vol. 7
	WAPS 62	Christmas Special
1973	WAPS 98	The Horse, The Man and His Son
	WAPS 78	
	WAPS 108	
	WAPS 138	Mo Tun Gbe De
1974	WAPS 148	
	WAPS 168	Fini Lokan...
	WAPS 188	Around The World
	WAPS 238	Ebenezer Obey and the InterReformers
	WAPS 248	Ota Mi Dehin Lehin Mi
1975	WAPS 278	
	WAPS 308	Edumare Mari
1976	WAPS 328	Murtala Mohammed
	WAPS 338	Operation Feed the Nation
	WAPS 358	Eda To Mose
	WAPS 378	Immortal Songs For Travellers
1977	WAPS 398	Adam And Eve
1978	WAPS 408	Igba Owuro Lawa
	WAPS 418	Oluwa Ni...
	WAPS 428	No Place Be Like My Country Nigeria
1979	WAPS 432	In The Sixties Vol. 1
	WAPS 438	Ode Yi Amilo
	WAPS 458	There Is No Friend Like Jesus
	WAPS 498	Sound Of The Moment
1980	OTI 488	Current Affairs
	OTI 508	Eyi Yato
1981	WAPS 528	What God Has Joined Together (Also OTI 528)
1982	WAPS 538	Celebration
	WAPS 558	Precious Gift
1983	WAPS 568	Ambition
	WAPS 578	Singing For The People
	WAPS 579	Greatest Hits Vol. 3
	V 2283	Je Ka Jo (45 rpm, also IOPS 001)
	OPS 002	Thank You ('Ose')
1984	OPS 003	The Only Condition To Save Nigeria
	OPS 005	Peace

	STERNS 1005	Solution
1985	OPS 006	Security
	OPS 007	My Vision
	SHAN 43031	Juju Jubilee

Ade, Sunny (b. Sunday Adeniyi, Oshogbo, Nigeria, 1946). A talented singer-composer-guitarist, Prince Sunday Adeniyi, the son of a Methodist minister, grew up in Oshogbo, Ondo State, before moving to Ibadan where, as a teenager, he joined a local comedy group. Shunning a grammar school education, he subsequently drifted to Lagos, finding employment with Moses Olaiya and his Rhythm Dandies – a well-known Lagos highlife band. But he was increasingly attracted to juju music and in 1964, inspired by the music of I.K. Dairo, he joined the legendary Tunde Nightingale – one of the early juju pioneers. Two years later, in 1966, after adopting the abbreviated name of Sunny Ade, he formed his own band, the Green Spots, thus launching a solo career. In 1967, he had his first hit single with 'Challenge Cup', a football song, and later the same year, he launched his first LP, *Alanu Loluwa*, on the Nigeria-Africa Song label. Altogether, Sunny Ade and the Green Spots released a total of 12 LPs on this label between 1967 and 1974 when, following contract hassles and a lengthy public court case, he decided to leave the company and form his own recording company – Sunny Alade Records linked to Decca in London. At the same time he changed the name of the band to the African Beats. They played a fast and spacey kind of juju music characterised by tight vocal harmonies and exquisite guitar work, backed by traditional talking drums and percussion. Ade has never been reluctant to introduce new instruments into the juju blend. Since 1974 Sunny Ade has released over 40 albums, as well as many singles and EPs. Each release added to his stature as the leading juju exponent, with lyrics reflecting his concern for the social problems of Nigeria. The majority of these records are widely available outside Nigeria and he reinforced his growing international reputation with successful tours of the USA, Europe and Japan. Starting with *E Kilo F'Omo Ode* in 1974, Ade has been able to maintain a prodigious recording output. Other classic LPs of the 1970s include *The Late General Murtala Mohammed*, *Synchro Chapter 1* and *The Royal Sound*. By the end of the decade each new release was guaranteed to sell in excess of 200,000 copies. Having thus secured his domestic reputation, Sunny Ade attempted to crack the international market by signing with the British company Island in 1982. Three LPs, *Juju Music*, *Synchro System* and *Aura* subsequently appeared in a blaze of publicity as the band embarked on an international tour to promote juju music. However, sales did not match Island's expectations and in 1984 they dropped Sunny Ade.

A further setback occurred in 1984 when, following a successful tour of Japan, dissension set in among the musicians. Ade dissolved the band and started a new outfit known as the Golden Mercury. His most recent releases mark a return to the style which earned Ade the title 'Minister of Enjoyment'. A devout Christian, Ade now lives and works in Lagos.

1970	KOO1 LP	Vintage King Sunny Ade
	LPAS 8006	The Master Guitarist
1971	LPAS 8010	Sunny Ade Vol. 4
1974	SALPS 1	E K'ilo F'Omo Ode
1975	SALPS 3	Sunny Ade and the African Beats Vol.2
	SALPS 4	The Late General Murtala Mohammed
1976	SALPS 5	Sunny Ade Live Play
1977	SALPS 7	Synchro Chapter 1
	SALPS 8	In London
	SALPS 9	Sound Vibration
1978	SALPS 11	Private Line
	SALPS 14	FESTAC 77
	SALPS 15	The Golden Mercury of Africa
1979	SALPS 16	The Royal Sound
	SALPS 17	Searching For My Love
1980	SALPS 20	Orimi Ja Fun Mi
	SALPS 23	Eje Nlogba
1981	SALPS 24	Juju Music of the 1980s
	SALPS 25	The Message
	SALPS 26	Check 'E'
1982	SALPS 27	Ariya Special
	SALPS 28	Juju Music (Also ILPS 9712)
	SALPS 30	Maa Jo
	SALPS 32	Ijinle Odu
	IPR 2054	The Message (45 rpm)
1983	SALPS 35	Ajoo
	SALPS 36	Bobby
	SALPS 37	Synchro-Series
	SALPS 38	Conscience
	ILPS 9737	Synchro System
1984	SALPS 39	Aura (Also ILPS 9746)
	SALPS 40	Explosion
	SALPS 42	Togetherness
1985	SALPS 44	Gratitude
	SALPS 46	Otito (The Truth)
	SALPS 48	Saviour

Adewale, Segun (b. Oshogbo, Nigeria, 1955). Juju singer and guitarist, Segun was born into a royal Yoruba family. He was first exposed to music through his father's amateur guitar-playing. However, his father objected to Segun's choice of a musical career and so, on completing his secondary education, Segun left home for Lagos where he became an apprentice musician with Chief S.L. Atolagbe and his Holy Rainbow. Struggling to keep body and soul together, Segun received encouragement from the great I.K. Dairo, who taught him the elements of composition and arrangement. In 1973 Segun formed his own band, the Superstars, and released the album *Kogbodopa Finna-Finna* before the band collapsed. He returned to big time music the following year by joining Prince Adekunle and the Western Brothers Band, a top juju band, as singer and composer. This band proved to be one of juju's best outfits and toured the UK in 1976. This experience fired Segun's ambition and in 1977 he left Prince Adekunle to form a new outfit, Shina Adewale and the Superstars International with his close friend, Sir Shina Peters. The band lasted three years, releasing a total of nine LPs on the Welkadeb label. However, despite the success of these records and the band's growing popularity, it became increasingly difficult to operate with two leaders and in 1980 Adewale and Peters split. Segun reformed the Superstars International and set up his own record label under the management of Ola Kazzim, owner of Mut-Mokson Records. Segun completed the series of Verse Records before starting a new chapter in his own career with the release in 1981 of *Ope Ye Baba*. This album, containing the hit song 'Olugbala Salabomi', confirmed Segun's reputation as a rising star of juju music. Over the next five years, Segun continued to produce a series of polished and progressive LPs including *Boomerang* and *Ase*. In 1984, Segun signed a contract with Stern's African Records in London, then under new management. Their first collaboration led to the best-selling album *Play For Me*. By this time, Segun had perfected his own style of juju, a modern blend comprising elements of funk, jazz, juju, reggae and afrobeat. Yo-Pop, described as 'kick and start' music, jumps straight into action, avoiding the slower build-up of Obey or Ade. Backed by the 20-piece Superstars, Segun continues to record and perform at his own nightclub in Nigeria. In 1985 he released his second Stern's album, *Ojo Je*, a compilation of material already released in Nigeria. In 1985, he returned to the UK for three consecutive performances at the prestigious Edinburgh International Festival.

1978	WKLPS 2	Verse 2
	WKLPS 4	Baba Wa Loke A Dude
1980	WKLPS 8	Superstars Verse 5
	WKLPS 9	Irawo Tiwa Lo Dode
1981	SARPS 1	Olu Orun Awa Bupe
1982	SARPS 3	Endurance

	SARPS 4	Boomerang
1983	SARPS 5	Ase (Amen)
	STERNS 1003	Play For Me
1984	SARPS 7	Atewo Lara
1985	STERNS 1109	Ojo Je
	MCY 001	Yo-pop 85
1986	OKLP 171	Glory

Abiodun, 'Admiral' Dele (b. Bendel State, Nigeria). Singer composer and guitarist. With a musical career stretching back 20 years, Abiodun is one of Nigeria's top juju musicians although he is not himself a Yoruba. As a youth he was excited by the school of music established by Nkrumah in Ghana and, with his school tuition fees, he left to work and study in Ghana, where he played bass with several highlife bands before returning to Lagos. In 1969 he introduced Sweet Abby and the Tophitters Band, playing a new mixture of highlife, juju and rock. The following year he introduced his own style known as Adawa (Independent Being) – a fusion of juju and Afro-beat. During the 1970s he released three singles, two EPs and over 20 LPs on the Olumo label. Abiodun made use of 'Hawaiian' steel guitar and claims to have been the first to introduce the instrument to juju music. A tour of the UK in 1974 helped establish his international reputation. In 1981 he released the impressive *Beginning of a New Era*. Following a bleak period he then released *Ma Se'ke* in 1983. More recently the Tophitters have released a mini-LP on Earthworks, titled *Confrontation*. Released at the same time in Nigeria was the juju-funk-soul record *Oro Ayo*.

1981	ASLP 001	Beginning of a New Era
	ASLP 002	E O Fura
1982	ASLP 003	1000 Miles
1983	ASLP 004	Ma Se'Ke
	OPPS 56	Adawa Super 5
1985	MWKS 3002	Confrontation
	ASLP 005	It's Time For Juju Music
1986	ASLP 006	Oro Ayo
	SHAN 43032	Adawa Super Sound
	SHAN 43037	Prince of Juju

Fashola, Kayode. The Music Makers, led by Kayode Fashola, became one of the most popular juju outfits during the 1970s, playing a rootsier, less sophisticated style than Obey or Ade.

1975	TYC 25	Volume 2
1976	TYC 62	Volume 6
	TYC 141	Volume 8

Adekunle, Prince. Originally named the Western Brothers Band, the Supersonic Sounds, led by Prince Adekunle, proved to be a prolific recording band and a fertile training ground for juju stars of the 1980s. The band were extremely popular in and around Lagos and toured the UK in 1976. Segun Adewale is the most famous musician to have graduated through their ranks.

1975	MOLPS 4	Ope Ni Fun Olowa
1976	MOLPS 6	London Special
1977	MOLPS 8	Oba Oyebade Lipede
1978	MOLPS 25	
	MOLPS 37	Oju Ko Le Ti Eniti

Bakare, Ayinde and his Inner Circle Orchestra.

1975	AJR 1037	Oladipo Egbo

Nightingale, Tunde and his Western Top Hitters.

1974	TYC 1	Tanife, Kani, Woro Vol. 2

Akintade, Francis and His Great Brothers Band. Based in Ondo state, they perform a style of juju which originated in Ondo in the 1950s and is today called 'Woro'.

1980	EKLP 090	Woro in the 1980s
1984	SDP 033	Oj'Omo Sowon

Aniwashawun, Idowu.

1975	TYC 44	Explosive
1976	TYC 61	African Cup Winner's Cup 1976

Dayoson, James. Dayoson, active in the 1970s developed a new juju style blending juju and funk.

	WAPS 226	Ibere
1980	LRCLS 23	One People One God
	LRCLS 24	Face To Face

Various

1980s	6122 N7	Femi Akinyemi: Egungun Riot
	EKLP 096	Suberu Oni (Re-issue from 1960s)
	POLP 87	Wale Abiodun and His Black Beetles: Oya

	Kajoo (Born in 1950, 'Handsome' Wale was born into a musical family. Uses the full juju line-up with the addition of moog synthesisers.)
LRCLS 45	Micho Ade: Ariya
POLP 106	Emperor Pick Peters and his Senior International Band. The band started in 1974
M 2404	Yommy Akins and His Melody Sounders: Oro Nigeria

Owoh, Orlando (b. Owo, Oyo State, Nigeria, early 1940s). Singer, composer and guitarist, Orlando Owoh plays a style of Yoruba palm-wine music known as 'toye'. Owoh is one of the few Yoruba musicians who has stuck with highlife throughout the juju boom. His music and lyrics are very down to earth and are largely preferred by an older generation of listeners. He started his musical career in 1960 playing bongos with the Fakunle Major Band in Oshogbo before transferring to Kehinde Adex. He subsequently moved to Lagos where he was taught to play the guitar by Fatai Rolling Dollar. Between 1967 and 1970 he fought on the Federal government side during the Civil War. After the war, he returned to music, forming his own Omimah Band and releasing his first hit song 'Oriki Ilu Oke'. Thereafter Owoh established a reputation with a succession of popular albums on Decca and constant touring of western Nigeria. In 1976 he reorganised the band, renaming it the Young Kenneries, while continuing to tour widely and record prolifically. Following a dispute with Decca over royalties, Owoh recorded a few albums for Electromat but soon returned to Decca to release another series of albums on their new Afrodisia label. However, he remained unhappy with the company and in 1981 finally parted company to record with Shanu-Olu. He then produced a series of outstanding albums whose saucy and provocative lyrics endeared him to the Nigerian public. With over 40 LPs to his credit, Orlando Owoh and the Young Kenneries remain one of Nigeria's most popular outfits. In 1983 Decca re-released some of Owoh's clasic songs from the 1960s on an album entitled *In The Sixties*.

1972	WAPS 36	Labalaba Fara W'eiye
	WAPS 50	In Great Britain
	WAPS 51	Ire Loni
	WAPS 179	Ajo Ko Dun Bi Ile
	WAPS 201	Ire Loni
	WAPS 220	Ero Ki Yeye Mi
1975	WAPS 247	Ajanaku Daraba
	WAPS 317	Okiki Ojo

1977	WAPS 379	FESATC 77
	DWAPS 2131	Igba Funfun Lere Wa
	DWAPS 2136	Easter Special
1979	SOS 36	Money For Hand Back For Ground
	SOS 46	Apartheid
	SOS 56	Chief Olademeji
	SOS 86	Oremi
1980	SOS 106	Ileya Special
1981	SOS 126	Ganja Part 2
1982	SOS 146	Ko Se Mani Labirin
1983	SOS 096	Ganja
	SOS 166	Lai Ku Egiri
	DWAPS 2187	In The Sixties
1984	SOS 186	Asotito Aiye
1985	SOS 196	Dance Music From West Africa

Fuji Music

During the 1980s, the juju music of the Yoruba of Nigeria made an international breakthrough due largely to the efforts of Sunny Ade, Ebenezer Obey and Segun Adewale. However, back home in Nigeria, it was the less westernised fuji music of Barrister and Kollington which was making the running. The style first emerged during the 1970s as a development of various traditional Yoruba forms like Apala, Sakara and Waka. Fuji assimilated various elements from each to transform what had initially been a religious and philosophical form into a secular and highly popular style. At first, fuji was widely regarded as an aberration from other neo-traditional styles. It was said that all you needed to get started was to adopt a queer name and round up four drummers, four singers and a gong player. But, of course, there was more to it than this. Over the last decade fuji has proved its staying power and expanded its horizons to develop a growing international appreciation for its fluent drum patterns and captivating vocal arrangements. Originally a synthesis of pre-Islamic Arabic culture and indigenous Yoruba traditions, traditional music was strongly influenced by the early nineteenth-century Fulani jihad of Uthman Dan Fodio and the re-Islamisation of south-west Nigeria. Islam took a strong hold amongst the Yoruba and when the Christian missions began to advance inland during the mid-nineteenth century, they failed to match the influence of Islam. Today, more Yoruba owe allegiance to Islam than to Christianity and this is reflected in the popularity of leading Muslim musicians.

But what was perhaps most important to the development of a distinctive

Muslim Yoruba tradition was the incompatibility of Christianity with existing forms of religion. Those who converted to Christianity were obliged to abandon traditional arts altogether given the inseparable links between traditional arts and traditional religion. Islam proved altogether more tolerant, to the extent that Muslim musicians not only continued to participate in traditional 'pagan' ceremonies but in time became their chief guardians. While western-educated Yoruba Christians moved into the professions and the civil service, Yoruba Muslims tended to concentrate in the commercial sector, thereby making more money to spend on ceremonies and social functions – and on the patronage of musicians.

By the early twentieth century, in the eyes of many Yoruba, traditional music was more or less synonymous with Muslim music and despite the disapproval of a few Muslim leaders, the most widespread view was that music was acceptable if put to proper use. For this reason, the orthodox Arabic music of the rest of the Muslim world remained the norm inside the mosque, with traditional Yoruba music being confined to social activities like weddings and religious festivals. For example, during the Id-El-Fitr and Id-El-Kebir, drum orchestras would be hired to accompany believers on their way to and from the mosque and to entertain them during the festivities. The quality and duration of the performance would often reflect the wealth and prestige of the patron. Thus, even from the early days, praise singing was an important aspect of the musical repertoire. Other styles would be played when welcoming pilgrims back from the Haj, or to rouse Muslims for an early morning meal prior to the day's fast during Ramadan.

The most popular instrument remained the dun-dun tension drum and while many of the rhythms and patterns owe more to local tradition than to Islam, the introduction of the iyalu talking drum produced a more spiritual tone, giving the music a specifically Muslim feel.

Ishola, Haruna (b. Haruna Ishola, Ibadan, Nigeria, 1918; d. 1983). Apala singer-composer, record company owner and 'King of Apala'. Alhaji Haruna Ishola dominated the musical style he helped popularise for over three decades. Apala music developed amongst the Yoruba Muslims and can be considered a form of neo-traditional music. Characterised by the use of the Iyalu talking drums to accompany one or more vocalists, Apala emerged as a distinct form of music in the mid-1920s. It was usually performed by amateurs who got together to wake people during the period of fasting. Later it was taken up by professional musicians who enlarged the instrumental base with drums of the dun-dun family and the agidigbo – a large hand piano. By the 1940s Apala had largely lost its earlier religious overtones and had become a music of entertainment. By the 1950s Haruna Ishola and his Apala Group had emerged as the leading exponents of this comparatively new style, releasing countless singles and at least 26 LPs on the Decca West Africa label. Such success made Ishola a wealthy and influential musician and in 1979 he was able to open his own 24-track recording studio – Phonodisc – at Ijebu-Igbo near Ibadan. Haruna Ishola died in 1983 at the age of 65. Such was his contribution to the development of Nigerian music that many top musicians later recorded songs in his memory. The majority of Ishola's records are no longer available but a few of his last recordings were released in the USA and can still be found.

1960s	WAL 1018	Apala Songs
1970s	SRPS 26	Ire Owo Pelu Omo
	SRPS 27	Bisimalai Rabana Oluwa
	SRPS 33	Eyin Ti Nperi Wa
	SRPS 36	Egbe Omejaiyejaiye Shagamu
	SRPS 37	Oluwa Wikan Loba
	SRPS 39	Late Mathew Toye
	SRPS 41	Onise Nsise
1980s	PHA 24	Oluwa Kii Binu
	N4	Egbe Oredegbe
	DWAPS 2144	Gboti Oloti Le
	NEMI 0049	Haruna Ishola and His Apala Group

Omowura, Ayinle, and his Apala Group. Omowura was the second ranking Apala musician who recorded some 15 albums, including several released posthumously. After his death in 1982, his younger brother Dauda took over the leadership of the band which is now known as the Ayinle Omowura Memorial Band. They visited the UK in 1985 and released a cassette on the World Circuit label entitled *Apala*.

1970s	NEMI 0002	Ayinle Omowura & His Apala Group: National Census
	NEMI 0024	Challenge Cup
1974	NEMI 0065	Ire Wale de
	NEMI 0110	Akigbo Wo Awon
	NEMI 0218	Abode Meca
	NEMI 0254	Owa Tuntun
	NEMI 0344	Ise Ile Lonbawan de'ta
	NEMI 0388	Egbo Tuntun
	NEMI 0417	Ati D'Ariyo
	NEMI 0422	Eyia Ose Lu Wa
	NEMI 0460	Omi Titun Ti Ru
	NEMI 0480	Epi Kipagun D'Ale
	NEMI 0507	Kinniun Subu Lule Ioko
	NEMI 0515	The Late Alhaji Omowuro and His Apala Group
	NEMI 0565	Orin Faaj

Barrister (b. Sikiru Ayinde, Lagos, Nigeria, 1948). Yoruba fuji singer composer, responsible for introducing fuji music to the Nigerian public. Nicknamed Barrister by his fans, Sikiru was born in Lagos where he attended the Muslim Mission School at Odiolowo before progressing to Yaba Polytechnic in 1961. However, since the age of ten, Sikiru had been singing in 'Were' competitions – a Muslim style of music performed usually during the Ramadan celebrations. Lack of funds forced him to leave school in 1963 and he worked briefly as a stenographer before joining the army. Even during the Nigerian Civil War (1967-70), Sikiru kept up his interest in music, acquiring a sound knowledge of Nigerian traditional instruments. When he left the army, he immediately resumed his musical career, coming under the management of Nigerian-African Songs Ltd, with whom he released three singles, two EPs and 12 albums. Throughout the 1970s, Barrister and his band – the Supreme Fuji Commanders – struggled to perfect the fuji sound. Working from a 'Were' beat, Barrister added touches of juju and apala as well as elements of Yoruba traditional blues. The result was the criss-cross rhythm of amplified percussion which gave commercial value to what had previously been purely Islamic music. As the originator of fuji, Barrister termed his music 'percussion conversation'. By the 1980s, Barrister and his 25-strong Fuji Commanders were established as one of Nigeria's top acts with a string of hit records which seriously threatened the hegemonic position of juju as the main recreational music of the Yoruba.

1982	SKOLP 18	Iwa
	SKOLP 19	Ise Logun Ise
	SKOLP 20	E Ku Odun
	SKOLP 21	Ijo Olomo
1983	SKOLP 22	Nigeria
1984	SKOLP 23	Love
	SKOLP 25	Military
	SKOLP 27	Fuji Vibration
	SKOLP 28	Destiny
1985	SKOLP 30	Superiority
	SKOLP 32	Fertiliser
	OLPS 1325	Elo Sona

Barrister, Wasui. Alhaji Chief Wasui Barrister and his Talazo Fuji Commanders Organisation. In 1984 a second Barrister appeared on the Nigerian fuji scene to rival Alhaji Sikiru. The similarity of names even extends to that of his group. The younger Barrister has released several albums since 1985 of which *Elo Sora* and *Talazo Disco* were the best received.

LRC 05	Oloriki Meta
OLPS 1323	Tala Disco 85
OLPS 1325	Elo Sora
OLPS 1331	Ori
OLPS 0311	Talazo Disco

Kollington (b. Ayinla Kollington, Ibadan, Nigeria, 1953). Fuji singer-composer, Kollington ranks second to Barrister in fuji popularity. Initially he appeared in no hurry to get anywhere, releasing several unspectacular albums in the mid-1970s on the EMI label. However, in 1978, Kollington suddenly changed his approach, added the bata drum (making it the focal point of his music) and rechristened the band the Fuji 78. With a distinctive new sound, he soon emerged from the shadow of Barrister and so began several years of intense rivalry between the two fuji giants. With a slightly faster rhythm than Barrister, and a sharper lyrical attack on social injustice, Kollington soon established a devoted following. He continued to release several more albums on the Olumo label before establishing his own company in 1982. Since then, every release has confirmed his stature in the Nigerian music business. His lyrics became more critical as the Nigerian economic crisis deepened; attacking politicians while praising teachers, condemning public waste and profligacy and praising the arrival of a new military government. The rivalry with Barrister is now a thing of the past; the popularity of fuji and the size of the market guarantee a future for both.

1975	NEMI 075	Ayanga Baba Yin
1978	NEMI 0298	Africa-Apartheid
1981	ORPS 125	Alakora Ofe Keni Keji Odin
	ORPS 132	Ajodun Ominira Nigeria
1981	ORPS 201	
1982	KRLPS 1	Motun De Pelu Ara
	KRLPS 2	Asiko Lo To
1983	KRLPS 3	Oro Idibo Nigeria
1983	KRLPS 4	Kolawole O Ku
	KRLPS 5	Nigeria Kole Ku
1984	KRLPS 6	Ijoba Ti Tun
	KRLPS 7	Owo Tuntun
	KRLPS 8	Ite Lorun
	KRLPS 9	Knock-Out Special

Omoge, Madam Comfort (b. Ilititun, Ondo State, Nigeria, 1929). Asiko singer and composer, Comfort Omoge and her Asiko Ikale group occupy a unique position in the Nigerian music scene. Playing an updated version of an older style, known as Ere Aboba Asiko, Madam Comfort and her 17-piece percussion orchestra play only traditional music on purely traditional instruments, unadulterated by any western influences or studio effects. Madam Comfort was educated at the local authority school in Ilititun and with the encouragement of others entered the music business at the age of 17. However, until the 1970s she remained an amateur, devoting most of her time to her husband, the Oba of Igbodigo, and their seven children, Then, in 1972, encouraged by her popularity not only in Ondo but throughout western Nigeria, she formed the Asiko Ikale Group, in the process revitalising Asiko music as a popular modern form. She released her first LP in 1976, on the Decca label and followed up this initial success with a string of hit albums. With the revival in the 1980s of other neo-traditional styles like fuji, apala and waka, Madam Comfort was able to consolidate her national appeal with further successful releases.

1976	WAPS 296	Biri
1977	WAPS 385	Ore Mi
1978	WAPS 419	Agbala Woma
1979	WAPS 423	Olorun Mi Iwo
	DWAPS 2112	Gbo Ohun Awon
1980	DWAPS 2139	Ile O Magbagbe
1981	DWAPS 2140	Munene Munene
1982	DWAPS 2167	Eni Lobe Ko Jeba
1983	DWAPS 2180	Ona Orun Ji
	DWAPS 2191	Nigeria Settle
1985	DWAPS 2235	Adeleke Special
	DWAPS 2240	Eni Odun Joba Keyo

Abeni, Queen Salawa (b. Nigeria, 1965). A waka singer-composer who by the age of eight had established a local reputation as an outstanding vocalist. A child prodigy, she released her first LP, *The Late Murtala Mohammed*, in 1977. Singing in Yoruba and backed by her New Waka Group, she soon gained national fame with her hard-edged vocals against a typical waka backing of talking drums and percussion. She followed up her initial success with a series of 12 LPs on the Leader record label. Her more recent releases are now widely available outside Nigeria. In 1984 she suffered a setback when her backing musicians, then known as the Waka Modernisers, left her to join rival waka star Kubarat Alaragbo. However she soon bounced back to have a massive hit with *Indian Waka* in 1984.

1976	LRCLS 006	Late Murtala Mohammed
	LRCLS	Iba Omode Iba Agba
1977	LRCLS	Ise Logunse
1978	LRCLS	Ijamba Motor
1979	LRCLS	Enibasun Koji
1980	LRCLS	Orin Tuntun

1981	LRCLS	Irohin Mecca
1982	LRCLS	Ile Aiye
	LRCLS	Omi Yale
1983	LRCLS	Ija O Dara
1984	LRCLS 34	Ikilo
	LRCLS 36	Eni Tori Eleku
	LRCLS 40	Challenge Cup 84
1985	LRCLS 44	Adieu Alhaji Haruna Ishola

Alaragbo, Kubarat. Kubarat is a new sensation on the Nigerian waka scene. With her Waka Reformers, a traditional group with the important addition of trap drums, she has produced several high-powered LPs for Olumo and Leader Records. She now poses a formidable threat to her more established rivals.

1982	ORPS 136	Awa Omo Olumo
1983	ORPS 141	Ija Pari Kollington Ati Barrister
1984	LRCLS 50	Adija Ti De
1985	LRCLS 53	Repercussion

Highlife

There is less confusion about the origins and growth of highlife in Nigeria than about either juju or other, older, Yoruba styles. Quite simply, highlife arrived in Nigeria in the early 1950s, following the successful tours of the country by the Ghanaian highlife king, E.T. Mensah. All leading Nigerian highlife musicians acknowledge their debt to Mensah and his Tempos, although it must be said that both Yorubas and Ibos had similar indigenous palm-wine styles on which to graft the highlife rhythm. Two early palm-wine stylists included G.T. Onwuka and Israel Nwoba,who played box guitar accompanied by bottles, clips and congas. By the 1950s indigenous highlife bands emerged in the wake of E.T. Mensah, including Aderi Olariechi from Owerri and Okonkwo Adigwe. In western Nigeria, dozens of musicians switched from either native blues or western dance music to cash in on the highlife boom stimulated by Mensah's frequent tours. Bobby Benson, Sammy Akpabot, Victor Olaiya, Roy Chicago, Victor Uwaifo, Rex Lawson, E.C. Arinze and Zeal Onyia were among the early pioneers of Nigerian highlife.

Sadly, many of these classic highlife bands released their songs on fragile 78 rpm shellac discs, few of which are still available. However, Nigerians seem to be very conscious of their musical heritage and unlike many other African countries still enjoy these classic highlife sounds. As a consequence several record companies continue to re-release older material and it is to be hoped that many more will appear in the future. Other stars of the 1950s and 1960s would include Prince Kayoson Dosumu, who combined highlife with Yoruba native blues, Charles Iwegbue and his Archibogs, Odus and his Morning Star Orchestra, the African Girl's Star Band, Eric Akaeze and his Agazas, Ude Ihesiulo and the City Stars of Aba, the Ekwuaro Brothers, the Music Makers, the Olu Right Time Orchestra, Otokiti and the Seven Brothers, Leonard Okala and the Moonshine Dance Band led by Sunday Irabor.

Highlife suffered badly during the Nigerian Civil War. Juju took over among the Yorubas and it was only in eastern Nigeria, among the Ibos, that highlife not only survived but positively flourished to the extent that by the 1970s and 1980s, with the decline in popularity of highlife in Ghana, it was really only the Ibos who were continuing to develop this important musical tradition. Stars of the 1970s included Celestine Ukwu, Osita Osadebe, the Peacocks, Paulson Kalu, the Orientals, the Ikengas, Oliver De Coque, Prince Nico Mbarga, Kabaka, Warrior and the Super Negro Bantous. Many of these musicians took highlife beyond either the dance band or guitar band formula to develop new highlife styles with strong congolese and Makossa overtones. Today, in eastern Nigeria, there are literally hundreds of highlife bands performing to enthusiastic audiences and hoping to make a commercial breakthrough with one of the major recording companies such as Rogers All Stars.

In the years before E.T. Mensah introduced modern highlife, Lagos audiences listened to the konkoma dance bands of the Ijaw. The music they played was universal, apart from the high-pitched kit drum. But when E.T. hit Lagos in the early 1950s, standards changed. His music was new, his instruments those of western bands while his musical standard was first class.

In the words of the West African Review, 'One result of Mensah's visit was that Nigerian band leaders realised that the best way to learn new techniques on these instruments was to join bands in the UK. Bobby Benson, Willy Payne, Layeni and others soon left for the UK to join dance bands there and acquire a polish and technique that was impossible in Nigeria. Also popular at this time was another kind of dance music under the title of "Agidigbo", popularised by a number of orchestras, among whom the most notable were the Racho Boys Orchestra and the Rio Lindo Orchestra.' These orchestras did not last long, although their language was Yoruba. During this period, ballroom dancing was basically a comparatively new introduction to Nigerian social life. On their return these musicians started to incorporate these new ideas and in time Nigerians began to write tunes that soon surpassed all other dances in Nigeria. 'In the beginning the tunes were those that E.T. Mensah had introduced, but before long Nigerian compositions had been composed and while the dance remained basically the same, a distinctive Nigerian stamp was incorporated to the kind of music played by Bobby Benson, Willy Payne, Victor Olaiya and others.' But what must not be forgotten is the diffusion of record players and the fact that this led to a rise in the standard of musicians and the incorporation into their repertoires of the best of western dance standards.

There can be little doubt that highlife is one of the major music styles of Africa and that it has both influenced and fed off other African styles. As such, it will surely emerge from its current downswing to excite music lovers throughout the world once again.

Olaiya, Victor (b. Victor Abimbola Olaiya, Ijebu, Nigeria, 1920s). Singer-composer and trumpet player, he is known to his fans as the 'Evil Genius of Highlife'. Victor Olaiya started his career with Bobby Benson playing a variety of waltzes, quicksteps, boleros, cha chas and highlifes. However, following Mensah's tour of Nigeria in 1952, Olaiya decided to depart to form his own highlife band. The band was named The Cool Cats, and during the 1950s Olaiya's reputation grew with a series of highlife hits. In 1960 he was chosen to represent Nigeria at the Independence celebrations. By this time he had renamed the band 'The All Stars' and both Victor Uwaifo and Fela (Ransome) Kuti passed through his ranks in the early days. During the highlife decline Olaiya, a Yoruba, was one of the very few Nigerians who persevered with highlife and who continued to make a living from this style. By the 1970s he was running his own club in Lagos – The Papingo – while remaining a leading member of the various Musicians Unions being established in Lagos. By the 1980s Dr Victor Olaiya was fronting the ten-piece International Stars, playing the length and breadth of Nigeria while maintaining his reputation with a succession of revitalised highlife classics.

1960s	POLP 66	In the Sixties
	13 403	Olaiya's Victories
	420 001	Afro-Rhythm Parade Vol. 2
	420 014	Afro-Rhythm Parade Vol. 7
1970s	POLP 073	Highlife Reincarnation
	POLP 96	Country Hard O!
1980s	POLP 102	Highlife Giants Vol. 1

Benson, Bobby (b.1920s, Ikeredo, Ondo; d.1983). African composer, singer guitarist, sax player and bandleader, Benson started his career playing ballroom and swing music in Lagos bands. In the early 1950s, following several influential tours of Nigeria by E.T. Mensah, he switched to highlife. This was the golden era of highlife and at the forefront stood Bobby Benson and his Combo – an 11-piece band featuring a seven-strong horn section, double bass, guitar and percussion. Like all big African bands the Combo spawned a number of other groups, helping to establish the reputations of Victor Olaiya, Chief Billy Friday, Zeal Onyia and King Pagoe. Famous hits from the 1950s and 1960s, when the band was at its peak, include 'Taxi Driver' and 'Freedom, Yes Sir'. Nicknamed 'Pa Bobby', Benson was keen to defend the interests of Nigerian musicians and their music. He was the first president of the Nigerian Union of Musicians (1960) and although this union later split, Benson was instrumental in healing the schisms to create the Performing Artistes Association of Nigeria in 1981. The Nigerian Civil War of 1967-70 dealt a serious blow to Nigerian highlife with many musicians returning to the east, and juju music gaining a strong following in western Nigeria. Benson, Roy Chicago and Victor Olaiya were among the few who continued with highlife throughout the 1970s. Occasionally available outside Nigeria is the album *Caban Bamboos*. Bobby Benson died in 1983 and as a mark of respect, several records were released in his memory, including Sunny Ade's *Bobby* (1983).

1960s   420 005   Caban Bamboos

Campbell, Ambrose. Yoruba drummer, guitarist and leader of the West African Rhythm Brothers highlife band. In 1946, the West African Rhythm Brothers band was formed in Nigeria by students and servicemen as a musical reaction to the western ballroom dance music of the war years. Under Campbell's leadership this indigenous-music dance band was established with an instrumental complement of various drums, shekere, gongong, guitar and mandolin. In an article published in *West African Review* (Nov 1952), guitarist and band secretary Ignatius Oke stated the band's intentions to bring into the limelight the intricacies of the different tribal tunes of Nigeria. 'The diversity of folk songs is a measure of our culture, of our beliefs; and our spiritual affinity, and hence to those heroes who have had their halcyon days, and are no more; and perhaps also as a measure of our greatness, and the glory that will be forever Africa.' The Rhythm Brothers went on to record a string of 78 rpm hit records and became one of the top highlife bands. After settling in London, where he earned a reputation in the jazz club scene, Campbell released his first album, *Highlife Today*, on Columbia in 1968, with British-based musicians from the West Indies, India and Europe playing jazz instruments in a multicultural fusion style of highlife.

1968   SX 6081   Ambrose Campbell & His Emergent Music:
                        Highlife Today

Lawson, Rex (b. Calabar, Eastern Nigeria, 1930s). Singer, composer, trumpeter and bandleader, Rex Lawson was born to a Kalabari father and an Ibo mother and went on to become one of Nigeria's greatest bandleaders. He could perform in all the major Nigerian languages but it was one song, in Yoruba, called 'Sawale' which really captured the hearts of all Nigerians. He started his career as a twelve-year-old when he approached Lord Eddyson, leader of the Port Harcourt based Starlite Melody Orchestra and offered his services as a 'band-boy'. Eddyson recognised the potential in Lawson's trumpet playing and placed him under the supervision of Sammy Obot, who later became the leader of Ghana's famous Uhuru Band. Lawson's talent flourished and when the band arrived in Lagos for a season of shows, Lawson left to continue his apprenticeship with the great highlife bands of the 1950s. During the years that followed, Lawson practised his trade with such luminaries as 'Pa' Bobby Benson, Roy Chicago, Victor Olaiya and Chris Ajiko. This was indeed the golden age of Nigerian highlife and in 1960, the year of Independence, Rex Lawson decided to form his own band. It was originally known as the Nigeraphone Studio Orchestra but the name was later changed to the better-known Mayor's Dance Band. Rex adopted the title 'Pastor' (later promoted to Cardinal), and set out on an illustrious solo career. Supported by an 11-piece dance band, Rex Lawson soon developed a distinctive sound, releasing hit after hit on the admiring Nigerian public. These included 'Jolly Papa', 'Oko', 'Yellow Sisi' and 'Gowon Special'. Rex Lawson died suddenly in 1976 at the peak of his fame and popularity. His band continued under the name Professional Seagulls, but the golden days of highlife had passed and although they continued to release several more LPs, the magic was gone. The majority of Rex Lawson's compositions were originally released on 45 rpms, few of which can now be found. None the less, such was the popularity of his music that his family, in conjunction with Polygram Nigeria are on the verge of signing an agreement which will allow all of his recorded output to be reissued for a younger generation of listeners.

1960s	420 019	Dancing Time No. 3
1970s	POLP 061	Greatest Hits
	PRL 13408	Rex Lawson's Victories
1980s	AGB 001	The Highlife King in London
	AGB 002	Love M'Adure Special
	AGB 003	Victories Vol. 2

Onyia, Zeal. Trumpeter from Nigeria who became one of the country's best loved musicians. Also played in Ghana.

| 1977 | TRL 110 | Zeal Onyia Returns. |

Ukwu, Celestine (b. Celestine Obiakor, Eastern Nigeria, 1940, d. 1979). Singer, composer and guitarist, Celestine first came to public notice at the age of 20 with the Paradise Rhythm Orchestra based in Enugu and run by Mike Ejeagha. After four years he moved on and formed his own band, the Music Royals, based in Onitsha. However, the Civil War started the following year and since so many talented artists came from the East, the style as a whole went into decline. But by 1970 the war was over and Celestine relaunched his career, renaming his band the Philosopher's National. They started recording in the early 1970s with a succession of popular highlife albums on the Phillips label. By this time Celestine had evolved his own style, playing a softer, more gentle-paced highlife. Perhaps what accounted for his success was his successful blending of keyboards, accentuated vocals and even the occasional use of pedal steel guitar. Under his direction, the Philosophers developed one of the most distinctive and popular of all Ibo highlife styles. By this time, the band was eleven-strong while the lyrics dealt with social evils, the need for peace and unity and, in general, the philosophical aspects of life. In 1976 Celestine Ukwu released his most popular album ever, *Igede Fantasia*, containing the hit song 'Money Palaver'. Sadly, Celestine died in 1979 at the very peak of his powers. Polydor released two of his albums posthumously but they only served to remind his fans of a talent lost. It has been said that if Rex Lawson ruled highlife in the 1960s, then it was Celestine Ukwu who ruled the 1970s.

1973	PL 6361 048	Tomorrow Is So Uncertain
1974	PL 6361 055	Ibo Abu Chi
	PL 6361 075	Ndu Ka Aku 1975
	PL 6361 109	True Philosophy
	PL 6361 111	Ejim Nk'onye
1976	PL 6361 159	Igede Fantasia
	POLP 091	Uru Gini
	POLP 093	His Philosophies

Osadebe (b. Stephen Osita Osadebe, Atani, near Onitsha, Nigeria, 1936). Singer, composer, guitarist, with over 30 albums to his credit, Osadebe is one of Nigeria's leading highlife musicians. His career started in 1959 when he joined Stephen Amache's Band, later moving on for a short spell with the Central Dance Band. In 1964 he established his own band, the Soundmakers International, with whom he still performs. Strongly influenced by the traditional Ibo highlife of the 1950s and 1960s, Osita has refused to adulterate his music with other styles and sounds, preferring to remain loyal to the highlife tradition. This loyalty to highlife is matched by his loyalty to the Phillips/ Phonogram/Polygram record company for whom he has recorded for over 20 years. By the late 1970s Osadebe had established a reputation as highlife leader and in 1981 he received a gold disc for the 1981 LP *Onu Kwulonjo*. Osadebe also released a series of albums dedicated to various social clubs which flourish amongst the Ibo. *People's Club Special* sold in excess of 40,000 copies. In 1982 Osita composed a song of welcome to mark the return to Nigeria of Emeka Ojukwu, the exiled Biafran leader. The same year, he also dedicated a song to Jim Nwobodo, Governor of Anambra State. By the mid-1980s, Osadebe was at the peak of his popularity, marking 750,000 record sales with the exellent LP *Osondi Owendi*.

1970s	PL6361015	Commander-In-Chief Stephen Osadebe
	PL6361024	Stephen Osita Osadebe and Nigerian Sound Masters
1974	POLP 001	Osadebe 75
1975	POLP 004	Osadebe 76
1976	POLP 007	Osadebe 76 Vol. 2
1977	POLP 010	Osadebe 77 Vol. 1
	VOLP 0077	FESTAC Explosion 77
1978	POLP 017	Osadebe 78
1979	POLP 032	Arum Achoro
1980	POLP 048	Osadebe in the 80s - Oyolima's Vol. 1
	POLP 052	Agbalu Aka No Ano
1981	POLP 056	Onu Kwulonjo, Okwue Nma
	POLP 058	Ony Bili - Ibeya Ibili
	POLP 060	Nke Onye Diliya
1982	POLP 070	People's Club Special
	POLP 074	Onye Ije Anatago
	POLP 075	Onye Agonam
	POLP 077	Ogbahu Akwulugo
	POLP 089	Igakam Ogonogo
	SPOSA 09	Jim's Special
1983	POLP 092	Okp'uzo Enweilo
	POLP 101	Onye Kwusia
	POLP 105	Onyeine Ewetaro
1984	POLP 120	Osondi Owendi
	POLP 125	Makajo

Mbarga, Prince Nico (b. Nicholas Mbarga, Abakaliki, Nigeria, 1950). Singer, composer and guitarist, Nico was born in Nigeria to a Cameroonian father and a Nigerian mother. He grew up in Cross River State amongst the Etura people. He first mastered the traditional wooden xylophone before starting his musical career in various high school bands. In 1969 he and his family fled to Cameroon to escape the Civil War and Nico soon joined a hotel band – the Melody Orchestra – with whom he served his musical apprenticeship. He started on Conga drums, moving through trap drums, bass and rhythm guitar before finally settling on lead guitar. In 1972, together with other musicians he returned to Nigeria and started performing regularly at the Plaza Hotel in Onitsha. Playing a type of music called panko, a combination of highlife, congo and makossa, Prince Nico had his first hit single in 1973 with 'I No Go Marry Papa'. This success was followed by a series of singles which failed to register. Then, in 1976, Prince Nico and his Rocafil Jazz released the song which would make him a household name throughout West Africa and which even today remains one of the all-time classics – 'Sweet Mother'. Sung in Pidgin English to enhance its international appeal, the song remained a best seller for over two years, establishing once and for all Prince Nico's reputation. Over the next few years Nico attempted to emulate the success of 'Sweet Mother', releasing a total of ten LPs. Each maintained a consistently high standard of modern dance music but he failed to recapture the mass market of the mid-1970s. None the less, despite his failure to repeat the success of 'Sweet Mother', Prince Nico has done extremely well out of his musical career and now owns a hotel/nightclub in Onitsha and the Sweet Mother Hotel in Calabar. In 1983 Prince Nico lost several of his musicians who, coming from Cameroon, were forced to leave Nigeria in compliance with the Aliens' Expulsion Order. Since then he has been trying to rebuild his band.

1975	RAS	Man Don Tire
1976	RAS 6	Sweet Mother
1977	RAS 8	Musicline
	RAS 10	Free Education in Nigeria
1978	RAS 14	Good Father
1980	RAS 18	No Die No Rest
1981	RAS 30	Family Movement
	RAS 35	Cool Money
1981	PNM 1001	Music Message
1982	RAS 40	Polygamy
	POLP 85	Let Them Say
1983	RASLPS 040	The Best of Prince Nico and Rocafil Jazz
1984	Round 5007	Sweet Mother

Coque, Oliver de (b. Oliver Sunday Akanite, Nigeria). Singer, composer, guitarist. Little is known about Oliver de Coque prior to his emergence in the mid-1970s with a unique blend of Ibo highlife known as the Ogene Sound. Characterised by Oliver's vibrant lead guitar, the Expo 76 Ogene Super Sounds quickly established themselves at the top of the highlife hierarchy with a succession of smooth and flowing hits on the Olumo label. A colourful character, Oliver de Coque is affectionately known by his fans as Oliver de Coke and even Oliver de Fanta. In 1982 he established his own Ogene label releasing several more albums. As one of the top highlife acts in Nigeria, Oliver maintains a hectic schedule of live dates, playing for and praising the many social clubs in eastern Nigeria.

1976	ORPS 48	Ogene Super Sound
1977	ORPS 68	Oje Mba Ewilo 1978

	ORPS 78	Sound Ogene
1979	ORPS 94	Jomo Kenyatta - Hero Of Africa
	ORPS 100	I Salute Africa
1980	ORPS 108	Identity
1981	ORPS 118	Ugbala
1982	ORPS 124	Udoka Social Club of Nigeria
	OGRLPS 1	Ekwueme Social Club of Nigeria
	ORPS 129	Opportunity
1983	ORPS 130	Nnata Chief Emeka Odumegwu Ojukwu
	OGRLPS 2	Anyi Cholu
	OGRLPS 3	Omumu Onye
1984	OGRLPS 4	Ogene King of Africa

Peacocks Guitar Band International. Led by Raphael Amarabem, the Peacocks are one of Nigeria's rootsiest highlife bands, playing in a full hard style reminiscent of Ghana's best guitar bands.

HNLX 5096	Smash Hits
HNLX 5099	Ejiogu
NEMI 0566	Ije Nde Mma

Orientals. Highlife Band from eastern Nigeria. The original Orientals, led by three brothers, Dan Satch, Warrior and Godwin Kabaka, became perhaps the most popular highlife guitar band of the 1970s. Formed in the early 1970s and featuring the combined guitar and vocal talents of the Opara Brothers, the band toured regularly and released a number of outstanding dance tracks on over 20 albums. However, the band was always beset by leadership problems and the first to leave was the guitarist Godwin Kabaka Opara who, in 1977, hived off from the main group to form Kabaka International Guitar Band. The Orientals continued under the joint leadership of Dan Satch and Warrior, while Kabaka pursued a successful solo career, releasing over a dozen albums featuring Kabaka's new blend of Ikpokrikpo highlife. The lyrics remained typically Ibo, reflecting the lessons to be learned from traditional wisdom and culture. Then, in 1980, the most serious split occurred when Warrior, an outstanding vocalist, left to form his own outfit – Dr Sir Warrior and the (Original) Oriental Brothers. Like Godwin before him, Warrior was able to establish a successful solo career, releasing over a dozen hit albums in the space of five years. Indeed, the very success of the two brothers fuelled rumours that these divisions were a marketing ploy and not really the result of personal animosity. Meanwhile, after a period of some confusion, with both bands working under the name Orientals, the original Orientals, under the leadership of guitar wizard Dan Satch, resumed their careers, releasing several more hit albums and thrilling dance fans throughout the country. Despite the splits, all three hands continue to match popular expectations while sales do not seem to have been affected by the changes. In 1985 Warrior led his band to London for highly acclaimed performances at the Commonwealth Music Festival.

Orientals

1974	DWAPS 44	Orientals Special
1975	DWAPS 59	Nwa Ada Di Nma
1977	DWAPS 71	Murtala Mohammed
	DWAPS 2020	Aluta Agbogho
	DWAPS 2023	Origbu Onye Ozo
	DWAPS 2024	Ugwu Manu Na Nwanne Ya
1978	DWAPS 2057	Ibezim Ako
	DWAPS 2065	Nwanne Awu Enyi
	NEMI 0382	Onye Shi Mu Na Ya
1979	DWAPS 2146	Best of Oriental Brothers
	DWAPS 2071	Onye Egbula...
1980	DWAPS 2090	Obi Nwanne
1981	DWAPS 2158	Udo Ka Nma
	DWAPS 2176	Onye Ije
1983	DWAPS 2193	Onye Nwe Ala
1984	DWAPS 2204	Ihe Eji Aku Eme

Kabaka

1977	DLPS 004	Izu Kamma Na Nneji
	DLPS 010	Ijeuzoije Amunkpa
	DLPS 011	Ewu Nla Ala...
1978	DLPS 015	Onye Mere
1979	DLPS 017	Ewu Nga Onye Eze...
1982	DWAPS 2112	Onye Man Ka Nma
	DWAPS 2141	Ego Di Nkpa
	DWAPS 2142	Nwanme Di Namba

Dr Sir Warrior

1980	DWAPS 2099	Onye Oma Nmanu
	DWAPS 2117	Hapun Mebiri
	DWAPS 2130	Ndo Ma Ike
1981	DWAPS 2157	Jide Nkeji
1982	OTI 2130	Onye Obula
	DWAPS 2130	Ndo Ma Ike
	DWAPS 2157	Jide Nkeji
	DWAPS 2130	Onye Obula
	OTI 2130	Ndo Ma Ike
	DWAPS 2164	Ihe Onyeche
1983	DWAPS 2175	Onye Ije

	DWAPS 2197	Ugo Chinyere
	DWAPS 2188	Agwo Loro Ibeya
1984	DWAPS 2207	Ndi Ji Ego

Ikengas, Ikenga Super Stars of Africa. An Ibo highlife band led by Vincent Okoroego and formed in the mid-1970s. They are still one of the most popular outfits in Nigeria and although their records sell well abroad they have so far failed to cash in on their popularity with either international tours or record contracts. They play a style of highlife known as Ikwokirikwo, a more modern blend incorporating elements of congo music. Lyrically, they tend to follow standard Ibo themes such as praising social clubs and commenting on Nigerian current affairs.

1976	SP 2109	Peace Movement Social Club
1979	OT 005	Destruction
1980	DWA 2114	Nke Onyw Asoa
1981	RAS 2	Ikenga Go Marry Me
1982	RAS 12	Late Celestine Ukwu Special
	DWAPS2068	Onye Weli We
1983	RASLPS048	African Unity
	DWAPS2150	Nwa Enwe Nne
1984	RASLPS056	Ikengas In Search of Peace
1985	RASLPS065	War Against Indiscipline

Imo Brothers International. Based in Owerri and led by Fiddey Onwuneme, alias 'Babwire', the Imo Brothers remain one of Nigeria's top highlife bands. Like the Ikengas, they also play a modern type of highlife called Ikwokirikwo as well as another style known as Oyorima.

1980	DWAPS 2027	Imo Brothers International Band
	DWAPS 2042	Agu Di Nura Etee
1981	DWAPS 2060	Ego Ni Nwa
	DWAPS 2093	Olee Ihe Giowu
1982	DWAPS 2133	Onye Wo Onye Oma
1983	DWAPS 2156	Akaraka
	DWAPS 2159	Uwa Ekwe Nmela
	DWAPS 2189	Kwutunmenu

Kuti, Fela Anikulapo (b. Fela Ransome Kuti, Abeokuta, Nigeria, 1938). Singer-composer, trumpet, sax and keyboard player, bandleader and politician. Fela Kuti remains Africa's most controversial musician who has continued to fight for the rights of the common man despite vilification, harassment and even imprisonment by the government of Nigeria. In the course of a stormy career he has established himself as a hero in the eyes of

many Africans; conquered the international market and released more
than 50 politically pointed albums. Born to Yoruba parents in Abeokuta,
Fela was strongly influenced by both his father and his mother, Funmilayo,
a leading figure in the nationalist struggle. His first musical venture came in
1954, when at the age of 16, he was introduced to Victor Olaiya by his friend
J.K. Braimah. During the 1950s highlife dominated the Lagos music scene
and Fela joined the Cool Cats as a singer. However, singing with Olaiya was
strictly a part-time profession and on completing his school certificate, Fela
took up employment in a government office. He lasted only six months
before persuading his mother that music could be a full-time career and
that he should go and study music abroad. Fela duly arrived in London in
1958 and enrolled at the Trinity College of Music. For four years he studied
musical theory specialising in the trumpet and marrying his first wife, Remi,
in 1961. It was during this period that he formed his first band, Koola
Lobitos, with J.K. Braimah who had also arrived in the UK to study law. On
his return to Nigeria in 1963 Fela worked briefly for Nigeria Broadcasting,
performing with his reformed Koola Lobitos. During these years, he
described his music as highlife-jazz, releasing several singles including
'Yeshe Yeshe' and 'Mr Who Are You'. But in 1966 the Sierra Leonean soul
singer Geraldo Pino arrived in Lagos, creating a huge stir which forced Fela
to reconsider his musical direction. For the next two years Fela flitted
between Ghana and Nigeria trying to redefine his music. Then in 1968 he
finally returned to Lagos and announced the arrival of Afro-beat. In 1969 he
departed for the USA where he spent ten months, releasing the single
'Keep Nigeria One' more out of financial necessity than from any pro-
Federal government sympathy. The band played a few shows in Los
Angeles but for Fela it was more a period of political awakening during
which he read widely on black history. He decided to return to Lagos and
shake up the scene with a new brand of politicised Afro-beat. He
established a communal compound in the Surulere suburb of Lagos (later
known as the Kalakuta Republic) and opened a new nightclub called the
Shrine. Finally he changed the name of the band to the Africa 70 and
started releasing a series of LPs which would transform Fela into the most
controversial musician in Africa. He started cautiously with *Fela's London
Scene* in 1970 but with the pace increasing he came to endear himself to the
Lagos public with a a remarkable succession of Afro-beat classics. In 1974
Fela and the Africa 70 entered a purple patch of music making which was to
see the release of 17 albums in the space of three years. However, his
constant attacks on military corruption and social injustice, underpinned by
tight Afro-beat backing, finally brought down the wrath of the military
government and in 1977 they attacked and burnt the Kalakuta Republic.
None the less, Fela continued with his outspoken attacks on the
government, becoming their most vocal and articulate critic. When the
civilians returned to power in 1979, Fela launched his own political party –

MOP (Movement of the People). He continued to attack waste, greed and corruption and carried his message abroad with tours of Europe and the USA. By the 1980s Fela was a musician of true international stature; an exceptional sax player, lyricist and big-band arranger and a thorn in the flesh of successive Nigerian governments. By this time, the band, now renamed Egypt 80 had grown into an 80-strong troupe, touring and recording at a prolific rate. The return of the military in 1983 did not bode well for Fela and in September 1984 he was sentenced to five years imprisonment on a spurious currency smuggling charge. He was only finally released in July 1986 following yet another change of government.

1970	HNLX 5200	Fela's London Scene
1971	HNLX 5090	Open and Close
	SLRZ 1023	Live With Ginger Baker (Also M 2400)
1972	EMI 008N	Shakara (Also EM 2305)
	JJLP 1001	Music of Fela; RofoRofo Fight (Also EM 2307)
1973	NEMI 0009	Gentleman
	EMI 062	Afrodisiak
1974	JILP 1002	Alagbon Close (Also EM 2313)
	EM 2309	Music of Fela; Question Jam Answer
1975	EMI 006N	He Miss Road
	SWS 101	Expensive Shit (Also EM 2315)
	ABRO 11	Noise For Vendor Mouth
	PMLP 1000	Everything Scatter
	PLMP 1002	Again, Excuse-O
	NEMI 0004	Confusion
1976	DWAPS2005	Upside Down
	SWS 1003	No Bread (Also EM 2382 – Unnecessary Begging)
	DWAPS 2023	J.J.D.
	DWAPS 2004	Yellow Fever
	PMLP 1001	Monkey Banana
	CRLP 511	Zombie
	CRLP 507	Kalakuta Show (Also EM 2320)
	LP 001	Ikoyi Blindness
1977	DWAPS 2033	Stalemate
	DWAPS 2035	Fear Not For Man
	KK 001	Sorrow Tears and Blood
	DWAPS 2026	Opposite People
	DWAPS 2039	No Agreement
1978	PMLP 1005	Shuffering and Shmiling
1979	SKLP 003	Unknown Soldier
	KILP 001	Vagabonds in Power

	K 203554	I.T.T.
1980		Authority Stealing
	PHD 003	Fela and Roy Ayers
1981	KALP 003	Coffin For Head Of State
	ARISTA	Black President
	SPART1177	Original Sufferhead
1982	EDP1547203	Alu Jon Jonkijon (double)
1983	LIR 6	Perambulator
1984	24 01293	Live in Amsterdam (double)
	PH 2000	Live in Amsterdam
1985	CEL 6109	Army Arrangement
		Greatest Hits
1986	DWAPS 2251	I Go Shout Plenty
1987	LONDP 28	Teacher Don't Teach Me Nonsense

Lijadu Sisters (b. Kehinde and Taiwo Lijadu, Nigeria). Singers and composers, the twins were born into a musical background, their father being an accomplished pianist. Since then the Lijadu Sisters have achieved an international reputation for their unique blend of various musical styles – including funk, traditional, disco and Afro-beat. Singing in Yoruba, and occasionally in English or Ibo, they first made their name as session singers. They released their first LP, *Iya Mi Jowo*, in 1969 following up with several more singles and EPs on the Decca label. Throughout the next decade they consolidated their success with a series of innovatory albums. In 1981 they featured prominently in the TV documentary 'Konkomba', and reappeared on the screen in 1985 in the British pop programme 'The Tube'. This international exposure led to an American release, *Double Trouble* featuring material culled from earlier albums.

1969		Iya Mi Jowo
1970s	DWAPS 2002	Danger
	DWAPS 2021	Mother Africa
	DWAPS 2046	Lijadu Sisters
	DWAPS 2089	Ore Elejigbo
	NEMI 0060	Kehinde L'o Gba Taiwo
1984	SHAN 43020	Double Trouble

Ejeagha, Gentleman Mike (b. Enugu, Nigeria, 1932). Mike Ejeagha played guitar as a child, singing folk songs in his spare time while attending St Patrick's school in Enugu. His first big band was the Paradise Rhythm Orchestra with whom he played guitar for three years before moving on to the Leisure Gardens Dance Band in Enugu. In 1964 he struck out on his own, forming the Rhythm Dandies, which later changed name to become the Premier Dance Band. He started his recording career in 1961 with a number of singles which established his name in the public mind before the Civil War caused the band, and many others, to split up. He reformed the group in 1971 and together they recorded their first LP for Philips, in 1974. A married man, he now lives with his family in Enugu and continues to attract appreciative audiences with his relaxed and pleasant Ibo rural music. His lyrics are full of proverbs and folk tales and he often appears on Anambra State Broadcasting and TV.

1970s	PL 6361074	Ude Egbuna
	PL 6361110	Onye Ndidi
	POLP 009	Akuko Na Egu
	POLP 013	Omenani Special
	POLP 018	Omenani Special Vol. 3
	POLP 027	Onye Oma Vol.4
	POLP 042	Elo
	POLP 051	Uwa Ngbede Ka Nma
	POLP 057	Onye Nwe Ona Ebe
	POLP 080	Ugo Mma
	PAN 528	Udoka Special

Maduka, Prince Morocco Maduka and his Minstrels. Based in Onitsha, Morocco Maduka is the leading exponent of a style known as Ibo blues, basically a percussion arrangement supported by vocals and lacking even guitars. Produced and marketed by Sammy Sparkle Records of Onitsha, Prince Morocco has proved so popular amongst the Ibo that in less than a decade he has released a dozen albums reflecting both the Ibo tradition of social club praise and wider issues of contemporary society.

1974	SSAS 002	Emebo Special
	SSAS 004	Eze Nzuzu
	SSAS 005	Nando Special
	SSAS 006	Njelite Special
	SSAS 010	Okwudili Special
	SSAS 011	Obioma Special
	SSAS 013	Enuigwe Special
	SSAS 017	Eze Aghugo
	SSAS 018	Anambra Division Social Club
	SSAS 023	Go Slow Onitsha
1983	SSAS 028	Austerity Measure

Okosun, Sonny (b. Benin City, Nigeria, 1947). Singer, composer and guitarist. Over the last ten years, Sonny Okosun has emerged as one of Nigeria's leading performers with a truly international appeal. Coming from a musical family, he was first inspired by Elvis Presley and Cliff Richard.

However, before turning to music professionally, Sonny first became an actor with the Eastern Nigerian Theatre. It was only in 1964 that he first picked up a guitar, forming his first group, the Postmen, two years later. During these early years Sonny played pure pop music until he joined Sir Victor Uwaifo as second guitarist in 1969. He stayed with Sir Victor for two years, learning his trade and accompanying Sir Victor on tours of Japan and Europe. But by the early 1970s Sonny was starting to develop his own style, a mixture of Bendel highlife and Santana rock, which he named Ozzidi after a traditional Ijaw God. In 1972 he set out on his own with a new group called Paperback Ltd – later changed to Ozzidi. However, the early rock influences remained and during the mid-70s Sonny started to experiment with an Ozzidi-rock-reggae fusion. He released his first 3 LPs in 1976-7, each of which sold in excess of 100,000. However, it was his fourth release, *Fire In Soweto*, which really captured the public's imagination, becoming a massive hit throughout West Africa and later being licensed to the OTI label in London. With his international reputation thus confirmed, Sonny went on to release a series of best sellers between 1977 and 1980. By this time Sonny Okosun was much in demand throughout West Africa, touring the region several times and travelling to Zimbabwe to perform at the Independence celebrations in 1980. With a penchant for protest songs and a strong sense of social injustice, Sonny widened his popularity during the 1980s with several overseas tours and further hit albums. In 1984 the band toured Cuba but it was in the USA that his rock/reggae fusion and trenchant lyrics made their greatest appeal. In 1985 he toured the USA to coincide with his first American release on the Shanachie label.

1976		Ozzidi
		Ozzidi For Sale
1977	NCC 3702	Living Music
	2C05882354	Papa's Land
1978	NEMI 0350	Holy Wars
	NEMI 0330	Fire In Soweto (Also OTI 058)
1980	NEMI 0550	Third World
	NEMI 0530	The Gospel of Ozzidi
1982	OTI 030	Mother and Child
	OTID 030	Mother and Child (45rpm)
1983	HMV 033	Togetherness
	HMV 036	Which Way Nigeria
1984	SHAN 43019	Liberation
1985	HMV 038	Revolution 2
1986	HMV	Africa Now or Never

Uwaifo, Victor (b. Benin City, Nigeria, 1941). Singer, composer, guitarist, flautist and keyboard player. A gifted musician and a former amateur wrestler, 'Sir' Victor Uwaifo has proved to be one of Nigeria's most resilient and inventive musical stars. By adapting the palm-wine styles of the mid-west and singing in Ibo and Pidgin, Victor has been able to develop new styles and dance rhythms with a facility which has maintained his popularity for over two decades. Victor arrived in Lagos in the late 1950s to complete his education. He led a number of school bands before joining Victor Olaiya's All-Stars in his spare time. In 1962 he won a scholarship to Yaba College of Technology and continued playing music in his spare time with the highlife band of E.C. Arinze. Then in 1964 he joined the Nigerian TV service and began to save money for his own instruments. The following year he formed his first band – the Melody Maestros – making three singles for Phonogram of which 'Joromi' became a massive hit, not only in Nigeria but throughout West Africa. During the next decade he released 8 LPs on Phonogram and well over a 100 singles, introducing a number of new dances – Akwete, Ekassa and so on – and thus establishing a truly national reputation. In 1969 Sir Victor and the 16-strong Melody Maestros represented Nigeria at the Black Arts Festival in Algeria. In 1970 he took the band on an extensive tour of th USA and Japan. His commercial success enabled Victor to open the Joromi Hotel in Benin City in 1971. In 1973 he toured the USSR and both Eastern and Western Europe, exciting audiences everywhere with his tight dance sound and exciting stage show. Throughout the 1970s Victor continued to tour West Africa with his new band, the Titibitis, consolidating his success with a series of best-selling albums. Sir Victor also played his part in training younger musicians with over 50 'graduates', including Sonny Okosun, going on to establish successful solo careers. By the 1980s Victor had established his own TV studio with his weekly half-hour show going out to all corners of Nigeria. He has maintained his popularity with several more best-selling albums including the classics *No Palava* and *Uwaifo 84*.

1960s	MEO 121	Sir Victor Uwaifo; Sahara All Stars Band
1969	PRL 13409	Sir Victor Uwaifo and the Melody Maestros
1977	BR 001	Laugh and Cry
	POLP 005	At the Crossroads
	M 2381	Jackpot
	POLP 046	The Best of Sir Victor Uwaifo Vol. 1
1979	RT 1	Roots
1984	POLP 099	Uwaifo 84
	POLP 111	No Palava; Delicate Lover
1985	POLP 139	Egwu-Ozo

Super Negro Bantous. Ibo highlife band led by Elah Elvis. They play in the modern highlife idiom with lyrics in Pidgin.

1977	RAS 11	People No Fit Understand
1981	RASLPS15	Travellers
1985	RASLPS047	Marriage Promise

Ekemode, Orlando Julius. Highlife veteran who started playing at the age of 13. In 1959 he joined the Modupe Dance Band as a jazz drummer before picking up sax and starting the Modern Aces in 1964. The following year he recorded the classic 'Jagwa Nana'. During the late 1960s he recorded seven LPs for Polydor. Toured Europe before settling in the USA in 1974, where he played with Masekela, composing the famous hit 'Ashiko'.

1968	POLP	Super Afro Soul
1984	AS001	Dance Afro Beat

Waza Rocafil Jazz. Led by Cameroon-born guitarist Jacob Nguni, this is a breakaway from Prince Nico's Rocafil Jazz, continuing with his 1960s style of social commentary, fast guitars and a highlife dance beat.

1979	RASLPS	Nigeria '79
1981	RASLPS	Bride and Bridegroom
1982	RASLPS033	Africa
1987	RASLPS060	Congratulations

Female Pop Singers

During the Nigerian boom period of the early 1980s a new phenomenon manifested itself in Nigeria – that of educated, professional young women seeking a seond career in the music business. No doubt inspired by the good fortune of Patti Boulaye, who won a British TV talent show, a flood of girls, mostly from eastern Nigeria, besieged the record companies. Of those listed below, all have studied overseas and several had careers in broadcasting.

Boulaye, Patti (b. 1954 Patricia Ngozi Ebigira). Actress and singer. Won the TV New Faces show in the late 1970s, settled in London and hosted her own TV show. She released two albums of pop and soul ballads. The second, *Music Machine* (1981) was more disco-orientated.

Onyeka (Onwenu). After studying journalism in the USA, Onyeka worked for regional and national TV in Nigeria until 1981 when she released her first album with the help of Sonny Okosun. It rose to No. 2 in the national chart. In 1984 she presented the controversial BBC TV documentary *A Squandering of Riches*, in which her own soft pop and Ibo folk music was featured. Her third album, *Morning Light*, produced in London by Keni St

George, was also a national hit.

EMI	Endless Life
AY 01	In the Morning Light

Onyioka, Oby. A history graduate of Rochester University, USA. Her debut was made with the album *I Want to Feel Your Love* (Phonodisk 1981).

Ifudu, Dora. Professional photographer and broadcaster. Her albums include *First Time Out, Twice As Much* and *This Time Around*.

Ulaefo, Martha. Radio producer, trained as an opera singer in Athens and London. Albums include *Love Me Now* and *Everlasting*.

Ibeto, Uche. Studied fashion in London, released *Sing With Me* in 1983.

Pip, Julie. Studied beauty in London. First album *Am Ever For You* (1984).

Essiens, Christie. Had a national No.1 hit with *Ever Liked My Person* (1983).

Musicians in London

Lawal, Gasper. Talking drummer, percussionist and composer, the Nigerian-born Gasper has been one of the stalwarts of the British scene for many years with his Drum Oro Band, and before that as a session musician in the 1960s with the Rolling Stones and Ginger Baker. His first album *Ajamase* was released in London in 1980, and re-released in 1983. Two songs, 'Kita Kita' and 'Oro Moro', were released as singles. Gasper is one of the founding members of the Black Music Association, London.

CAP 1	Ajamase
CAP	Abiosunmi

Allen, Tony. Drummer. Considered by many to be the finest kit drummer to come out of Africa, Allen helped to establish Afro-beat, as the driving force of the great Africa 70 band of Fela Kuti. He started out playing with Victor Olaiya's band and moved on to the Nigerian Messengers, Melody Makers and Fela's first group Koola Lobitos. He left Fela in the 1980s to become a session player in London guesting on Sunny Ade's *Aura* among other discs. He recorded his first Britsh release, the mini LP *NEPA* in 1984. He then moved to Paris to join the hi-tech outfit of Zairean Ray Lema.

| 1984 | MWKS 3001 | NEPA |

Ozo. London-based recording group of singer, composer and producer Keil St George, a Nigerian now based in London. They play a fusion of styles with a professed Buddhist intent.

BB SPLP01	Spirits of Africa
MAS 1202	Why Waste

Olatunji, Michael Baba. Yoruba drummer who moved to the USA and gained enormous popularity with his African drum ensemble. He records for Columbia.

R25 274	Drums, Drums, Drums
CS 8210	Drums of Passion
CS 9307	More Drums of Passion
CS 8434	Zungo-Afro Percussion
CS 8666	Flaming Drums

Osayomore, Joseph. Leading exponent of Benin highlife. As guitarist, flautist and vocalist, he leads the Ulele Power Sounds.

1982	EMOLP 01	Ulele in Transit
1983	SDP 020	Ororo No De Fade

Henshaw, Chief Nyang. Old-fashioned Efik highlife star. As a vocalist he led his band, the Top Ten Aces, through a successful career in the 1960s and 1970s.

POLP 107	Top Ten Tunes

Various

1983	DELP 8203	Alhadji Dauda Epo Akara: Iya Alakara
	DELP 8304	Alhadji Dauda Epo Akara: Ekun Odun
	DWAPS 2185	Adeolu Akinsanya: Babo Eto (Yoruba highlife)
1984	TRL 239	Mallam Issa Abass: Sawaba (Hausa lyrics, Congo highlife style)

Theatrical Performers

There is a strong tradition of theatre and comedy shows in Nigeria, and many plays and humorous sketches have been released on record.

DWAPS 2179   The late Ojo Ladipo (Baba Mero): Oju
                Asewo A Ja
ACLPS 002   Ola Balogun: Owo L'Agba (Money Power)

The Christian Tradition

Nigeria is today predominantly a Muslim country although successive regimes have stopped short at declaring the country an Islamic Republic. None the less, Nigeria contains a substantial number of Christians, particularly in the southern parts of the country, belonging to a variety of Christian denominations. During the early twentieth century a number of indigenous Christian churches were established, combining elements of western Christianity with elements from traditional religion. Known as the Aladura churches, they have largely superseded formal western churches amongst the Yoruba and Ibo. By the 1980s, many of these churches were releasing recordings of their own choirs and there are literally hundreds of albums available in Nigeria. Demand for this gospel music outside Nigeria is not great but several interesting recordings have become available over the last few years.

Obassey, Patty. Patty Obassey and his Charismatics is one of Nigeria's most popular religious musicians. A gifted composer and guitarist, he scored an enormous success in 1984 with *Nne Galu.*

1984   TRL 268   Nne Galu Nwamamiwota (Also POLP 112)

Ayo. Imole Ayo and the Christian Singers. One of Nigeria's most popular gospel choirs, this album was recorded to commemorate the death of Prophet Oschoffa – the leader of Nigeria's biggest Aladura church. Oschoffa was born in 1919 in Porto Novo and worked as a carpenter before turning to full-time evangelism in 1947. One of Nigeria's most influential leaders, he died in 1985.

1985   IMALP 006   The Great Prophet S.B.J. Oschoffa

Euba, Akin. One of Nigeria's leading composers and musicologists. Classically trained, he became Professor of Music at the University of Lagos before establishing his own music school in 1982. He has toured extensively, performing both in the USA and Europe. He has an active interest in Nigerian traditional music and is planning to release a series of compilation albums featuring the best of Nigerian music.

	BMI 003	Akin Euba: African Nativity

Others

1978	ALPS 1003	Brothers Lazarus and Emmanuel (Ibo Chorals)
1981	MOLPS 81	Choir of the Eternal Sacred Order of Cherubim and Seraphim (Yoruba Spirituals)
1982	POLP 081	Erasmus Jenewari and His Gospel Bells
1986	LRCLS 37	Celestial Church of Christ: Ijo Mimo

GHANA

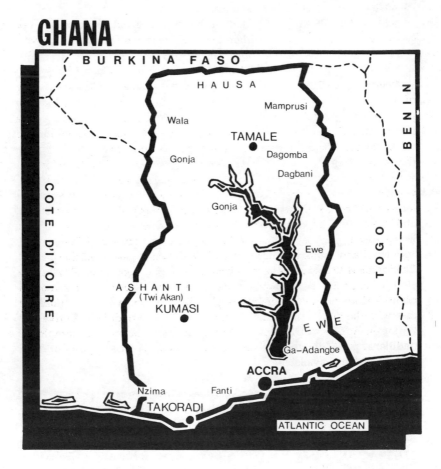

3
Ghana

With over 100 languages and ethnic groupings, Ghana possesses a wealth of traditional music much of which has never been recorded. What is also important to remember is that while traditional music continues to be performed and enjoyed by the rural population, it also has a foothold in the urban centres where it jostles with urban popular music for popularity. At the same time, it cannot be considered an archaic or static form in the sense that it is constantly evolving both in the rural areas and in the towns where it constantly enriches urban electric styles. The juxtaposition of the terms traditional and modern is therefore something of a false dichotomy and it would perhaps be more fruitful to consider Ghanaian music as a living whole, with a strong continuum between 'bush' and 'town' and traditional and popular. During the 1970s Ghana experienced the perfect illustration of this process in the phenomenon of a 'roots revival' whereby electric bands like Bunsu Soundz, Bassa Bassa and Hedzolleh returned to traditional idioms for contemporary performance. This was even more the case with the revival of Ga traditional music by neo-traditional outfits like Wulomei, Adzo and Dzadzeloi. The records listed below are examples of traditional music drawn from various parts of Ghana. The majority of them are still currently available.

1977	ATA 006	Anlo-Afiadenyigba Agbadza Group
1978	M 2341	Akom: Religious Music of the Akans
1985	AA 001	Bantama Kontire
	R 5016	Master Drummers of Dagbon
1986	AK 1	Dade Krama: Ancestral Music of Ghana
	VPA 8400	Ghana: Ceremonial and Commemorative Music
	TGS 130	Kakrabi Lobi: Xylophone Player From Ghana
	LPAM 032	Adowa
	KR 24	Agbadza
	ADSC86012	Yacub Addy
	ADSC86011	Ritual Music of the Yeve
1972	TGS 113	Mustapha Tettey Addy: Master Drummer

		From Ghana
1979	H 72082	Ancient Ceremonies Dance, Music and Songs of Ghana
	ETH 4222	Ewe Music of Ghana
	ETH 4240	Music of the Ashanti
	ETH 4257	Traditional Women's Music of Ghana
	ETH 4291	Ga Music of Ghana
	ETH 4324	Music of the Dagomba of Ghana
	ETH 785	Ghana Children at Play
	ETH 8858	Traditional Drumming and Dances of Ghana
	ETH 8859	Folk Music of Ghana
	ETH 8910	The Ghana Language

Highlife

Highlife music, originating in Ghana and Sierra Leone has proved to be one of Africa's most popular and potent forms of music. Highlife can be considered a fusion of indigenous dance rhythms and melodies and western influences, including regimental music, sea shanties and church hymns, which first emerged in the coastal towns of Ghana in the early years of the twentieth century. Early instrumentation varied from African drums to harmonicas, guitars and accordions. Early, 'proto-highlife' highlife styles included Osibisaba, Ashiko and Dagomba but by 1920 they had become collectively known as highlife. During this decade three distinct styles of highlife emerged – the ballroom dance band variety for the coastal urban elite, the village brass band variety and finally the 'low-class' rural guitar bands, playing a less westernised highlife for less-westernised audiences. By the 1930s, highlife was established along the West African coast with dozens of bands springing to life in Ghana, Sierra Leone and Nigeria. The influence of highlife was even felt as far south as the Belgian Congo (Zaire), where early rumba musicians can remember its potency. The basic form also spread inland to establish a popularity which was only restricted by the more northerly predominance of Islamic culture. During the 1930s and 1940s thousands of shellac 78 rpms were issued for the West African market and highlife began to establish an international reputation. Then, during the Second World War, swing was added to the highlife dance band repertoire and it took on its more modern sound. In 1948 E.T. Mensah and the Tempos emerged, going on to become the most influential highlife band of the post-war era. The band toured widely, making an enormous impact in Nigeria and spawning hundreds of imitators. The 1950s and 1960s became the golden age of highlife with bands like the Tempos, the Black Beats, the Uhurus and Broadway thrilling audiences in Ghana while bands like those of Bobby Benson, Rex Lawson, Victor Olaiya and Roy Chicago flourished in Nigeria. However, the rural guitar bands also continued to grow in popularity, producing in the 1950s an exciting new fusion of highlife and drama in the form of the concert party. Leading exponents of this style included E.K. Nyame, Onyina's Guitar Band, Kakaiku's and, more recently, Nana Ampadu and the African Brothers. By the 1970s highlife began to decline in popularity; juju music replaced highlife amongst the Yoruba in western Nigeria in the aftermath of the Civil War. Highlife did however survive in eastern Nigeria, finding a new lease of life in the music of Celestine Ukwu, Osita Osadebe and, more recently, in the music of Prince Nico, the Orientals and the Ikengas. Even in Ghana, highlife experienced a rapid decline with the arrival of disco music and the growth in 'copyright' bands, despite the best efforts of Konadu, C.K. Mann and the Sweet Talks to keep the music alive. By the 1980s, highlife was undergoing a major revival although the dance band style has largely vanished. Musicians moved abroad and with access to sophisticated recording equipment began to experiment with a number of modernised highlife styles. This was particularly the case with Ghanaian musicians based in the UK and Germany. For almost a century, highlife, in one form or another, has remained one of the most influential musical styles to have emerged in Africa.

Mensah, E.T. (b. Emmanuel Tetteh Mensah, Ussher Town, Accra, 1919). Trumpet-player, sax and bandleader, E.T. Mensah is known throughout West Africa as the 'King of Highlife' and is without doubt the single most influential musician in the history of highlife. Born the son of an amateur guitarist, E.T. entered Jamestown Elementary School where he joined the school fife band run by Teacher Lamptey. From this basic musical education E.T. moved on to High School where he studied organ and saxophone. On leaving school he helped form the Accra Rhythmic Orchestra with his elder brother Yebuah. By this time E.T. had picked up the trumpet and when the Second World War came to Africa (and with it, the arrival of thousands of British and American troops), E.T. joined forces with a Scottish sax player, Jack Leopard, in the seminal Black and White Spots, playing at Army camps and clubs in the Accra Region. During the war, swing music made its influence felt in Ghana and shortly after the end of the war, following spells with the Kumasi Philharmonic Orchestra and the Army Band, E.T. joined the famous Tempos Band, then under the joint leadership of Joe Kelly and Guy Warren. The band then entered a period of reorganisation and later, in 1948, E.T. launched the reformed Tempos under his own leadership. At the time they were Ghana's first and only full-time professional dance band. Four years later, in 1952, and featuring trumpet, trombone, saxes, double bass, drums, congas, bongos, clips and maraccas, E.T. and the Tempos made their first recordings for Decca. With songs like

'Donkey Calypso', 'Sunday Mirror', 'School Girl' and 'You Call Me Roko', the Tempos quickly established themselves as Ghana's top highlife band. Comprising Dan Acquaye, Julie Okine, Jimmy Hagen, Spike Anyankor and Spivack Doddoo, the 12-piece outfit displayed a mastery of many musical styles including highlife, calypso, charanga, cha-cha, congolese and meringue. They also sang, and thus communicated in a variety of languages including Twi, Fanti, Ga, Efik, Hausa, Ewe, English and Spanish. Yet it was as a disseminator of highlife that E.T. carved out an international reputation with frequent tours of West Africa (in particular Nigeria) influencing musical developments throughout the region. He also toured with Nkrumah, acting on occasion as the country's musical ambassador. The hits continued to flow throughout the 1950s and 1960s with a succession of singles and albums, few of which, sadly, are still available. The band also featured heavily on a series of highlife compilations released by Decca in the 1960s. Like all the great African bands, the Tempos also acted as a training school for younger musicians producing a number of spin-off bands as musicians graduated through the ranks to front their own outfits. Spin-off bands would include the Red Spots and the Rhythm Aces. At the same time new recruits continued to add to the Tempos repertoire, bringing in new elements of rhythm and blues, twist, rock and reggae. In 1969 E.T. released *The King of African Highlife Rhythm* on Decca, but by this time the golden era of highlife was drawing to a close. As the big dance bands of the 1950s and 1960s slowly disappeared, so too was E.T. forced to give up his professional music career and return to government service as a pharmacist. However, by the mid-1970s a highlife roots revival was under way and E.T. once more stepped into the limelight releasing the album *The King of Highlife Music* on the Afrodisia label in 1977. Altogether, E.T. Mensah recorded another six albums in the late 1970s of which only two were finally released. A second come-back was staged in 1982 when E.T. travelled to Nigeria to record. In 1986 his early material was re-released by RetroAfric on an album entitled *All For You*, which he followed up with gigs in London and Amsterdam.

1951	WAL 1001	E.T. Mensah and the Tempos
1952	WAL 1002	No. 2
1953	WAL 1003	School Girl
	WAL 1004	Ghana Festival
	WAL 1009	Tempos on the Beat
	WAL 1013	A Saturday Night
1962	WAL 1022	Tempos Melodies
1963	WAL 1032	King of the Highlifes
1969		The King of Highlife Rhythm
1970s	WAPS 20	Stars of West Africa (Compilation)
	WAPS 27	Mensah's African Rhythms

	WAPS 283	Dofo Dra
	WAPS 286	Afi Hei
1977	DWAPS 2013	The King of Highlife
1978		E.T. Mensah is Back Again
1982	POLP 102	Highlife Giants of Africa (With Victor Olaiya)
1986	RETRO 1	All For You (Re-release of classic material)

Highlife Dance Bands

The big dance bands flourished during the 1950s and 1960s in both Ghana and Nigeria. In Ghana, the leading bands played regularly in the major towns, now growing rapidly in population. Comprising a typical line-up of brass, vocals, percussion, drums, double bass and electric guitar, the bands could play a bewildering variety of styles reflecting popular demand although highlife itself remained the staple fare. The most popular styles were swing, calypso, cha cha, rumba, blues, meringue, twist, pachanga and kpanlogo. The lyrics were also delivered in a variety of languages including Twi, Fante, Ga, Efik, Ibo, Ewe and Hausa as well as English and Spanish. During the 1960s many dance bands suffered at the hands of the state bands who, by offering a regular salary and stable employment, attracted many of the best musicians away from the private highlife bands. Many of the large state corporations, from the Cocoa Board and the Black Star line to the State Hotels and the Builders Brigade, formed their own outfits. By the 1970s, hard on the heels of economic decline and an increase in the demand for imported music, highlife dance bands were steadily declining in number and popularity. The Tempos and the Uhurus staggered on but it was really only the Ramblers who survived as a viable musical unit. Sadly, very few records from the golden era of highlife are still available but I have tried to list below the leading bands and a few of their recordings. Now available only in private collections and sound archives, anyone lucky enough to come across any of these recordings will appreciate the beauty of these LPs. Of course the vast majority of dance band highlife was released on 78 rpms and from the 1960s onwards on 45 rpm. I have only attempted to mention those recordings available on LP.

Black Beats

WAL 1006	Black Beat Rhythms
WAL 1011	Tropical Rhythms
WAL 1021	Black Beats Encores
WAL 1029	Sweet Sound of the Black Beats

Broadway dance

WAL 1010	Happy Highlife Band
WAL 1025	Broadway Hit Encores
WAL 1035	Back to Broadway

Stargazers

WAL 1008	Stars Are Dancing
WAL 1014	Come To Kumasi: Ashanti Highlifes

Other leading dance bands would include The Red Spots, the Republicans, Globemasters, Melody Aces, Spike Anyankor and the Rhythm Aces, Black Santiagos, the Black Star Band, Bob Cole and his Music Makers, High Class Diamonds, Messengers Dance Band, the Modernaires, Eddy Okonto and his Top Aces, Bobby Pieterson and his Combo, Police Dance Band, the Professional Beach Melodians, Worker's Brigade Band No. 2, the Professional Uhuru Dance Band, the African Tones and even the Springbok Dance Band. The vast majority of these bands signed with Decca, recording in Ghana and sending the master tapes for pressing in the UK. Other labels active during the 1950s and 1960s would include Melodisc, Phillips Parlophone and RCA Victor.

Mensah, Kwaa. Known throughout Ghana as 'The Grandfather' of palm-wine highlife, Kwaa Mensah was taught guitar as a child by his uncle, the legendary Kwame Asare (aka Sam). Palm-wine music originated in Ghana at the turn of the century in Ghana's numerous coastal ports. Note in particular the influence of Kru fishermen who created the distinctive two-finger variety of guitar playing. One of the earliest recruits to the Kru style was Sam, who not only composed the highlife classic 'Yaa Amponsah', but was the first Ghanaian to record his music when he travelled to London in 1928 to release recordings for Zonophone. Kwaa Mensah, as nephew of Sam, inherited his role as perhaps Ghana's finest palm-wine guitarist. Based in Mankesim, the old Fante capital, Kwaa became a household name during the 1950s with his popular style. During the 1960s and 1970s his public profile dipped but many of his songs became hits when recorded by other bands. Indeed, many people thought him dead.

Born in Lagos in 1920, Kwaa was brought up in Cape Coast where he was taught guitar by his uncle. During public performances, Kwaa supported his uncle, playing clips. In time Kwaa moved on to the brass bands, playing the pati – a small local drum. Then during the late 1930s, Kwaa switched to Kon-Komba, introducing the guitar where previously brass had held front-line. In 1951, Kwaa formed his own guitar band, releasing over 400 78 rpms and becoming a national celebrity. Following the lead of E.K. Nyame, Kwaa then turned his guitar band into a fully-fledged concert party. The band made an appearance during the 1971 'Soul-To-Soul' concert in Accra but it was only in 1975, due to widespread cultural reawakening, that Ghanaians started to pay attention to their own cultural heritage. Kwaa Mensah was 'rediscovered' and in 1975 released his first album entitled *Wawo Christo*. On the strength of this cultural renaissance, Kwaa was invited to tour the USA in 1977, as a support act for Wulomei, Ghana's premier cultural troupe. On his return to Ghana, Kwaa Mensah played several live shows and became increasingly active in Musicians Union affairs. However, despite his experience and ability. Kwaa seems to have been forgotten by the current interest in African music. As they say in Ghana 'No condition is permanent'.

1975   LPAM 006   Wawo Christo

Kakaiku. Born in 1916, at Tarkwa in the Western Region, Moses Kweku Oppong died in 1986 at Tarkwa Hospital. As a child he attended the Aboso Methodist School, but music had already established a hold on his life, and at the age of 14 he left school to improve on his guitar playing. He continued to entertain people at all social occasions and in 1955 he started to record with Badu, and later Ambassador Records. He became extremely popular in Ghana and by the time of his retirement in the mid-1960s he had become a household name with over 200 compositions to his credit. He helped establish Ambassador Records as a force on the Ghanaian music scene and helped train dozens of new musicians including A.K. Yeboah and Oko. His use of proverbs and stories later helped inspire Nana Ampadu to maintain the guitar band style of highlife. He briefly returned to the limelight in the early 1980s, rearranging old songs for current consumption. However, his original musicians had disappeared and Kakaiku was left with only a reputation. He will be sorely missed.

Ramblers. The Ramblers International Dance Band was one of Ghana's longest running and most popular dance bands. Led by the tenor sax player, Jerry Hansen, the band was formed during the 1960s highlife boom. As a 15-piece orchestra, the Ramblers survived for over two decades. During the 1960s, the band established its reputation both in Ghana and throughout West Africa with a string of popular hits including 'Auntie Christie', 'Scholarship', 'Ekembi', 'Abonsam Fireman' and 'Eka Wo Ukoa'. The band released many LPs but their most successful, *The Hit Sounds of the Ramblers Dance Band*, is the only one which is widely available. During the 1970s, the Ramblers took up a residency at Ghana's prestigious Ambassador Hotel, thrilling audiences with their professionalism and the diversity of their repertoire. In 1974, in recognition of his contribution to the development of highlife, Jerry Hansen was elected as the first president of the Musicians Union of Ghana. The band continued until the early 1980s when the deteriorating economic climate in Ghana made it impossible to continue. Little money was available for entertainment, recording facilities were inadequate and public taste was changing. Jerry Hansen now lives in the USA.

1960s	WAL 1030	Fabulous Ramblers
	WAL 1031	Ramblers Encores
1968	WAPS 24	Dance With The Ramblers
	WAPS 25	Ramblers Dance Band
1970	WAPS 35	Doin Our Own Thing
1975	DWAPS 25	The Hit Sounds of the Ramblers Dance Band

Uhurus

1970	WAPS 31	The Professional Uhuru Dance Band

Compilations
Many of the best bands were recorded on a series of excellent compilations released by Decca. However, the only compilation still available is the LP *Akomko*, featuring many of the best dance bands. Originally recorded in the 1950s, these songs were re-released by Afrodisia in 1983.

1983	WAPS 281	Various Artists 'Akomko '

Ghanaba, Kofi (b. Guy Warren, Accra, Ghana, 1923). Master jazz drummer and composer, now known as Kofi Ghanaba, Guy Warren is perhaps the finest jazz drummer in Africa. Born in Accra and educated at the prestigious Achimota School, Guy took an interest in drums at an early age, familiarising himself both with traditional and jazz drums. One of his first bands was the Accra Rhythmic Orchestra with whom he played for a short time before visiting the USA in 1939. On his return to Ghana he played in a number of outfits catering for the servicemen who passed through Accra on their way to the war in the Middle East. In 1947 he was invited to join the Tempos dance band, who at that time were playing a mixture of ballroom, ragtimes and highlife. However, Guy's clear preference was for jazz and in 1948 he made his way to the UK where he joined Kenny Graham's Afro-Cubists, playing a latin-calypso fusion. After nine months he returned to Accra and to the Tempos, bringing with him new musical ideas as well as a selection of Latin percussion. During this period he also worked as a journalist, espousing the nationalist cause of Nkrumah and the Convention People's Party. However his eyes were set on the USA and after a brief stay in Lagos he made his way to Liberia where he stayed three years, continuing to experiment with Afro-jazz fusions and working in local radio. In 1953 he finally arrived in the US, settling in Chicago and pushing forward with his idea of introducing African music to the Americans. During the 1950s he released a series of revolutionary albums combining modern jazz with African percussion. These recordings are now rarely available. During his sojourn in the USA, Guy met and played with many of America's leading jazz musicians, helping to redefine their conception of jazz. In the 1960s he returned home but was so far ahead of his time that he played only the occasional show in Accra, preferring to lead the life of a recluse in his Achimota hideaway. He continued to amass an enormous library of music and during the 1970s prepared his autobiography (still unpublished). He has been described as the spiritual father of Afro-beat, inspiring a new generation of musicians to make greater use of Africa's indigenous musical heritage. It is almost impossible to do Ghanaba's career justice in these short paragraphs. I can only urge readers to search out his recordings and judge for themselves.

1950s	DL 4243	African Rhythms
	DL 8446	Africa Speaks - America Answers
		(Also available as LAT 8237)
		Africa Sounds
		Third Phase
1958	LPM 1864	Themes For African Drums

Highlife Guitar Bands

By the 1920s the guitar bands had established a variety of highlife music quite distinct from that being heard in the coastal cities. It was mainly found in the rural areas particularly in the Asante region and in the beginning struggled for acceptance alongside the more popular rural brass bands. Indeed, so popular were the brass bands that during the 1920s and 1930s no self-respecting rural town could be without its own brass band which performed at local ceremonies and on the key dates in the colonial calender – Empire Day, the King's Birthday and so on. However, by the mid-1930s, the brass bands were declining in popularity and the guitar bands, using acoustic guitars and local percussion, took over. The instruments were cheaper and more accessible while new fusions of local melodies and imported styles made it possible for every village to establish a guitar band. The musicians peformed in local languages and adapted traditional proverbs and stories to current events. The early guitar bands should also be distinguished from the palm-wine stylists, musicians who provided a musical accompaniment for the social activity of palm-wine drinking. Guitar bands flourished during the 1930s and 1940s, with hundreds of bands recording for a variety of labels. Occasionally, one of the major western trading companies would sponsor a band as a form of advertising their products. Early guitar band stars would include the Kumasi Trio, who released dozens of 78 rpms on the Zonophone label. Comprising guitar, vocals, castanets and occasionally clarinet, they established a successful professional career. Other early stars included Kofi Attah and his Trio on Odeon, Kakaiku's band, K. Gyasi, Sampson's Band on HMV, Osei Bonsu on the JVA series, Akompi's Guitar Band, Akwaboa's Band, Onyina's Guitar Band, Oppong's Band, the Royal Brothers and Yamoah's Band. In the early 1950s another important development occurred when E.K. Nyame formed the Akan Trio which for the first time combined guitar band music with comic theatre to produce the first concert party. This development finally established the credentials of the guitar bands, which had hitherto been considered as low class or 'bush' in contrast with the sophisticated urban dance orchestras. The 1950s and 1960s witnessed a flowering of the guitar bands as dozens of bands appeared, either operating on their own or in conjunction with a concert party. Leading concert parties included the Axim Trio, the Fanti Trio the Ahanta Trio, Appiah Adjekum's Band, the Black Star Trio, Bob Cole's Ghana Trio and the famous Jaguar Jokers. The full story of the concert party can be found in K.N. Bame's excellent study *Come to Laugh: African Traditional Theatre*. The bands toured constantly, bringing news and music to isolated rural communities. Leading guitar bands of this period would include the African Brothers, Akonaba's Band, Alex Konadu's Band, All Brother's Band, the Ashanti Brothers, City Boys, Cubana Fiesta Akonaba's Band, Alex Konadu's Band, All Brother's Band, F. Kenya's band, K.K.'s No. 2 Band, Kumapim Royals, Oketekyie's Band, Okukuseku's, Eddie Donkor and the Simple Seven, Sunsum Mystic Band, Yamoah's Band, Kofi Ani Johnson and the Parrots, Opambuo's Band, the Canadoes, Yeboah's Band, Vis-A-Vis, Nana Krah's, Atakora Manu's and Elder Osei Bonsu. By the 1970s, several important changes were underway. Ghana's economy was declining, making the professional musician's life much more difficult. Imported music was becoming increasingly popular and the majority of bands were forced to abandon original composition in favour of straight 'copyright'. However, guitar band highlife did not die completely. Many bands sought to modernise their indigenous sound while a few musicians, like Konimo, made a conscious attempt to return to the past and save what was left of the traditional musical heritage. Several outfits moved to Nigeria, to take advantage of the wealth of the oil boom and succeeded in keeping highlife alive and finding appreciative audiences in eastern Nigeria. By the 1980s, many of the musicians who had served an apprenticeship in either guitar bands or the dance bands were maturing as solo artists, reviving highlife rhythms and finding a new audience for the deceptive simplicity of the highlife beat. Recent successes in the basic highlife idiom would include Pat Thomas, Jewel Ackah, A.B. Crentsil, Thomas Frempong, Eric Agyeman, Adomako Nyameke, Nana Tuffuor, George Darko, Kantata, Charles Amoah, Hi-Life International, Rex Gyamfi, the Dutch Benglos, Teacher and His Africana, T.O. Jazz, C.K. Mann, F. Kenya and Andy Vans.

Nyame, E.K. (b. Kwahu, Ghana, 1927; d. Accra, 1977). By the time of his death in 1977, E.K. Nyame had established a reputation as the most popular guitarist and bandleader of his generation. A self-taught guitarist, he first played with an amateur band while at school before joining Appiah Adjekum's Band in 1948. Comprising guitar, concertina, drums and claves, the band would perform at major functions and ceremonies. During the day, E.K. was a clerk with a European company. However he was an ambitious musician and wanted to modernise guitar-band highlife by introducing notation and the training of musicians. So in 1950 he formed his own outfit – E.K.'s Band, comprising guitars, clips, bongos, jazz drums and fiddle bass. Two years later, he formed the path-breaking Akan Trio, a concert party which combined highlife music with slapstick comedy. The idea was an immediate success and set the standard for subsequent concert parties. In 1953 he was invited to travel to Liberia with President Nkrumah, performing at a number of state functions. The success of this tour and the growing popularity of the Akan Trio enabled E.K. to turn professional and devote his life to music. The concerts were initially staged in English but during the 1950s Twi steadily replaced English as the language of communication. Before and after the drama, the band would perform a variety of highlifes, ragtimes and calypsos to entertain the audience, generally ending up with a normal dance hall full of enthusiasts. E.K. started recording in 1951 having a major success with his first song, 'Small Boy Nye Me Bra'. During the next two decades, as E.K.'s popularity grew he recorded a phenomenal 400 singles on a variety of labels – Decca, Queenophone, HMV and latterly on Skanaphone. His most popular hits included 'Menia Agya Meni Na' and 'Maye Maye Meni Aye'. He continued to innovate with the guitar band context and devoted to his life to the development of highlife music. In the mid-1970s he recorded a number of his most popular hits on the LP *Sankofa* (Go Back and Retrieve). Then, suddenly, in 1977 E.K. died, but such was his influence and popularity amongst musicians and the public at large, that he was given a state funeral with over 10,000 people turning out to pay their last respects. Mention should also be made of E.T.'s longtime associate and friend, Kobina Okine (b. Abra Dunkwa 1924; d. 1985). Kobina played with E.K. throughout most of his career, composing many memorable highlifes including the all-time classic 'Tetteh Quarshie'. Sadly none of E.K. Nyame's recordings are currently available. Perhaps in the future, someone will recognise the genius that was E.K. Nyame and re-release a few of his golden moments.

1960s	420 012	E.K.'s Favourites
	420 020	More E.K.'s Favourites
1970s	STK LP001	Famous E.K.'s Band
1975	RAL 01	Sankofa

Kobina Okine

GAL 001   Kobina Okine

African Brothers International Band (Ghanaian highlife band and concert party formed in 1963, led by Nana Kwame Ampadu, b. Kwahu, Eastern Ghana). The African Brothers Band are now one of Ghana's top electric guitar bands comprising anywhere from 10 to 15 musicians. Four guitarists criss-cross to create a network of sound, backed by four percussionists and four vocalists, all underpinned by 'Ancient' Amuah on keyboards. They had their first big hit in 1967 with the single 'Ebi Tie Ye' (Some are Sitting Well), which was followed by a succession of hit singles, running to over 100 separate discs, before they released their first LP in 1971. The discography below starts in 1974 with the album *Locomotive*, which was their eleventh LP! They also continued to release singles at a prolific rate and by the the early 1970s had established themselves as Ghana's leading guitar band. Nana Ampadu in particular marked himself out as a singularly gifted guitarist, composer, arranger and social commentator. His entertaining and thoughtful lyrics established his reputation as a storyteller of the highest order. The band also continued to innovate with the highlife framework, introducing a number of new styles and dances including Locomotive, Afro-Reggae, Afro-Hili and Odonsan. Nana Ampadu is also very active in Musicians Union affairs and is determined to safeguard both Ghana's highlife heritage and the rights of musicians within it. The majority of records released by the African Brothers are rarely available outside Ghana but over the last few years his growing international popularity has led to several being available in the USA, on the Makossa label, and in the UK on the Stern's label. In 1984 he featured heavily on the British television series *Repercussions*, including film of the band performing in London. In recent years the band have made several overseas tours while continuing to record and tour the length and breadth of Ghana. The solid rhythms, tight harmonies and exquisite guitar work of this, one of Ghana's few professional outfits, continue to provide inspiration for younger generations of musicians.

1970s	LPJN05	Afrohili Soundz
1974	LPJN 08	Locomotive Train
1977	AB 001	Afrohili to the USA
1978	ABBI 023	Ode Nti
	JJLP 002	Enyimba di N'aba (also LP 7084)
	JJLP 003	Sanbra
	JJLP 005	Susana
1981	BNELP 01	Agatha
	MA 7080	Owuo Aye Me Bi
1984	MA 7087	Nketenketenkete

	ST 1004	Me Poma
	AB 004	Space Reggae Medley
	AB 005	Me Maame
1985	AB 006	Obi Doba
	AB 826	Obiara Ba Nnye
	MA 7088	Mede Wo Ka A
1986	AB 110	Osoro Siane

Konimo (b. Daniel Amponsah, Fuase, Asante Region, Ghana, 1934). Singer, composer and guitarist, 'Konimo' started music at an early age when he was introduced to church music by his family. By the age of 15 he was playing church organ. In 1940 he was sent by his uncle to study at the Presbyterian School in Kumasi where he was introduced to European classical music. In 1949 he transferred to Adisadel College in Cape Coast where he picked up the guitar and formed a school band. After graduation, he worked alternatively as a teacher and a music master in his village school, making an acquaintance with the various brass instruments which figured so prominently in the village brass band. However he soon moved to Accra, to the Medical Research Institute, during which time he made his first recording – the highlife song 'Go Inside'. In 1955 he returned to Kumasi, formed the Antobre Group, and played pop and highlife before starting to perform regularly on radio. However he also maintained a full-time professional career, joining the Chemistry Department at the University of Science and Technology in Kumasi in 1960. By this time Konimo had progressed to the Spanish guitar and was taking lessons in classical guitar. He subsequently won a scholarship to the UK, returning in the mid-1960s to record several songs with Dr K. Gyasi. In 1968 he translated several Asante ballads into English releasing them on an LP in 1968 – *Asante Ballads*. The following year he returned to the UK – to the University of Salford – during which time he prepared several programmes of music for the BBC External Service. On his return to Ghana he recorded several more songs with Dr K. Gyasi on the Essiebons label. By the 1970s Konimo had made a conscious decision to work within the palm-wine idiom of guitar highlife, leading a seven-piece acoustic ensemble featuring classical guitar, talking drum (atumpan), handpiano, gyama drum, gong and vocals. A skilled and knowledgeable musician, Konimo is only starting to receive the kind of international recognition which his musical talent so richly deserves. In 1983 he thrilled audiences at the Commonwealth International Music Village in London and in 1984 was featured prominently in the British TV series *Repercussions*. In the mid-1970s he released the classic album *Odonsan Nkoro*, which, sadly, is no longer available. Konimo is a rare musician who finds recording opportunities few and far between. His revitalisation of half-forgotten styles will surely achieve much more recognition in the future.

Mann C.K. (b. Charles Kofi Amankwaa Mann, central Ghana). As singer and guitarist, C.K. Mann became one of Ghana's leading highlife stars of the 1970s with the reputation of the man who kept highlife alive during the years of the rock and disco invasion. Formerly a seaman, C.K. started his musical career with Kakaiku's Guitar Band in the 1960s prior to establishing his own outfit, the Carousel Seven, in 1969. Playing modern highlife, he had his first hit in 1969 with the single 'Edina Brenya'. Then, at a time when the very survival of highlife was threatened by several forces – a declining record industry, a growth in 'copyright' bands and an influx of North American disco, C.K. Mann rejuvenated the Osode beat, a traditional Ghanaian recreational dance. He teamed up with the master vocalist Kofi Yankson and together they dominated the mid-1970s with a series of best-selling LPs. By the 1980s C.K. Mann was still popular and appeared on the highlife compilation *Roots to Fruits*. But it was difficult to match the success of the 1970s and since then little has been heard of one of Ghana's most influential musicians.

1973	EBL 6114	Party Time With Ceekay
1974	EBL 6126	With Love From C.K.
1975	EBL 6131	Funky Highlife
	EB 458	Menu Me
	EBL 6154	Go Mann Go (with Kofi 'Papa' Yankson)
1979	EBL 6196	Womma Yengor
	OS 101	Osode (With Bob Cole)

Asabia (b. Eugenia Asabia Cropper, Accra, Ghana, 1957). A singer and soprano sax player, Asabia was born into a musical family and entered the music scene at the age of 18 singing in a number of groups with her brother, the guitarist Eugene Cropper. Later, during a visit to neighbouring Togo, she did some sessions with Ghanaian musicians based in Lomé and so appreciative was the audience that she decided to embark on a professional music career. On her return to Accra she joined the Sweet Talks, with whom she sang for two years. During this period the band toured the Ivory Coast and Asabia established a number of important connections. When her contract with the Sweet Talks expired she joined the Black Hustlers with Smart Nkansah only to return to the Ivory Coast within a short period. During this tour she was spotted by the President of DiscoStock, a leading Ivorian record company, who immediately offered her a recording contract. The next two years were spent polishing her act and selecting material before she went into the studio to record her debut solo album. This proved to be one of the most popular albums ever to emerge from Ghana and is currently available on the American Makossa label. Entitled *Wamaya*, the LP showcased Asabia's exceptional voice and ability to turn it to a diversity nf matorial. Inspired by Konima, this album of 'refined highlife' made Asabia one of the most sought-after session singers in Africa. Despite a successful tour of Germany, Asabia prefers to remain in Africa, close to her roots.

1981   Wamaya

Crentsil, A.B. (b. Saltpond, Ghana, 1950). A.B. Crentsil enjoyed a comfortable childhood, attending the Methodist Primary School and the Rev. Clelland Memorial School, both in Takoradi. On leaving school, A.B. followed in his father's footsteps, taking up an apprenticeship as an electrician with the Ghana Railways. Yet while the Railways offered a stable future, A.B. had already demonstrated a talent for music and by the mid-1960s A.B. and a group of friends were playing semi-professionally at local funerals and weddings under the name the Strollers Dance Band. The instrumentation was rudimentary but the enthusiasm was there and after practising steadily the group was rewarded with a contract by the management of the Aboso Glass Factory. As a 'state band' the band took on the name the El Dorados, touring widely in Ghana under the auspices of the Glass Factory. The musicians received a steady wage but when inflation began to affect the real value of their salaries, A.B. and J.Y. Thorty moved on to form the nucleus of a new band, the Lantics, based at the Atlantic Hotel in Takoradi. By 1973 the musicians in the band were earning a steady c75.00 per month and took the opportunity to record three 45 rpms at Ghana Film Studios. In 1975, the band received a better offer from the new Talk of The Town in Tema. They renamed the band the Sweet Talks and so began the story of one of Ghana's most popular and successful highlife bands of the late 1970s. In 1975 they recorded their first LP *Adam and Eve* and followed up its success with several more best-selling albums. Now 11-strong, and featuring an exciting blend of dance-floor highlife and copyright music, the band toured widely in Ghana, even performing before the Head of State. Their success in Ghana led to Phonogram taking an interest and in 1978 they travelled to the USA to provide the backing tracks for a new Crusaders album. They finished the work in two weeks and took advantage of the extra studio time to record their all-time classic *Hollywood Highlife Party*. Sadly, at the very peak of their popularity, money wrangles brought the band to an end and on their return to Ghana, the Sweet Talks disbanded. Smart Nkansah left to form the Black Hustlers and later the Sunsum Mystic Band; Eric Agyeman left to pursue a successful solo career while A.B. was left to pursue very expensive court actions against the management and Phonogram. He tried to retain the commercial appeal of the Sweet Talks with a new outfit – the Super Sweet Talks – but litigation still held the upper hand and after experimenting with the Super Brains, he settled for the name Ahenfo Band which he retains until today. He recorded two more

LPS, *Adjoa* and *Afia* before causing a new sensation with *Moses*. Despite condemnation by the Ghana Christian Council, the album proved extremely popular and established A.B. as one of the most imaginative singers in Ghana. His career flourished and despite maintaining his roots in the Tema community he began to search for another international success, finding it with his first British release, *Tantie Alaba*. In 1985 he toured the USA and Canada releasing another classic album *Toronto By Night*. In 1986 he toured the UK and Europe with the Ahenfo Band and the concert party troupe – the Jaguar Jokers. Now at the peak of his powers, A.B. Crentsil remains one of Ghana's finest musical exports.

1977	MEZ 100	Adam and Eve
	MEZ 101	Kusum Beat
1978		M'Besiafo Nto Nsa
		Spiritual Ghana
	635 4034	Hollywood Highlife Party
1979	MAG 1	Mewo Road
	OFBLS 1020	Lord's Prayer
1980		Adjoa
		Afia
1983	ABC 001	Moses
1984	ERT 1004	Tantie Alaba
	ABC 002	The Masters (with J.Y. Thorty)
1985		Toronto By Night

Frempong, Thomas. Originally a drummer with the Sweet Talks, Frempong moved to London in the early 1980s, playing with a number of other Ghanaian musicians before releasing his first solo albums.

	DDP 006	Sansakroma
1985	ASR 20100	Aye Yi
1986	ASR 5010	Anansi Shuttle

Agyeman, Eric. Guitarist and composer, Eric Agyeman is regarded as one of Ghana's finest guitarists. Eric started in the guitar band style of highlife with Dr K. Gyasi and the Noble Kings in 1972 where he helped modernise the roots of highlife to develop the distinctive 'sikyi' highlife. In 1977 he left to join the highly successful Sweet Talks with whom he remained until 1979. He then pursued a solo career with his own Kokroko Band which was to bring him international recognition.

1980s	PMA 001	Kona Kohwe (with Thomas Frempong)
	BEBLOP 13	Highlife Safari
	EBLS 7111	Wonko Menko

Sunsum, Mystic Band. Formed by Smart Nkansah and Agyaaka in 1981, the Sunsum Band soon became one of Ghana's most popular highlife bands with a lively and direct approach to highlife music. Both Smart and Agyaaku had played with Yamoah's guitar band in the 1960s but while Agyaaku stayed in Kumasi with Yamoah, Smart moved to Accra to join forces with the Sweet Talks. With the demise of the Sweet Talks, they joined forces again to create the Black Hustlers before forming Sunsum in 1981. They owe their current popularity to their new blend of dance and guitar band styles. In 1984, they were featured in the British TV documentary *Repercussions* and performed several times in the UK.

1981		Gye Wani
1982	OBL 504	Emma Bekum Mmarima
1983	BEBLOP 17	Broken Heart
1984	ASA 1001	Odo (Love)

Thomas, Pat. Pat Thomas today ranks with A.B. Crentsil and Jewel Ackah as one of Ghana's finest singers. He served his apprenticeship as a vocalist in several of Ghana's finest dance bands including the Broadway Dance Band, Stargazers and the Great Uhurus before joining the government-sponsored Sweet Beans in the early 1970s. By the mid-1970s he was established as a solo artist of considerable stature and for the next decade consolidated his position with a series of classic highlife albums, often ably assisted by his old friend Eboe Taylor. By the mid-1980s he was on the threshold of an international breakthrough playing several shows in Europe before touring the USA backed by Herman Asafo-Agyei's Native Spirit.

1974	GAPO	False Lovers (with Sweet Beans)
1976	GAPO	Marijata
	GAPO 773	Asawa Do
1980	PAR 003	1980
1981	PAR 006	Sweeter Than Honey (with Eboe Taylor)
1983	ERT 1001	Asante Kotoko
1984	NAK 001	Mpaebo
	TONE 002	Oye Odo (with Eboe Taylor)
1985	NAP 001	Kumasi Asante Kotoko
	JAP 0101	Asanteman
1986	JAP 0102	Highlife Greats

Ackah, Jewel. Jewel Ackah is the third of Ghana's great contemporary highlife vocalists. Born in the Nzima region of western Ghana, he has consistently produced albums of the highest quality.

1975	GAPO 814	Fre No Ma Me
1981	PAR 001	Safari and Classical Highlifes
1982	PAR 005	Hallelujah
1983	KYK 005	Supa Pawa
1984	JA 001	Akaraka-Chi
	DRS 001	London Connection
1986	AS 4010	Electric Hi-Life

City Boys. Perhaps the finest Asante guitar band of the 1970s, the City Boys were formed in 1977 when Jackson Adofo, Elvis Yeboah and P.P. Lamptey were approached by B.K. Safo, proprietor of the Highlife Music Stores in Accra, to form a band for which he would act as agent and promoter. A deal was struck and within a few months they had recorded their first single entitled 'Odo Mu Nkyenkema'. It became an instant hit and was followed by several more popular dance singles. Although basically a guitar band, the musicians worked hard to develop and perfect new styles. Led by Jackson Adofo (aka the Black Chinese or Chairman Muo), a native of Kwahu and cousin of Nana Ampadu of the African Brothers, the City Boys are today one of Ghana's biggest attractions. Adofo was educated at the Obo Presbyterian School before moving to Accra to pursue a career as a lottery agent. However his interest in music remained and in 1977 he formed the City Boys. The rest, as they say, is history.

1981	LDR 2001	Nya Asem Hue
	LDR 2004	Odo Pa Baabi
	LDR 2008	Odo Nnidi Ntwen Me
1982	LDR 2014	Merefre No BJI
	1002	Owuo De Dom Ko
1983	SDX 2	In Nigeria

Ashanti Brothers. Led by Osei Vasco, the Ashanti Brothers are a twelve-piece guitar band formed in 1976. They began life as the Unity Stars playing regularly at a hotel in Aprebo, near Kumasi. Their first few singles were instant hits and in time they moved on to Phonogram who released their all-time classic cut – 'Manuu Me Mo'.

1977	6354 008	Wo Yonko Da Ne Wo Da
1982	RASLPS 039	Enoma Nkoweri
	KBL 04	Greatest Hits

Vis-a-Vis. Known alternatively as Tops Vis-a-Vis or Versatile Vis-a-Vis, this highlife guitar band is led by Isaac Yeboah and during the late 1970s and early 1980s became one of Ghana's most popular outfits, touring the country regularly and playing a combination of original material and copyright hits. After a series of hit singles, the band gained international exposure by signing for the New York based Makossa label. Sadly, however, they failed to capitalise on this opportunity and in time dropped almost completely from sight.

1970s	LYN 6225	Passage to Paradise
1980s	MA 7065	Obaa Mansah
	MA 7075	Maye Afafanto
	MA 7076	Obi Agye Me Dofo

Konadu, Alex. One of Ghana's most popular stars, known popularly as One Man Thousand or the 'Wonderful Alex Konadu', Alex is one of Ghana's most popular and active musicians. An exceptional guitarist and charismatic stage performer, Alex Konadu has, in a career spanning two decades, not only played every village and town in Ghana, but is beginning to receive the kind of commercial acclaim which his talent so richly deserves.

1970s	MA 7061	Abiba Nagoodey
	MA 7062	Kunkonuhunu
	MA 7066	Odo Ma Yenka Nkam
	MA 7068	Okafo Didi
	MA 7067	Asaase Ase
	MA 7071	Odo Beko Ma Obi Aba
	MA 7081	Obi Aba Wuo (Also KBL 039)
1980s	KBL 039	Konadu's Dance Band of Ghana
	KBL 100	Yere Wo Ato Mu Ate Ebi Awe
	KBL 101	Obi Aba Wuo (Alos MA 7081)

Manu, Atakora. Accompanied by the Sound Engineers, Atakora Manu has proved to be one of Ghana's most popular indigenous highlife stars of the 1970s and 1980s.

	MA 7074	Disko Highlife
	MA 7077	Afro-Highlife
1980s	LPAM 030	Adee Asika Ayo
	LPAM 050	Adofo Nko Gya Me
1985	PMA 004	Bre Bre Na Eye (with Agyeman and Tuffuor)

Djeni, Safohene and his Appollos. A Nzima speaking band from Western Ghana. Led by Bright Kwesi Mould (aka Safohene Djeni), they play a style of old guitar highlife seldom heard these days. Djeni, the 'Music Explorer', played with several of Ghana's top bands – Okukuseku's, Akompi's and Ahomomo's – before establishing his own guitar band. His style is simple and compelling and is equally appreciated across the border in Côte D'Ivoire.

		Sonla Wu Sonla Fe
		Nea Ye Boe
1979	SAD 001	Ema Enwozoa
1982	SMP 6031	Ghana

Redding, Ekow. Born in Kumasi, Ekow travelled widely in West Africa before settling in Liberia where he formed his own band – the Paramount Six. In 1963 he returned to Ghana where he played with a number of bands including Broadway (on sax and flute) and the Noble Kings. In 1969 he travelled to Germany where he established a new band known as the Kumbey Salleys. During this spell in Europe he picked up the guitar and when he returned to Ghana in 1973 formed his own outfit – Katakumbey.

1976	EBL 6142	Katakumbey

Wulomei. A Ga traditional percussion group formed in Accra in 1973. For the next decade Wulomei spearheaded the revival of Ga traditional music with their modernised folk music and exciting live shows. Formed by Nii Ashitey (ex-Tempos, Police Band and Brigade Band No. 2) and Saka Acquaye (Ghanaian composer and impresario) the band featured three female singers supported by acoustic guitar, three male vocalists, bamboo flutes and a substantial percussion section of drums, calabash, clips, gong and the giant frame Gome drum. They sang in Ga but by playing a mixture of neo-traditional styles – sea shanties, street songs and highlifes – they established a truly national reputation which extended beyond the Ga people to encompass all Ghanaians. They recorded their first LP in 1974 and followed it up with a number of best selling albums, including *Drum Conference*. In 1976 they embarked on an ambitious 45-day US tour. Further releases on the Polydor label confirmed their status as the most successful of the Ga folk bands. Their success encouraged many other musicians to follow their example and by the late 1970s Ga folk bands could be found performing in most of Accra's major nightspots. Amongst those who followed Wulomei (fetish priests) are Dzadzeloi, Adzo, Bokoor, Blemabii, Suku Troupe and Agbafoi.

1974	AGL 009	Wulomei: Mibi Shi Dinn
1975	AGL 002	Wulomei: Walatu Walasa
	AGL 007	Ablade: Ablade Bii
1976	P 2940001	Wulomei: Drum Conference

| 1978 | | Dzadzeloi: Two Paddys Follow One Girl |
| 1981 | DZ 101 | Dzadzeloi: Napoliata |

Eyison, Joe. Born in 1933, Joe Eyison started playing music in 1958, turning professional in 1963. A gifted singer, he is better known as a composer, writing songs for all the best Ghanaian musicians, from E. T. Mensah and E.K. Nyame to the Ramblers and C.K. Mann. A humorous and often bawdy writer, Joe Eyison is today entirely neglected by the record-buying public. On the album listed below he is supported by the GBC Dance Band with vocals courtesy of Pat Thomas.

| 1974 | EMI 01 | Old Hits Vol 1. (including Auntie Christie) |

Pelikans, Eboe Taylor and the Pelikans. Attempted to 'cross-over' with a blend of highlife and disco during the mid-1970s. Eboe, one of Ghana's most accomplished musicians and a first-class producer, played out a long apprenticeship with the Stargazers, Broadway and Uhurus. Recently, Eboe has been working with one of Ghana's best vocalists – Pat Thomas.

| | ABLS 01 | Eboe Taylor and the Pelikans. |

Various

	EBL 6133	Gyedu-Blay Ambolley: Simigwa (A huge hit)
	LPAM 019	Akwaboa's Int. Band: Maye Kom
1975	6354 013	T.O. Jazz: Yenegoro Akatin (Akan folklore)
	SRLP 003	T.O. Jazz
1976	ILPS 9446	Eddie Quansah: Che Che Kule (One of Ghana's finest trumpeters, Eddie signed with Island and returned to Ghana in the late 1970s. He made an impressive impact with his tight arrangements before moving to Australia.)
1976	DWRS 7702	Andy Vans: Osor Nye Asaase
1977	GEMA 6621	B.B. Osei with the Noble Kings: Yako Aba (on this album, recorded in Berlin, Osei runs through many of Dr K. Gyasi's best songs)
	NK 000	Dr K. Gyasi and the Noble Kings: In Europe
	EBL 6117	K. Gyasi and the Noble Kings: Sikyi Highlife
1977	6354 013	Teacher and His Africana: Odo Gyae (Philips)
1982	KBLS 2005	Kumapim Royals: Time Changes
1983	KBL 2010	Kumapim Royals: Pe Me Seyee
	MA 7063	Kumapim Royals: Nsekuro

1981	MA 7078	Elder Osei Bonsu: African Child (A gifted guitarist, supported by Nana Tuffuor on organ)
	GAB 001	Nana Tuffuor: Highlife Romance
	KAM 001	Nana Tuffuor: Ye Wo Asaase (With Eric Agyeman)
1983	EBLS 6224	Yamoah's Band: Fa Asem Kye
1983	OBL 50	Adomako Nyamekye: Ka Nea Maye (1st LP)
1984	YEB 002	Adomako Nyamekye: Ano Plan (both albums recorded with the help of Smart Nkansah and the Sunsum Band)
	PAR 002	F.K. and O.P.K.'s Band: Abraham
	ASR 1010	A.K. Yeboah's and K.K.'s No. 2 : Nde Yen Da
	PN 07	K.K.'s No. 2 : Nde Yen Daa
	MA 7070	Akwasi Yeboah's Band: Obataan (Good Mother)
	KBL 111	Nana Krah's Band: Mintumi Ntease (Supported by Vis-A-Vis, Nana Krah released this hit album in the early 1980s. He was born in Cape Coast in 1945, joining the Noble Kings in 1964. In 1968 he formed his own outfit – The Ambassadors – but they soon collapsed and Nana moved for a spell with the Kofi Ani Johnson and the Parrots before establishing his own band.)
1985	WK 30363	Dutch Benglos: So So Kyen Kyenn (The Dutch Benglos, formed in the mid-1970s quickly established themselves as one of Accra's top club bands.)

Compilations

| 1983 | A DRY 1 | Various: Guitar and Gun (Featuring Genesis Gospel, Salaam, F. Kenya, Supreme Christian Singers, etc.) |
| 1985 | A DRY 6 | Guitar and Gun Vol.2 (Featuring Blind Dzissan, Baptist Disciples, F. Kenya, Adinkra, Wofa Rockson, etc.) |

These two compilations, recorded at the Bokoor Studio, outside Accra, bring to the Western public the most authentic, indigenous and imaginative music being played in Ghana today. More than records released in the West, they represent what Ghanaians listen to today.

Guitar Bands in Nigeria

Although Okukuseku was the most prominent Ghanaian band to find fame and fortune in Nigeria during the oil boom of the late 1970s and early 1980s, many other Ghanaian bands also made the short journey to Nigeria. The majority stopped off first in Lagos before moving on to Eastern Nigeria where their brand of highlife guitar playing found a more appreciative audience. It would be almost impossible to catalogue all the LPs released by Ghanaians working in Nigeria since the majority recorded for obscure small labels whose products have seldom reached a wider market. None the less, those listed below are perhaps representative of the rootsy highlife style which found such widespread acceptance in Eastern Nigeria. By the mid-1980s, many of these musicians had returned to Ghana in the wake of the 1983 and 1984 Aliens' Expulsion Order. There can be no doubt that while highlife was undergoing a decline in popularity in Ghana that these highlife bands helped keep the genre alive and that on their return to Ghana they helped revitalise one of Africa's greatest dance styles.

Canadoes. Singing in Twi and Pidgin, the Canadoes arrived in Nigeria in 1979. Led by Big Boy Dansoh, and playing a blend of meringue and highlife, they not only established a market amongst Nigerians but retained a substantial Ghanaian following. By the mid-1980s they had become one of West Africa's most popular guitar bands following the critical success of their hit LP *Fine Woman*.

1980	RASLPS 010	Oga Sorry
1981	RASLPS 031	Fine Woman
1982	RAS 38	Never Lose Hope
1985	OJILP 047	Afaa Boatemah

Opambua. Another great highlife band led by Nana Agyeman Opambua. They also sing in Twi and Pidgin and during the early 1980s became one of the hottest Ghanaian outfits in Nigeria.

1982	RASLPS 032	Kiss Me and Smile
1984	RASLPS 054	Come Cool My Heart
	MA 7060	Medofo Nantew Yie

Various

1981	SMART 01	Kuul Strangers: Paddle Your Own Canoe
	RASLPS 022	Original Beach Scorpions
1982	CYLP 011	Odoyewu Int. Band: Monkey Chop
	CYLP 014	Apollo Int. Band: Jealousy
1984	RASLPS 053	Golden Boys Band of Ghana 'I Don Tire'

(Twi Highlife led by Henry Maliki Baah)
JRS 020   Citistyle Band of Ghana: Oya

Okukuseku, International Band of Ghana. One of Ghana's best highlife guitar bands, Okukuseku was formed in Accra in 1969 when two close friends, Kofi Sammy and Water Proof, joined forces. Kofi Sammy, singer and composer, began his career with Kakaiku's guitar band playing in the palm-wine style of highlife before moving on for a spell with K. Gyasi and His Noble Kings. Water Proof, a stage actor, had served his apprenticeship with E.K. Nyame's No.1 Band and although neither he nor Kofi played the guitar they eventually came together to create Okukuseku's No.2 Guitar Band. In 1969 they recorded their first song 'Osona Ba' at the Ghana Film Studios but after year they moved north to Kumasi after a fruitless search for instruments and equipment. In Kumasi they were able to borrow the necessary equipment from Ambassador Studios with whom they recorded several more singles. These proved to be sufficiently popular to persuade the chairman of Ambassador, A. Kwesi Badu, to lend them the equipment. Over the next decade Okukuseku's toured widely and released more than 60 singles, establishing their reputation as one the most popular and professional bands in Ghana. During the early 1970s they recorded their first two albums before economic recession and limited recording facilities occasioned their removal to Nigeria where, in 1979, they entered a new phase in their career. They were initially based in Lagos where they recorded two more albums, but their brand of rootsy highlife found a bigger audience in the east and in 1981 they moved to Onitsha to record with Rogers All Stars. They continued to play Asante highlife, singing in Twi, but in time they began to add songs in Pidgin and Ibo as well as adding various Nigerian highlife inflexions to their music. The band proved to be extremely popular in eastern Nigeria, adapting to local tastes without compromising their popularity back in Ghana. Finally, in 1985 the band returned to Ghana, in an effort both to renew their musical roots and take advantage of the relative prosperity of Ghana. They settled in Koforidua and although no new record has come from them since then, they have been very active touring the country, thrilling audiences with their sophisticated and exciting brand of highlife.

1970s	LPEX 001	Agyanka Due
	LPAM 004	Bosoe Special
1979	MLP 502	Okponku Special
1980	JKA 005	Original Kekako
	RAS 007	Yebre Ama Owuo
1981	RASLPS 017	Okukuseku
	RASLPS 026	Suffer Suffer
1983	RASLPS 030	Take Time

1984	RASLPS 045	Black Beauty
	RASLPS 052	Odo Ye De

Highlife in London

The Ghanaian highlife scene in London has deep historical roots, with Ghanaian musicians playing in London as early as the 1920s – often with other Africans and West Indians. There was another period of creative fusion during the late 1930s, 1940s and early 1950s (usually associated with Ambrose Campbell) but it was not until the 1970s that Ghanaian musicians made a really serious impact on the British commercial music scene. The first band to make the important breakthrough was Osibisa who in the early 1970s established Afro-rock on the British scene. Another period of growth occurred in the early 1980s when many talented Ghanaian musicians made their way to London in search of better recording facilities and greater commercial opportunities. However, while these attractions made London a suitable base for new fusions of African and European music, the main reason underlying this flowering of highlife in London remained domestic. For as the Ghanaian economy declined and musical opportunities dried up, many Ghanaian musicians left the country not only for the UK but also for Nigeria, Ivory Coast, Germany and the USA. The arrival of so many musicians in western countries proved most fortuitous – there was a general revival of interest in the music of Africa while, for the first time, talented and professional musicians were available to maintain the the momentum.

Osibisa. An African pop/Afro-rock group formed in London in 1969. Osibisa remain one of the most commercially successful African groups of all time with their unique blend of 'criss-cross rhythms'. Osibisa was the brainchild of Teddy Osei, sax player, flautist, singer and drummer. Born in Kumasi, Teddy qualified as a building inspector before turning to music and forming his first band, the Comets, in 1958. The following year the band had a huge hit in Ghana with 'Pete Pete' from the album *Afro-Rhythm Parade 1*. In 1962 Teddy decided to move to London and after several years of hardship was awarded a scholarship by the government of Ghana to study music. He also formed his own band – Cat's Paws – and started to develop his musical ideas of breaking down black music into its constituent elements and building from there. In 1969 he invited his brother, Mac Tontoh (trumpet and flugelhorn) and Sol Amarfio (drums and bongos), over to London and in time Osibisa was born. Mac Tontoh was an experienced musician who had graduated through the Comets and the Uhurus while Sol, another old friend, was a graduate of the Stargazers and the Rhythm Aces. The central core of three Ghanaians were joined by a Nigerian, Lasisi Amoa on sax and congas and three West Indians, Spartacus R, Wendell

Richardson and Robert Bailey on bass, guitar and keyboards respectively. The combination proved to be an immediate success, recording their first hit single 'Music For Gong Gong' in 1970. This was followed by a period of outstanding musical creativity during which time the band released six hit albums and made the British top ten with three outstanding singles – 'Sunshine Day', 'Dance the Body Music' and 'Coffee Song'. The band became the best-known African band in the UK and by the mid-1970s they were ready to consolidate their success on the international market. Since then, there are few countries which Osibisa have not visited. Highlights include tours of Japan, India and Australia. They have also played widely throughout Africa, including a prestigious appearance at the 1977 FESTAC, and a special performance at the Zimbabwe Independence celebrations in 1980. Despite many changes in personnel, the central core of three Ghanaians has remained steady. Graduates of the band who have gone on to establish successful solo careers include Spartacus, Kiki Gyan, Alfred Bannerman and Herman Asafo-Agyei. The band still play regularly to enthusiastic audiences around the world but the recording output has declined since the heyday of the 1970s. Recent offerings include *Celebration* and the excellent live album *Live At The Marquee*, featuring many of their best-loved songs – 'Woyaya', 'Sunshine Day' and 'Music for Gong Gong'. In 1983 Teddy Osei and Mac Tontoh collaborated with an all-star Ghana line-up on the highly acclaimed album *Highlife Stars 1*.

1970s		Osibisa
		Heads
		Happy Children
		Welcome
		Black Magic Night
		Ojah Awake
1983	CEL 6703	Celebration
1984	CBR 1035	Live at The Marquee

Hi-Life International. Formed in 1982 as a seven-piece band, Hi-Life International picked up the mantle of Osibisa to become London's best loved and most professional highlife band. Led by guitarist Kwabena Oduro-Kwarteng, the band quickly established a reputation as a hard-working and far-travelled band – more than living up to their motto 'travel and see'. Comprising Kwabena on lead guitar and vocals (ex-Ranchis), Kofi Adu on drums (ex-Boombaya, Ojah Band, Alpha Waves and Pigbag), Sam Ashley on congas (ex-Sankofa and Aklowa), Herman Asafo-Agyei on bass and vocals (ex-Bassa Bassa), Stu Hamer on trumpet (ex-Dizzy Gillespie) and South African Frank Williams on sax, Hi-Life released their first LP on the London based Stern's label in 1983. Playing an exciting blend of highlife, soukous and kwela, Hi-Life excited dance floor fans in the UK before embarking on a successful series of European engagements. In 1984 their first LP was licensed to Rounder in the USA and in 1985 they followed up the success of their first release with their second album and a 45 rpm. The band played at several international festivals during 1985 and represented African music at the International Youth Year celebrations in Greece. Since then the band has undergone several personnel changes with Frank Williams leaving to form his own highly successful outfit Kintone with District Six guitarist Russell Herman. The band are often joined on stage by Alfred Bannerman, the Osibisa guitar virtuoso. In 1986 Herman Asafo-Agyei left to form a new outfit, Native Spirit, which toured the USA as backing band for Pat Thomas.

| 1983 | ST 1002 | Travel and See |
| 1985 | ST 1006 | Na Wa For You |

By the 1980s there were many Ghanaian musicians in London, playing in a variety of styles for an increasingly domiciled Ghanaian community and reaching out to make an impact on the public at large. What I have presented below are only those bands who succeeded in making LPs. Countless 45 rpms were released as each group of musicians sought to stamp a distinct identity on the London market. There was at the same time a great cross-over of musicians with key individuals performing on a number of albums and thereby influencing the overall direction of highlife in London.

1983	ST 1001	Malcolm Mohammed Ben 'African Feeling'. (Formerly the music director of the African Brothers, his first solo album was acclaimed as a critical success. First LP on Stern's label.)
	STMSH 0183	Rex Gyamfi 'Sweet Lady'. (This first recording was followed up by a cassette-only release,' Hi-Life For You' - a major success on the Ghanaian market.)
1984	EBUS 1	George Lee's Anansi 'Anansi'. (Vintage Afro-jazz from Ghana's finest sax-player.)
	RR 001	Mighty Rossy 'Highlife Africana'
	RR 002	Mighty Rossy 'Happy Birthday'
	OBS 001	Baffour Kyei 'Odo Mpa So' (Ghanaian singer born in Kumasi in 1947, graduated from the Ashanti Police Band to pursue solo career in the UK.)
1985	AFRB 1001	Redcap James 'Plays Broadway and Uhuru'. (A gifted pianist, Redcap was formerly

director of the Ghana Prisons Service.
Featuring Thomas Frempong and Smart
Nkansah, this album comprised a
reworking of classic highlife hits.)

	NAB 5001	Nana Boamah 'Party Time'
	DDP 005	Kofi Asamoah 'Oberima Nkwan Yede' (A gifted guitarist, fronting a big highlife band.)
1986	AB 100	Asare Bediako 'Lovers Highlife'. (Featuring Kofi Adu, Herman Asafo-Agyei, Karl Bannerman and Ema Rentzos on keyboards, this LP proved to be one of the most successful Ghanaian albums of 1986.)
	AMP 1001	Kwabena Boateng ' Me Dofo Wuo'. (The first release of Asaase Records, run by Kwabena Oduro-Kwarteng, Boateng is a guitarist from the school of Konadu and Ampadu.)

Burgher Highlife

During the late 1970s, many Ghanaians made their way to Germany, amongst them several talented musicians. In time, they began to produce a very sophisticated, hi-tech variety of highlife which was eventually dubbed 'Burgher Highlife'. Leading exponents of this new dance-floor music included George Darko, his former band Kantata and Charles Amoah. Popular throughout Europe while retaining domestic audiences, Burgher highlife proved that highlife could be successfully modernised without compromising the basis of the style.

Darko, George (b. Akropong, Ghana, 1951). Now an accomplished guitarist and composer, George Darko started his musical career as a fontonfrom drummer before switching to acoustic guitar during his school days at Okuapem. On leaving school, he first worked as a printer to earn money to buy his first electric guitar. In 1970, having mastered both bass and rhythm guitars, he joined his first band – the Reborn Avengers. In 1972 he transferred to a pop band, the Soul Believers, playing music heavily influenced by Santana, Hendrix and Booker T. He then moved on to the 4th Dimension with whom he recorded the highlife classic – 'Ye Da Nampa Aba'. By this time, Darko was based in Kumasi where he took guitar lessons from the master musician Konimo. It was during these years that he learnt the 'Yaa Amponsah' style of highlife. During the rest of the 1970s he played with a number of bands in Ghana, always seeking to blend his two major influences – the guitar styles of Konimo and George Benson. Finally, in

1979, he left Ghana in search of better studio facilities. He settled in Berlin where he linked up with several other Ghanaian musicians in a short-lived outfit called Fire Connection. The group re-emerged later as Bus Stop, comprising Lee Duodo (vocals), Sometimer (bass), Jagger (drums), Bob Fiscian (keyboards) and Stephen Mills on sax. In 1983 they released their first LP, *Friends*, featuring the classic highlife hit 'Akoo Te Brofo', an international blend of highlife and funk. The track attracted a great deal of attention and later in 1983 the band released a reworked version of the song in English entitled 'Highlife Time'. In 1984 the band toured the UK and the USA, releasing a compilation album on the English label, Oval. The band also visited Ghana, performing before enthusiastic audiences and selling large quantities of records. Sadly, at the peak of their popularity, several members of the band quit to form a new group called Kantata. George Darko continued with his hi-tech highlife, scoring again in 1986 with the smash hit album, *Money Palava*. Kantata also continued in the same style, releasing several albums of dance floor music.

1983	RRK 15011	Friends
	GEMA ST33	Highlife Time
1986	AB 001	Money Palava
1984	OVLP 508	Kantata; Asiko
1986	LMI 5301	It's High Time Now

Asiedu, Nana (Big Joe). Musician and producer. Joe started his musical career in 1968, playing percussion with Psychadelic Alien, a funk-highlife band. In 1972 he partnered Alfred Bannerman and Kofi Adu in Boombaya, and later joined Pat Thomas's group Sweet Beans. In 1977 he moved to Germany with George Darko, in the group that eventually became known as Bus Stop. In 1980 he was in Lagos, training as a studio producer with Tabansi Records. Following further work with Darko and Pat Thomas, Joe inaugurated his Nakasi label, releasing Thomas's records, Osei Kofi's, Gospel Music and the Senegalese, Diamond Shake.

Religious Music

Christianity has in general terms played a significant role in the social history of Ghana. From the beginnings of Christian evangelisation, the influence of the various churches has often been a decisive factor in the development of religion in Ghana. In an earlier section I noted the importance of Christianity not only as a source of musical inspiration but as a training school for musicians. There can be no doubt that the Christian religion played a significant role in the development of highlife music. However, as colonialism developed, and with it the formation of a Christian educated elite, the impact of religion on music declined as Ghana experienced a nationalist revolution based on a return to specifically Ghanaian cultural phenomena. Thus, the 1960s and 1970s saw the era of privately owned and managed highlife bands. The mood was one of optimism for the future and with the declaration of a republic in 1961, Ghana seemed to be pursuing a more secular path. As a result, religion played a less significant role in social life than during the early colonial period. But by the late 1970s the situation was changing rapidly. As the economy entered its well-documented decline, religion, fetish and witchcraft entered a period of growth. One of the indications of this trend was the rapid growth of indigenous church membership and the increase in the number of 'gospel' bands. As resources moved from private to institutional hands, so too did one of the principal means of financing music. Many bands were created by indigenous churches and were provided with instruments and ready markets in the process. In a sense, during the late 1970s and the early to mid-1980s, highlife adopted a distinctly religious flavour.

1979	WW 111	F'Eden Church of Ghana: Yesu Kristo (Known as the 'pulpit masters', the band started in the 1960s.)
	EBLS 164	Western Melodic Singers: Tsetse Bo (A big band based in Sekondi. Formed in 1968, they are led by Prof. Bilson.)
	EBL 6124	Western Melodic Singers: Womme Yensor
1981	APL 1	U.G.O.: Amen
1984	BAEM 001	Born Again Gospel Band; 2,000 Years Ago (Big gospel band, formed in 1982 – 3rd release.)
	A DRY 5	Genesis Gospel Singers: N'tutu (Formed in 1980, they are one of six bands from the Christo Asafo mission, founded by Prophet Kojo Safo.)
1985	ABA 151	Yaw Sarpong: My Special Prayer. (Featuring guitars percussion and vocals, the Peace Prophet was recorded and released by Ambassador Records.)
	OM 001	Rev. Michael Osei-Bonsu: Hallelujah
1986	RSB 005	Prof. Kofi Abraham Gospel Band: Tie Me Mobro
	SRT 944	Advent Heralds: Nebuchadnezzar

4

Sierra Leone

Situated on the extreme west corner of Africa, Sierra Leone is home to a great variety of ethnic groups including the Mende and the Temne (the two largest ethnic groups) and the Mandingo, Fula, Karanko, Susu, Yalunka and Limba. With both a Christian and a Muslim population, the musical traditions of Sierra Leone are vast and varied but little known outside the country. What is even more disturbing is the recent collapse of the indigenous music industry, after a glorious three decades of record making which put Sierra Leone on the West African music map. Today very few discs come out of Sierra Leone with the result that many of the country's top musicians now operate from other countries. Luckily however, Sierra Leone is one country where musicologists have been extremely active and although few records are currently available, we have at our disposal a great wealth of published information about the country. The principal sources utilised in what follows include N. Ware, *Popular Music and African Identity in Freetown Sierra Leone*; W. Bender, *Songs by Ebenezer Calender in Krio and English* and C. Van Oven, *An Introduction to the Music of Sierra Leone*.

Religious music in Sierra Leone is divided into the formal Islamic music and the formal Christian music including church choirs, organists and soloists. Secular music emerged from the various ethnic groups but by the early twentieth century western-type popular music occasions were in evidence. Between the wars, the Royal West African Frontier Force Band dominated the music scene although it was really the Second World War which led to a dramatic increase in nightlife. Early stars included the Mayfair Jazz Band, the Blue Rhythm Band, Ralph Wright and his Melody Swingers, Charles Mann, the Njala Symphonic Orchestra and the band of the RWAFF. During these years, music was mainly disseminated by the overseas service of the BBC and the powerful, American-built transmitter in Brazzaville. However some local products had appeared during the 1930s – fragile shellac discs featuring local Temne and Mende musicians as well as imports from the Gold Coast. The most popular styles, quite distinct from the large urban dance orchestras, were the palm-wine style and maringa – an indigenous style similar to Caribbean merengue. During the 1950s, one of the most popular maringa musicians was Ebenezer Calender, of whom

SIERRA LEONE/LIBERIA

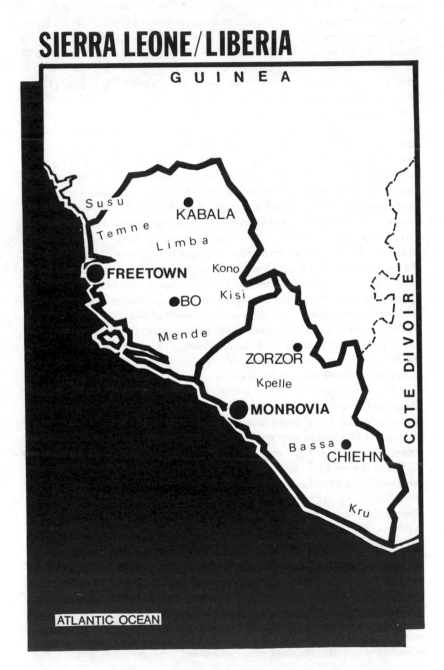

GUINEA

Susu

Temne

Limba

KABALA

Kono

FREETOWN

Kisi

BO

Mende

ZORZOR

Kpelle

MONROVIA

COTE D'IVOIRE

Bassa

CHIEHN

Kru

ATLANTIC OCEAN

more below.

By the 1950s amplification and electric instruments had arrived in Sierra Leone and a younger generation of 'pop' stars took the stage playing a Sierra Leonian version of highlife. One of the most famous of these bands was the Ticklers, who played music similar in style to that of the Ramblers of Ghana. We should also mention the Police Orchestra – a big band with female vocalists, drummers and brass players.

Independence came in 1961 and Sierra Leonians enjoyed their new freedom by importing large numbers of Nigerian (Olaiya) and Congolese (Dr Nico) records. Western pop music also made enormous inroads in the music market with Cliff Richard, the Beatles and Elvis Presley finding large and appreciative audiences. Indeed they served to inspire a new wave of local musicians who adapted their songs to suit local tastes. The first real 'pop' band, the Heartbeats, was formed in 1961 by Gerald Pine although others like the Red Stars, and the Golden Strings soon followed. Gerald Pine was perhaps the most influential musician of the 1960s. He started playing pop music but the initial conception was soon changed to embrace rumbas, cha chas and Latin music – causing Pine to change his name to Geraldo Pino. By the mid-1960s the band had also incorporated soul music (picked up in neighbouring Liberia) and it was for this style that Pino became famous throughout West Africa, touring Ghana and Nigeria with enormous effect, influencing a new generation of musicians including a youthful Fela.

Another popular style during the 1960s was 'Milo jazz' which grew out of the traditional goombay rhythm – named after the lead drum. However, maringa remained the staple fare, with the singers often accompanied by improvised instruments. Leading maringa musicians of the 1960s included Ebenezer Calender and the Rokel River Bóys. But by the 1970s, things were changing in the Sierra Leone music scene. Several musicians started to drift abroad, while western pop music declined in popularity to be replaced by more African sounding bands. The Afro-Nationals, led by singer Patricia Koroma, the Cisco Kid Dance band, Sabanoh 75, Dr Dynamite and his African Rhythms, Chris Na Case and the Masokoloko Dance Band introduced new repertoires, making use of indigenous rhythms and ballads. The various Police and Army bands also continued to entertain music lovers while student bands played at school functions. Sadly, by the end of the decade, this exciting music scene was in decline, reflecting the economic hardships suffered by the country as a whole. Many more musicians moved abroad while the local recording business totally collapsed. Bootleg tapes dominated the market with Sierra Leonian music making little or no impact on the international scene. The only exceptions to this trend were the Afro-Nationals, who released several albums in the late 1970s and enjoyed a solid reputation in the USA. Similarly, in London, promoter Aki Dean released several highly acclaimed dance 45s on the Rokel label. Finally, there was Bunny Mack who enjoyed enormous international success with his best selling album *Let Me Love You*.

Traditional Music

OCR 558 549	Sierra Leone: Traditional Music
ETH 4322	Music of the Mende of Sierra Leone
ETH 4330	Music of Sierra Leone

Modern Music

Calender, Ebenezer (b. Sierra Leone, 1912). Composer, guitarist and singer, Ebenezer started his musical career on the gombe drum (a large bass drum) before forming his own outfit featuring gombe drum, two frame drums, guitars, flutes and recorders. Singing in Krio and English he soon became the leading exponent of maringa music. Originally a carpenter by profession, he became the most popular musician in the country during the 1950s and seemed to be personally known to almost everyone in Freetown. His songs related to everyday life, special events and questions of social behaviour. He released many 78 rpms on the Decca label including such popular hits as 'Jollof Rice', 'Double Decker Bus', 'Baby Lay Your Powder On', 'Vulture Has No Certificate' and 'Do Your Thing, Leave Mine'. Between 1960 and 1984 he worked with the Sierra Leone Broadcasting Service as Director of Traditional Music, playing occasionally with his Maringa Band on both TV and radio. Sadly, none of his music is currently available, but in 1986, many of his records, along with the entire collection of Radio Sierra Leone, were transcribed on to tape by the German author and musicologist Wolfgang Bender. Perhaps some of this magnificent music will now be released.

Rogie, S. E. Sooliman Rogie was born and brought up in Sierra Leone, growing up during the formative years of highlife. An outstanding palm-wine guitarist, he learned to play guitar at an early age, following in the footsteps of two great guitarists – Ekundaio and Joboynor. He supported his musical career by working as a tailor but by the 1960s, with his guitar technique and smooth baritone voice he had produced several hit records which endeared him to the Sierra Leonian public. Several of his early masterpieces have since been re-released on the R & G label. Singing in four languages he achieved great success with songs like 'Go Easy With Me' and 'Koneh Pehlawo'. However, his greatest hit was 'My Lovely Elizabeth' which was covered by countless musicians and is known all along the West African Coast. The song was picked up by EMI and marked a major development in Rogie's recording career which had hitherto been confined to makeshift studios. By 1965 Rogie had assembled a fully-fledged band, the Morningstars, who accompanied his acoustic guitar with electric instruments and indigenous percussion. His local popularity gave him the basis to travel abroad and in 1967 he visited Liberia where he recorded several tracks at the Phillips studio. He also played before several heads of state and in the 1970s travelled to the USA where he released the album *African Lady*. Currently the career of one of Africa's brightest stars is undergoing something of a revival.

| 1975 | ROGI R1 | African Lady |
| 1976 | ROGI R2 | The 60s Sounds of S.E. Rogie |

Mack, Bunny (b. Cecil Bunting MacCormack, Freetown, Sierra Leone). A successful singer and composer, Bunny Mack started his musical career playing harmonica and penny-whistle as a child. He then progressed to the banjo, singing in church choirs before finally picking up the guitar. He then formed his own group, the Daverns, who appeared on radio several times although Bunny was careful to keep his name off the air due to parental displeasure. Then in 1966 he adopted the stage name Kenny Marso and formed a new band known as the Soundcasters. In 1967 the band travelled to the UK, releasing several singles before Home Office problems forced a move to Germany. For the next decade Bunny continued with his music but with little success until in 1979 he teamed up with fellow Sierra Leonian and producer Aki Dean. Aki had already produced the Afro-Nationals and had very definite ideas about how to promote 'cross-over' music. They first recorded 'Shake Your Battie' but it was the second single, 'Funny Lady/Discalypso' which finally established Bunny Mack's name amongst dance fans everywhere. In 1981 Bunny released his first LP, *Let Me Love You*, which became an enormous international hit, in the West Indies, in Europe, in Nigeria and reaching number one in Nairobi. Bunny made use of the best session musicians around, including Alfred Bannerman, George Lee, the late Jake Sollo and Papa Mensah. His new disco-funk-calypso fusion caught the public's imagination and in 1982 Bunny followed up with his second album, *Supafrico*.

| 1981 | Let Me Love You |
| 1982 | Supafrico |

5
Liberia

Liberia is the oldest independent state in Africa. It lies between Sierra Leone, Guinea and Ivory Coast, bordering the Atlantic Ocean. The main ethnic groups of the forested interior regions are the Kpelle and the Bassa, while Manding people now occupy the savannah regions, and along the coast the Kru are dominant. During the nineteenth century, however, there was a great influx of freed slaves from America and in 1847 this 'Americo-Liberian' elite established the first independent government. They remain the dominant social class and have retained strong commercial and cultural links with the USA. Of the indigenous peoples, the Kru have lived in Liberia and the Ivory Coast longer than most. They are traditionally fishermen and sailors and, as such, they have established themselves along the West African coast. Many Kru served in British and American ships and they have been credited with the spread of Pidgin English. According to John Collins, Kru sailors were actually the source of the highlife guitar style which was taken up in Ghana and spread throughout Africa. He points out that the thumb and forefinger picking style (similar to the kora fingering technique) used by the sea-faring Liberians was disseminated along the West African coast. The first Ghanaian artiste to record guitar highlife, Kwame Asare in 1926, was reportedly taught to play by a Kru seaman.

Contemporary Music

The most recent review of the Liberian pop scene comes from Collins, whose article in *Africa Music* magazine (24, 1985) provides the information below. In addition to the palm-wine highlife music, brass bands playing quadrilles, foxtrots and calypsos were the other ingredients in popular Liberian music during the the pre-war years. Since then, however, the musical ambience has been very American. Local highlife bands did exist but only in the less salubrious bars, and it was not until the 1960s that local music was first recorded in Monrovia, the capital city. Of the musicians to have achieved national reputations Collins lists the following: Jones Dopoe; John Dweh; Yatta Zoe, the first female star with over two dozen singles released; Morris Dorley, who mixes merengues, rumbas and highlife with his Sunset Boys; Music Makers, set up by veteran Jerome Paye, Danny Moore, who sings in the Vai language; Kruboy Emmanuel Koffa, exponent of Darze music, using drums, harmonica, musical saw (!) and percussion. Others include Robert Toe, a highlife playing soldier, Lofa Zoes, another army man, Fatu Gayflor, a singer and dancer with the National Troupe, the Afro-rock group Oxygen and their spin-off the Humble Rebels. Ciaffa Barclay and O.J. Brown are other recently recorded artistes. Many of those mentioned represent the first generation of musicians to utilise Studio 99, an eight-track studio opened in 1984 by Faisal Helwani, the Ghanaian-born producer who recorded 36 cassette albums in his first year of operation. Cassettes, rather than vinyl products, account for almost all the recorded music on sale within the country. In 1986 Corina Flamma-Sherman, a singer of funk-style numbers, was voted Best Female Singer in the Radio France International 'Discovery' awards.

KR25	The Africanas. Music of Liberia
LPM 2345	Afro Disco Band
EMC3294	Miatta Fanbulleh (A female singer of some repute, occasionally based in London.)

SENEGAL / THE GAMBIA

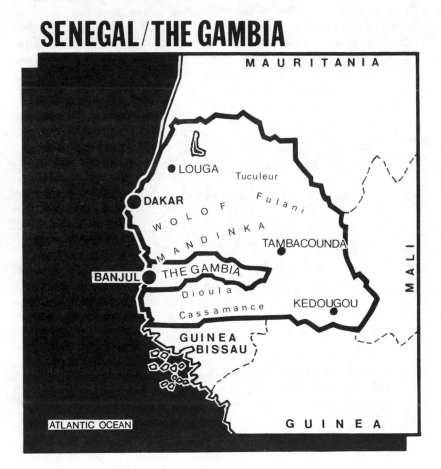

6
The Gambia

The Gambia is one of Africa's smallest countries, yet its musical output is substantial. Its traditional musicians, particularly the kora-playing griots (praise singers and oral historians) of the Mandinka people, have been heard frequently in the west, both on record and through personal appearance. Within the Gambia the music of the kora is dominant. This 21-string harp-lute (Africa's ultimate guitar) is exclusive to the Manding people whose territory stretches from Mali to Guinea, and the historical development of the musical style is discussed further in the chapter on Mali. Suffice to say that within the Gambia there is a surfeit of kora musicians (jalis) and visitors to the country are soon made aware that the ubiquitous kora is the symbolic sound of the Gambia. The National Troupe, which plays for tourists, villagers and for the Banjul elite, once contained seven kora players, with balafons, drums, xalam, molo lutes and singers and dancers. Most of the music, however, is played by soloists for important patrons whose praises and genealogy the griots deliver with energy. Wolof and Jola griots of the area rely more on percussion instruments and drums. While there are women griots who sing, no women play instruments other than percussion sticks or bells.

One of the finest kora players of recent times, who died in 1983, was Alhaji Bai Konte, famous not only throughout his own land but who also introduced kora music to international audiences in USA, Russia and Europe. Bai Konte was born in 1920 in western Gambia, but his father had come from Mali and Bai was able to combine the two styles of kora playing into something powerful and sublime. Following the release of an album on Rounder in the early 1970s Bai Konte began to tour extensively, later to be joined by his two sons Dembo Konte and Malamini Jobarteh. Since his death these two have recorded together and often visit Europe. Other major kora musicians to have found an audience in the west include Amadu Bansang Jobarteh, Jali Nyama Suso and Kausu Kouyate, who plays a much rarer 23-string instrument.

1970s	R 5001	Alhaji Bai Konte: Kora Melodies from The Gambia
	SNTF 666	African Journey,Vol 1 Roots of The Blues

	SNTF 729	Jali Nyama Suso: Songs from The Gambia
	EDM 101	Amadu Bansang Jobarteh, Master of the Kora
1982	VX 1006	Konte Family: Mandinka Music
1985	STERNS 1010	Malamini Jobarteh & Dembo Konte.Jaliya
1987	FMSL 2009	Dembo Konte and Kausu Kouyate: Tanante

Popular Music

In the Gambia traditional music is strong and rich, and so is the popular music of the region, most of which is now of Senegalese origin. Musicians are obliged to record cassette releases in the studios of Dakar, as Gambia's only recording facility is the very basic studio at Radio Gambia in Banjul. Youssou N'Dour with Super Etoile, and Super Diamono are the most popular bands, but even they admit that the inspiration for the creation of an electric pop music came from the Gambian group Ifang Bondi, the ex-Super Eagles of Banjul. They were the first outfit to blend the traditional rhythms with progressive electric sounds. While their influence and the band itself survives, Ifang Bondi have not achieved a great deal of financial reward. In 1979 Ifang Bondi recorded their debut album *Saraba*, a progressive sound which introduces phased and fuzzed guitar and heavy percussion with a Wolof atmosphere. In recent years the group has been based in Europe, with only four of the original members remaining.

Bubacar Jammeh, who had travelled to Germany in 1975, released his first record in 1983, while in 1978 another self-exiled Gambian set up the Mandingo Griot Society in America. He is Foday Musa Suso, a descendent of the original kora player and a man with an extensive repertoire. Suso's jazz-blues griot fusion was a fascinating attempt to enter the international jazz scene. His later recording, *Watto Sitta*, with Herbie Hancock guesting, was an electro-griot blend in a very hi-tech style. Other Gambian groups popular on the home front have been Karantaba, Kulanjang and Manding Kelepha.

1978	FF 076	Mandingo Griot Society
	FF 269	Mandingo Griot Society: Mighty Rhythm
1979	GRIOT	Ifang Bondi: Saraba
1983	LPH 2366	Ifang Bondi: Mantra
	JR I06	Bubacar Jammeh: Kiang Jennyerr Kulumba Vol.1
1984	CEL 6103	Mandingo: Watto Sitta

Part III
Francophone West Africa

COTE D'IVOIRE

7

Côte d'Ivoire

Côte d'Ivoire (the Ivory Coast) is a melting pot of peoples and cultures. The west and south of the country is the home area of the Dank; the Akan occupy the centre and East; in the north we find the Senoufo and Lobi while in the north-east we find the Bambaras who have their cousins in both Mali and Guinea. The philosophy, conception and performance of music of course varies between the various cultures although, almost inevitably, certain features, like the mask, remain cross-cultural. Instrumentation is also similar in different parts of the country although the drum, in different forms, remains the major instrument in all parts. As in the rest of Africa, music is utilised on a variety of occasions with each form having its own traditional place in the society. Sacred dances should not be performed outside their proper context while more specialised music – for circumcision, medicinal purposes and so on – also have their precise place in social life. But as with most of Black Africa, the older forms and traditions no longer demand the respect and attention to detail which marked earlier eras.

Urbanisation and the introduction of electric instruments have both played their part in the gradual, even imperceptible changes in recreational music. In this respect, the modern music of Côte d'Ivoire has had to fight hard to assert itself. During the 1960s it had few stars who were generally known only within ethnic areas. Foreign competition, whether from America, Cuba, the Caribbean, France, Britain, Ghana or Zaire tended to dominate the music scene. More recently however, Ivorian stars have worked hard to prove their cultural heritage and have recently begun to spread their appeal into neighbouring countries. Modern Ivorian music really started in the 1960s. The Bete and the Atche proved to be the most astute musicians in the country, producing more stars and bands than other ethnic groups. This can be partly explained by the love of these two groups for singing and dancing while other ethnic groups tended to regard musicians in general as social failures, people too lazy to be farmers or not good enough to be educated. This was not an unusual attitude in Africa where musicians were often regarded as womanisers, wasters and people not to be taken seriously. Indeed, the history of modern music in Africa is redolent with this attitude that musicians were somehow unworthy of consideration and that the worst thing that could happen to parents was for their offspring either to become or become involved with musicians. The most popular bands during the 1960s were Yapi Jazz, Anoma Barou Felix and his Ivoiris Band from Adzope, N'Douba Simon from Abiousso, Les Souers Comoe from Prikro and the band of Napounou Amedee Pierre from Soubre in the mid-west. Amedee Pierre played local music during the 1960s and later, in the 1970s made even more popular sounds such as the 'Soklokpeu' and 'Dope'. He rose to fame with a song called 'Bon Café de Côte d'Ivoire'. Fax Clark, from Tabou in the south-west, had a big success with 'Akpongbo'. A trumpeter, his sound was taken up by musicians throughout the country and although originally a Baule sound, it was enjoyed by the public throughout the country. Mamadou Doumbia was another pioneer from the north who chose to dwell on the subject of male-female relationships. Finally, in the late 1960s François Lougah returned from France with a single entitled 'Pekoussa' which was typical of his native Lokota region in the mid-west. He retained his popularity with a prolific recording output and exciting stage performances. The 1970s witnessed the emergence of new bands and stars while a few of the older groups managed to retain their popularity. The Grands Columbia D'Adzope, led by Okoi Seka Athenase, from Affery in the south-east, rose to fame with their songs in Atche while focusing on women's infidelity, hypocrisy and proverbs. They also sang a number of love songs which for Akans was unusual. Later they turned to the more congolese influenced sound known as soukous or cavacha (kabacha) which was then more fashionable and sold better. Appiah Moro and Les Cantadores were just two of the bands from Bongouanou in the east who became popular amongst the Agni playing this style. Another singer popular amongst the people was Gueli Jean from Guiglo in the west. He was the first Guere to sing in his native language for a national audience. Another, more local, success came from Les Rossignols d'Ananquie of Adzope, who were never famous like Les Grands Columbians but made a name in the Atche region. In 1978 another singer rose to national prominence with a single entitled 'Trahison'. Named Eba Aka Jerome from Abiousso, he sang about the infidelity of women (seemingly a favourite theme amongst Ivorians). Perhaps the most famous of all Ivorian singers was Ernesto Dje-Dje from Daboa in the mid-west. He first emerged in the 1970s and remained popular until his death in 1983. He was responsible for bringing Ziglibithy to the fore. This is a Bete dance rhythm which he sought to modernise, thus demonstrating to fellow Ivorians that they should make increasing commercial use of their indigenous musical heritage. Ziglibithy was a highly rhythmic dance which Dje-Dje mastered completely. He would stop and dance sideways, shaking his shoulders to an irresistible sound which found appreciative audiences across the country. His style inspired dozens of other musicians with such hits as 'Zibote' and 'Aguisse'. He was amongst the first to export Ivorian music to neighbouring countries, making an impact in Burkina Faso, Togo and Zaire.

The next major star to make an impact was Daouda, a TV technician, who rose to fame in 1977 with a humorous song about 'mammy-wagon' buses, which were then about to be abolished in Abidjan. Since then his career has moved on to an international level with hits in Paris, and in London with the Stern's album *Le Sentimental*.

The twin brothers Doh Albert and Houon Pierre, also made the the charts in 1978 singing about social problems. With a father from Guiglo in the west and a mother from Abiousso, Doh sang in Anwi while Pierre sang in his father's tongue. During the 1970s several Ivorian musicians returned from Paris to play for their countrymen. N'Goran Jimmy Hyacinthe eventually settled in Côte d'Ivoire after his band, Bozambo, collapsed. In 1982 he decided to modernise the 'goli', a Baule dance, and was seen on TV dressed in Baule cloth and performing original music. Since then he has become one of the best producers in West Africa.

Another 'returnee' was the singer Obui Maufelui from Anyama who played local Atche music, singing about social problems and dealing with them in a light-hearted way. Bally Spinto was another who returned after several years abroad, becoming exceptionally popular in the early 1980s. Generally speaking, the 1980s saw a revitalisation of Ivorian music. It became more respectable in the eyes of the public and a hit parade chart was established on national radio leading to the creation of a national music award – the 'Belier d'Or'. Bally Spinto took the title in 1982 with an album entitled *Taxi Sognon*. Meanwhile Dje-Dje's hard work also brought its rewards, making him the country's leading musician. The Ziglibithy sound was taken up by another Bete singer, Jean Baptiste Zibodi, who explored other Bete styles such as Akoukou – a popular Bete dance which has been taken up by other musicians.

Then Alpha Blondy appeared – perhaps the country's most popular musical star and a guaranteed earner of foreign exchange for the country. Born in the north, Alpha rose to prominence in 1982 with the hit single 'Brigadier Sabari' and the second hit 'Opération Coupe de Poine' about a police crackdown on Abidjan gangsters. Specialising in reggae, Alpha quickly established an international reputation in Africa and Europe with his thundering reggae beat, his stylish appearance and his amazing live shows where, during 'Opération' he imitated in gesticulation someone being beaten by police officers.

Of the female Ivorian singers Aicha Kone is the most famous. Born in Odienne in the north of the country, she has a fine soprano voice and sings in Bambara, making it easier for her music to be appreciated in neighbouring countries. She first hit the national scene in the late 1970s with several hits including 'Degny Keleny'. However it was her 1982 album with Jimmy Hyacinthe which really established her national reputation. The second major female star is Jane Agnimel from Dabou in the south of the country. She started her career singing with L'Orchestre RTI, then under the musical direction of Manu Dibango. In the wake of these two stars are several new talents including Virginie Gaudji from Gagnea, who had a major success in 1982 with a song produced by the Malian producer Boncana Maiga, and Dianne Solo.

Côte d'Ivoire has always proved to be a country open to external musical influences and in many ways this has stunted the development of an indigenous Ivorian sound.   During the 1960s, the Ivorian market was dominated by the music of Zaire with Franco, Dr Nico and Rochereau in the forefront.   Then, towards the end of the decade, Ghanaian highlife made substantial inroads in the market before the arrival of American soul music in the form of James Brown took the country by storm. At the same time, the Beatles also found an appreciative audience while the love songs of metropolitan France maintained a steady position. The Zairean musical invasion continued throughout the 1970s with even leading musicians like Okoi Athenase being forced to play soukous or 'cavacha' to retain an audience. The mid-1970s witnessed an extraordinary growth in the market for Kenyan music, while the Afro-beat of Fela, particularly 'Lady' and 'Shakara' swept the country.   Even Sir Victor Uwaifo and Ebenezer Obey managed to cash in on the popularity of Nigerian music. By the late 1970s, reggae and its superstars had started to influence popular taste in Côte d'Ivoire. Throughout these two decades Ivorian music languished in the background, leading Dibango to comment that while the country had many good musicians it had no music. This was of course a vast exaggeration, but in the sense that the country had not yet produced a truly Pan-African star, his sentiments are understandable.

The musical invasion of Côte d'Ivoire was not restricted to musicians from other African countries. Cuban music had long been popular and by the late 1970s the Antillean music of bands like Coupe Cloue was finding a ready market. The impact of disco music also served to push Ivorian styles even further into the background. But by the late 1970s and the early 1980s the situation was changing rapidly.   Dje-Dje, Spinto and Lougah all began to rediscover their musical roots and during a period of extraordinary musical creativity returned to the Ivorian cultural heritage for musical inspiration. A new era of awareness dawned in the country with new dances and rhythms emerging everywhere. Public appreciation of their efforts in turn provided these musicians with a record market to exploit. Traditional idioms and instruments were increasingly utilised to establish a distinctly Ivorian sound. Sadly, the Ivorian record industry failed to match the development of the music and by the mid-1980s not only were the leading musicians making the trek to Paris to record but foreign music was making something of a comeback. But the talent is there and it only remains to be seen whether record industry executives are prepared to support the musicians and thus expose the living vitality of music in Côte d'Ivoire to a wider international market.

Traditional Music

1962	OCR 34	MusiqueBaoule-Kode
	OCR 48	Musiques Gouro
	OCR 52	Musiques Dans
	ETH 4476	The Baoule of Ivory Coast
	SOR 6	Côte d'Ivoire – Musique Baoule
	BM30L 2308	Music of the Senufo
1978	824 806	Ensemble Nationale de la Côte d'Ivoire Vol.1
	824 807	Ensemble Nationale de la Côte d'Ivoire Vol.2

Contemporary Music

1976	SAF 50036	François Lougah: Au Zaire (Accompanied by Les Redoubtables with Tabu Ley.)
	SMP 6030	Francois Lougah: Benediction
1977		Ernesto Dje-Dje: Zibote
		Ernesto Dje-Dje: Ziglibithy
1978	DIS001	Eba Aka Jerome et L'Orc Sanwi Star: Trahison
1978	SAF 50069	Coulibaly Notin: 18th Anniversaire de l'Independence de Côte d'Ivoire
	SAF 61010	Coulibaly Notin: 18th Anniversaire de l'Independence de Côte d'Ivoire
1978	360 012	Orc. De La RTI (The official orchestra of Radiodiffusion Télévision Ivorienne. Directed by Manu Dibango, this big band plays both classics and some original compositions – including 'El Manicero'.)
1981	DS 0808	Okoi Seka Athanase et Les Grands Columbians
1985	OSA 2085	Okoi Seka Athanase de L'Adjomake: Special Mix 85 (Okoi plays a lilting dance music with strong soukous overtones. His most recent recording featured the combined talents of Jimmy Hyacinthe, Jimmy and Fredo and Prospero.)
1982	BK 001	Luckson Padaud: Vol.1 Bithye
	SHA 0036	Luckson Padaud: Vol.2 Agnon-Nouke

1983	AR 002	Luckson Padaud Hommage a Ernesto Dje-Dje
	ZIB 001	J.B. Zibodi: Wazie Meo
		(Rhythm guitarist and singer, he followed in the style of Dje-Dje but his use of sophisticated recording equipment and occasional use of reggae beat carries him beyond the master of Ziglibithy.)
1983	WAM 793010	Aicha Kone: Aminata
	KS 434	Aicha Kone: La Chanson de la Chance
1984	REF 1227	Tony Blesson: Hon Sio Mai Gnin
	K 4240	Anouman Brouh Felix 'Sacoche'
		(Poet and philosopher – he has made it his task to protect the national culture.)
1984	SAS 055	Jane Agnimel: Zoum (Talented female singer, she sang with Dibango and Bebe Manga. She has toured widely in Africa, releasing her first LP in 1980.)
1984	SHA 041	Blissi Tebil: Ziglibithy – La Continuité
		(A fast, up-tempo album with the curious jerky feel associated with the genre – slightly slower than the best Makossa.)
1984	SK 84001	Tina Dakouri: Inoneka-Nokeka
	TAN 7003	Maître Gazonga: Les Jaloux Saboteurs
	TAN 7004	Meta and Feza: Surprise
1985	ASLP 991	Manana Antoine: Amour Cherche Amour
1985	PRD 9008	Kassiry: Afrika (Sophisticated Afro-funk jazz.)
1985	425 004	Woya: Kacou Ananze
1985	TAN 7013	Ismael Isaac et Les Frères Keita: Liberté
		(A new big band, includes hit single 'Mandela'.)
1985	PMA 003	Willy Darling: Joe (Ivorian vocalist based in Kumasi where he recorded this reggae album with the help of Eric Agyeman and Nana Tuffuor.)
1986	LS 89	Jimmy Hyacinthe: Retro
	CEL 6777	Nyanka Bell: If You Came to Go
		(Following up on her 1984 single hit 'Ami-O', here accompanied by members of the Antilles group Kassav.)

| 111 281 | Fifi Dallo: Oh Africa! (Born into a family of Ivorian griots, Fifi moved to Paris where she recorded this with Rigo, Diblo and Armando from Zaire.) |

Daouda. (b. Tou Kone Daouda, Abidjan, Côte d'Ivoire). A singer and composer, Daouda was born in Abidjan of Burkinabe parents. He began his career as a TV technician. He was however also a talented amateur singer and guitarist whose big break came when he was overheard practising in the studio and was invited to appear on TV and make a record. In 1976 he released his first single 'Les Gbakas d'Abidjan'. The public demanded more of his sweet soukous and so he turned to music as a full-time career releasing his second single, 'Le Villageons', in 1977. A gifted lyricist, Daouda introduced Ivorian audiences to his unique mixture of soukous, makossa and local rhythms. In 1978 he released the first version of *Mon Couer Balance*. Several more LPs followed in quick succession as Daouda established his national reputation. However, his biggest breakthrough came in 1983 with the international release of a reworked version of his first LP on the London based Sterns label – *Le Sentimental*. With the help of Souzy Kasseya, Alhadji Toure, Jimmy Hyacinthe and Jimmy and Fredo (one of Africa's hottest horn sections), the album was an instant hit in the francophone world. In 1985 he released the long-awaited *La Femme de Mon Patron* with the help of several Cameroonian musicians. Now based in Paris, he has established a truly international reputation.

1978		Mon Coeur Balance
1979		Vive La Musique
1980		Le Margouillat
1982	SA 3000005	Le Salsa
1983		Le Sentimental
1984	ST 1008	Le Sentimental
1985		La Femme De Mon Patron

Glou, Emile. Comedian, dancer and singer. Emile Glou was born at Guiglo and started his career in 1967 after four years experience with the Ivorian national ballet. In 1970 he started his own troupe, touring Africa and visiting Paris in 1976. With this success, he was able to start his own theatre company which toured several European countries during the late 1970s.

| MRC 003 | Musiques, Chants et Rythmes de Côte d'Ivoire |

Bozambo. An early African supergroup, Bozambo was formed in 1966 in Abidjan by five young men including Jimmy Hyacinthe, Rato Venance,

Georges Ouedrago (from Upper Volta), Adel Dabo and Coco Jean-Pierre. The band was ambitious and in an effort to conquer the European market they moved to Paris. However talent alone was not enough and they moved on to Munich where they spent four years playing the clubs. In 1976 they returned to Paris to make their first LP. The band released several more LPs but their lack of commercial succes forced them to split up in the late 1970s.

1976	CL 02	M'babila
1977	CLS 05	Africa

Blondy, Alpha (b. Sedou Kone, 1953, Dimbokoro, Côte d'Ivoire.) African reggae singer-composer. At high school he created an Afro-rock band Atomic Vibrations, then moved to Liberia to improve his English and from there he progressed to the USA, spending two years studying trade and English at Columbia University. He recorded six reggae numbers in Jamaica but had no money to release them. On his return to Côte d'Ivoire his parents committed him to a psychiatric hospital for two years because of his Rasta beliefs. He continued to sing and prepare English translations for Ivorian TV. Following a TV appearance in 1982 he was given the chance to record his first album, *Jah Glory*, released in June 1983 to become a massive hit all over West Africa, with videos, tapes and T-shirt merchandising. Several songs became standards. In mid-1984 he released a single 'Rasta Poue!' and later came the LP *Cocody Rock* on the Pathe-Marconi label. Following this enormous hit, he played to 60,000 people in Paris. He sings in Dioula, English and French, with a strong Rasta flavour to his delivery of African proverbs. In 1985 Alpha Blondy sustained his magic with the hit album *Apartheid is Nazism*, re-released in the UK by Sterns in 1986. Following his 1986 recording *Jerusalem* he announced a personal crusade to unite his Rasta philosophy with the Moslem culture of his people. In 1987 he received the first 'Senghor' award as the best male singer in francophone Africa.

1983	Jah Glory
1984	Cocody Rock
1985	Apartheid (Also STERNS 1017)
1986	Jerusalem (Also STERNS 1020)

8
Mali

Mali, a savannah state of the western Sahel, has a long and glorious history usually associated with the ancient Mali kingdom of Mansa Musa. The Mali empire benefited from its central position on the trans-Sahara routes as an inland entrepot for the slave, gold, salt and commodity trades. A variety of ethnic groups occupy the present Mali nation state including the Dogon, Peul, Mandingo and Songhai. An ancient history, an Islamic veneer and French colonialism have all combined to produce a great cultural and musical diversity. The Dogon, for example, live on a plateau and are closely related to the Mandingo. Traditionally farmers, their entire life is related to a vast cosmology which inspires and directs their activities. Relative isolation and the strength of their beliefs have contributed to the development of a unique art form. Utilising drums, bells, flutes and horn trumpets, their music is both recreational and functional – 'the essence of their music is to stir souls'. The other ethnic groups likewise developed their own style of music and several records are available which demonstrate the variety of these musical traditions.

The Mande-speaking peoples have, however, remained dominant. The old empire lost its unity in the fifteenth century and reverted to several small states, with the Bambara people near the Guinea-Mali border and the Mandingos to the west as far as the Gambia. Manding society retains the traditional craft groups or castes, which often have ritual responsibilities as well as their professional obligations. Prominent among these are the musician caste of jalis (dyelia). Famous names associated with jaliya, such as Konte, Kouyate, Jobarteh (Diabateh) and Suso are now becoming familiar in the west. Jalis are griots who maintain the oral literature of the people including the histories of the ancient empire and family genealogies. The mandingo griots use two of the most beautiful and evocative instruments in Africa – the kora, a 21-string harp/lute and the balo (balafon or xylophone). The power of a griot is assessed by the quality and accuracy of his narrative. When applied to praise song this makes a griot an indispensable ally to the rich and famous. Tradition, however, gives griots the status of virtual beggars in their own communities, but knowledge of ritual and custom keeps them close to the secrets of sorcerers and as 'wizards' their influence is great. Today griots are widespread throughout

MALI

the region. Their music remains largely untouched by western influences but listeners can often discover connections with blues and jazz patterns. There are two strains of music from the Bambara and Mandingo although both use the same instrumental language. The first, which retains original inflexions and is considered 'cool', is meditative yet physically involving, with an undeniable swing often driven on by the resonant tone of the balafon. The music style found in The Gambia is more flamboyant, virtuoso with less insistence on the ensemble and more individual expression.

By the mid-twentieth century various external influences had begun to affect the development of traditional music. Western instruments became available while Cuban and congolese music helped shape the modern urban sound. Mali became independent in 1960 and in a demonstration of Pan-African solidarity joined the Ghana-Guinea union. State socialism played a part in the development of music with the creation of officially sponsored bands.

Today Malian music encompasses the entire range of musical expression. The griot tradition is maintained in both traditional and modern music. Batourou Sekou Kouyate and Bazoumba Sissoko, 'The Old Lion', are among the most popular. Other artistes combine traditions by adapting new songs to traditional airs. Fanta Sacko, for example, has established a national reputation at a young age with her Jamana-Kura (New Age), a genre in which Mokontafe Sacko enjoys a similar reputation. Fanta Damba, Ali Farka Touré and Sory Bamba also occupy this musical middle ground. Finally there are the urban electric groups of the 1970s and 1980s. The best-known bands are the Rail Band and the Ambassadeurs but there are hundreds of other guitar bands in the major urban centres.

Traditional Music

	OCR 33	Les Dogons: Les Chants de la Vie
1980s	OCR558 662/663	Ousmane Sacko and Yiakare Diabate: 'La Nuit des Griots' (As husband and wife, they have toured Europe several times. Two of Mali's outstanding singers, they demonstrate many varieties of Malian music. Sacko, who also plays guitar, is a balladeer well known for his soaring melodies and haunting voice. Their repertoire includes not only traditional songs about the Malian past but also new material.)
1970s	BM 30L 250	Les Mandingues: Le Mali Des Steppes et Des Savanes
	BM 30L 2502	Les Peuls: Le Mali du Fleuve
	BM 30L 2503	Les Songoy: Le Mali des Sables
	BM 30L 2504	L'Ensemble Instrumental du Mali
	BM 30L 2505	Cordes Anciennes: Batourou Sekou Kouyate
	BM 30L 2551	Musique du Mali: Fanta Sacko
	BM 30L 3552	Musique du Mali: Bazoumana Sissoko 1
	BM 30L 3553	Musique de Mali: Bazoumana Sissoko 2
	CV 1272	Musique Folklorique du Monde 'Tombouctou'
	VP 8326	Epic, Historical, Political and Propaganda Songs of the Socialist Government of Modibo Keita (1960–6) Vol. 1. (Kora music with extensive footnotes in Italian.)
	VP 8327	Epic Speeches Vol.2
	RS 1221	Racines Sall: Special Chants Religieux

(Born at Kayes, Racines entered an Islamic school at the age of five, learned the Koran by heart and attended Islamic conferences with his father. He developed a passion for religious music and many of his compositions were aired on Radio Mali. In 1978 he launched his own artistic troupe.)

MAO 1040   Sandaly and Nmawa Kante: Foudou. (Backed by the Ambassadeurs Internationaux, Sandaly and Nmawa are two great composers of the famous family 'Griotte du Mandingue'.)

SAF 50077   Sidiki Diabate: Rythmes et Chants du Mali

Bamba, Sory. Sory Bamba is regarded as the moderniser of Dogon folklore. Born in the south-east of the country, Sory has adapted folk traditions using modern instruments and arrangements.

1979	SAF 50097	Sory Bamba; Mayal
	SON 8203	Faux Galant
	SON 8206	Yayoroba

Monkontafe Safo

SAF 50012	Farafina Moussou
SAF 5002	Special
SAF 50033	Mali Balon Tan Nau
SAF 50059	Badialo Siby (with traditional ensemble)

Damba, Fanta. Born in Segou in Mali, Fanta Damba is known to her many admirers as 'La Grande Vedette Malienne'. She was born into a well-known family of griots and started singing as a child. Singing in Bambara, she started recordings in the early 1960s, marking herself out as one of the leading interpreters of Mali's oral traditions. She has been married twice and has five children. Her first husband was a guitarist while her present husband acts as her manager. During the 1960s she released many singles which established her reputation as a regional as well as a national star. In 1975 she formed her own folk group to accompany her on stage and is now often joined on stage by her two daughters, Nana and Aminata. Whether singing solo, or accompanied by kora and/or guitar, she continues to extend her international reputation with fresh recordings. She has also recorded several albums with the Malian kora master, Batourou Sekou Kouyate.

1960s	BM 30L 2506	La Tradition Epique
1970s	SON 8201	Loterie Nationale (with Sekou Kouyate)

	SON 8202	Hamet
	ESP 7518	Mamadou Magadji
1976	KLP 1041	Mamaya
	SON 8205	Ousmane Bamara (with Sekou Kouyate)
1977	SON 8210	Samega 1980s
	CEL 6637	Bahamadou Simogo

Kouyate, Sekou Batourou. Perhaps the most famous of all Malian kora players.

	KR 28	Keme Bourama
1976	KLP 1041	Mamaya

Farka, Ali Touré. Malian singer-guitarist who plays in a neo-traditional style which many people consider to be the closest thing to blues to have originated in Africa. For this reason, his rootsy blues sound has found appreciative audiences amongst blues lovers throughout the world.

SAF 50013	Bandolobourou
SAF 50016	Ali Farka Touré
SAF 50020	Special
SAF 50032	Biennale
SAF 50060	Yer Sabou Yerkoy

Ambassadeurs, Les. Big band from Mali formed in early 1970s. The story of Les Ambassadeurs Du Mali cannot be separated from that of Salif Keita (vocalist and composer) and Kante Manfila (guitarist, composer and leader of the Orchestra). Salif Keita was born in Djoliba and educated in the capital – Bamako. He started the career with the Rail Band, one of the most prestigious of all Malian bands which received government sponsorship in an effort to safeguard the development of Malian culture. In 1973 Keita left the Rail Band to join Les Ambassadeurs and, with the help of Manfila, extended the repertoire of the band by adding local rhythms and melodies to their existing Congo-Cuban sound. The results can be heard on the three excellent albums from 1977 on the Safari label. By 1977, the reputation of Keita and the band had extended beyond the confines of Mali and in the same year Keita was given a national award by President Sekou Touré of Guinea. In reply, Keita composed what was to become his most successful song, 'Mandjou', telling the history of the people of Mali and paying homage to Sekou Touré. This was soon followed by 'Primpin' which also became a hit throughout West Africa. In the wake of these successes, Keita and Manfila left Mali for Abidjan, capital of Côte D'Ivoire and the music capital of francophone West Africa. By this time Keita was determined to crack the international market and he duly renamed the band Les

Ambassadeurs Internationaux in recognition of his growing stature. Featuring Keita's stunning voice, fluent guitar and sax solos and an unmistakably overall Islamic sound, the band became one of the most popular in the region. Sadly however, tension developed between Keita and Manfila and they eventually parted company with Keita forming a new outfit – Super Ambassadeurs. More recently, Keita has been performing regularly in Europe, playing to appreciative audiences and enhancing his reputation as one of Africa's most gifted singers.

1977	SAF 50014	Les Ambassadeurs Du Motel
	SAF 50030	Les Ambassadeurs de Bamako Vol. 1
	SAF 50031	Les Ambassadeurs de Bamako Vol. 2 1980s
	CEL 6635	Djougouya
	CEL 6640	Best of The Ambassadeurs
1984	CEL 6717	Tounkan
	CEL 6721	Mandjou
	ROUND 5013	Dance Music From Mali
	DS 7986	Les Ambassadeurs Internationaux.

Keita, Salif

| 1987 | 240751 | Soro (Keita's first solo album. Also STERNS 1020.) |

Kouyate, Ousmane. An agriculturalist by training, Ousmane now plays guitar with Les Ambassadeurs. He has made two LPs, including *Kefimba*, featuring members of Bembeya Jazz from Guinea. He performs regularly with Salif Keita in Europe.

| 1985 | OK 8010 | Kefimba |

Super Djata. Led by Zani Diabate, Super Djata is currently one of the hottest bands in Mali with a growing international reputation.

| 1985 | MM85 1001 | Super Djata |

Rail Band. Along with Les Ambassadeurs, the Rail Band of the Buffet Hôtel de La Gare de Bamako is one of Mali's most popular bands. Now 14 strong, the band was founded in 1970 with the sponsorship of the Ministry of Information. Through the hotels division of the National Railway Company, a permanent venue was secured for the band at the Station Hotel in Bamako. Singing in Bambara,   a Mandingo language understood in Mali, Guinea, the Gambia and parts of Senegal, the band adapted both traditional kora and balafon rhythms and Islamic vocal styles to the demands of modern urban pop music. Like the majority of bands in Mali, the Rail Band depended heavily on government support. Private bands were forced to buy their own equipment while the irregularity of power supply made runnng a private band an extremely risky business. However, while state sponsorship helped alleviate these problems it also brought with it interference in the day-to-day management of the band's affairs. In 1975, the Rail Band made a successful tour of Nigeria, pressing five LPs on their return. Despite many personnel changes, including the arrival and departure of Salif Keita, the band continued to entertain Bamako music fans throughout the 1970s. By the 1980s the band had established a secure reputation throughout francophone West Africa and in 1985 made their international breakthrough with their first British release.

1970	BM 30L 2605	Sunjata
1975	HNLX 5146	Soundiata
	KLP 1040	Kandoun
1970s	KLP 1042	Concert Rail Band du Mali
	KLP 1043	Melodias Rail Band du Mali
1979	LS 24	Quedraogo Mamadou et L'Orch. Super Rail Band
	LS 25	Affair Social
1985	ORB 001	New Dimensions in Rail Culture

Maravillas. L'Orchestre Maravillas De Mali was formed in 1965 when a group of Malians studying music in Cuba organised a performance for the Guinean Embassy in Havana. Playing a mixture of Latin styles, including cha chas, montunos and boleros, the band often appeared on Cuban TV and toured the island regularly. However the band did not neglect its African roots as is apparent on the Radio Mali album.

| 1985 | EGR 6112 | Radio Mali |

Super Biton. Another hot band from Bamako, Super Biton have been in existence since the early 1960s. They have toured extensively in West Africa and since 1983 they have made three visits to Europe under the leadership of trumpeter Amadou Ba.

| 1983 | TAN 7008 | Balandzan |
| 1986 | BP 13 | Super Biton de Segou |

Ama Maiga

| 1983 | 79426 | Ama Maiga (Contemporary kora fusion) |

GUINEA—BISSAU/GUINEA

9
Guinea

Guinea's relative isolation from the rest of Africa during the years of Sekou Touré's presidency has meant that very little research has been conducted into the country's culture. Situated on the coast of West Africa, it is bordered by Côte d'Ivoire, Mali, Senegal and Guinea-Bissau and completely surrounds the two smaller republics of Liberia and Sierre Leone. Inevitably, given the arbitrariness of colonial boundaries, Guinea straddles several distinct cultural and ethnic divisions, sharing its people and culture with its close neighbours. Specific mention should be made of the Malinke (the Mandingo) and the Foulah in the north of the country, whose musical culture is so rich and influential that several observers have dubbed northern Guinea, along with Mali and Senegal, as comprising the 'Golden Triangle' of West African music. This generalisation is particularly pertinent in relation to the kora traditions of West Africa.

Other major ethnic groups in Guinea include the Susu, the Kissi, the Toma, the Guerze, the Baga and the Dialonke. Each developed a distinct musical culture, a few of which are represented on record. These cultures utilised a variety of instruments; drums, balafons, guitars and koras to which were added the usual selection of western instruments – keyboards, electric guitars, jazz drums and brass.

Guinea came under French colonial rule towards the end of the last century. However when France offered to establish a larger francophone community for its colonies in West Africa, Guinea alone refused and became the first independent state in francophone Africa. Under the leadership of Sekou Touré, Guinea pursued a radical path in comparison with its neighbours and with the help of Nkrumah of Ghana and economic assistance from the Soviet bloc established a reputation as a progressive and radical state. However the sudden departure of the French caused severe problems for the country. The French stripped the country bare, burning all office files, throwing weapons in the river and generally trying to cripple the fledgling state. But these acts of wanton destruction only served to stiffen the resolve of the Guinean people. E.T. Mensah and the Tempos visited Conakry, the capital, only a few weeks after the departure of the French and it is perhaps worth recounting the recollections of one of the Ghanaian musicians.

My impression of the town was that the people were determined. They were working for months without pay, although food was being supplied by the Army and the Police. Yet we couldn't see any sign of grievance. Stealing had actually disappeared. The country had been left naked and the little that someone had, if you stole it, you were a saboteur.

During the late 1950s, the most popular music in the major cities – Conakry, Kankan, Kindia, Labe and N'Zerekore – was the cha cha, the bolero and the samba. However, very few Guineans performed in the modern bands and in most of the hotels and clubs the musicians were all European. As a result, French music was widely played, with negative effects on the development of a modern Guinean musical culture. However, with Independence, modern musical styles emerged, using amplified electric instruments. Dozens of bands sprang up, among them Bembeya Jazz, Les Amazones and Les Balladins. New influences appeared, including Ghanaian highlife, perhaps reflecting the strong relations existing between Nkrumah and Sekou Touré. In 1959 Ghana, Guinea and Mali established a regional union which they hoped would pave the way for a truly Pan-African Union. For its part, the ruling party in Guinea – the PDG – played a central role in the development of a contemporary national musical culture. It founded and directly sponsored several bands, including Les Amazones, and helped establish a national recording company with whom the majority of Guinean musicians record. Finally, in an effort both to unite the nation and encourage the development of Guinean traditional music, the PDG organised annual musical festivals where regional musicians came together in Conakry to compete for prizes. With a strong and lively traditional culture and a distinct modern musical style, Guinea is in the forefront of modern African music. It remains to be seen whether changes in the style of government, following the death of Sekou Touré, will lead to a more commercial approach to the development of modern Guinean music.

Traditional Music

1953	LDM 30107	Music of the Toma of Guinea
	CPTX 240746	Escale En Guinée
	LDM 30116	Music From West Africa: Mandinka and Baule Music
	LDM 30113	Music Malinke du Guinea
	SAF 50034	Bah-Sadio: Folklore Peu (accompanied by guitar)
	SAF 50053	Fode Youla: Soleil du Guinea (Songs and dances from Guinea and Sierra Leone.)
	SLP 33	Les Rythmes et Les Chants Sacrés

SLP 43	Folklore et Ensembles Instrumentaux
SLP 42	11th Festival National Des Arts et De La Culture.
SLP 25	Trio Federal de Pointe (A compilation featuring Kebendo Jazz, Horoya Band and Niandan Jazz)

Kouyate, Sory Kandia. Known as 'The Itinerant Ambassador of African Song', Kouyate started his career as a singer and dancer with Ballets Africaines before moving on to join a bigger cultural group known as Djoliba National. He then took up a position as artistic director of the Ensemble Instrumental et Choral de la Voix de la Révolution. He remained with them for a decade while working simultaneously with Keletigui et Les Tambourins. With an outstanding tenor voice, he was awarded the first prize in 1970 by the Charles Cros Académie in Paris. He subsequently linked up with two other musicians to tour Africa, playing in many countries and picking up aspects of traditional culture wherever they went. He also performed regularly with a much bigger band, Les Tambourins, with whom he collaborated through his close friend, Keletigui. Les Tambourins at that time featured Kouyate Dieli Sory, regarded by many as Guinea's best balafon player. Kandia has released several albums including the classic three-volume *L'Epopée du Mandingue*, recounting the medieval history of the Mandingo people.

1970s	SLP 12	Grand Prix du Disque
1970	SLP 2	Tara
	SLP 36	L'Epopée du Mandingue Vol. 1
	SLP 37	L'Epopée du Mandingue Vol. 2
	SLP 38	L'Epopée du Mandingue Vol. 3

Bembeya Jazz. Formed in Beyla, Guinea, 1961, Bembeya Jazz have played a central role in the musical development of post-colonial Guinea. The band, or more properly orchestra, fluctuates in number between 15 and 25, and comprises a basic line-up of electric guitars, horns, vocals and percussion. The sound they produce is unique in Africa – a sophisticated blend of indigenous musical styles, Congo influences, Islamic traditions and the genuine Cuban rumba. The band was founded by Aboubacar Demba Camara in 1961, becoming the offical Guinean National Orchestra in 1966. As band-leader, composer, arranger and custodian of Guinea's national traditions, Aboubacar's untimely death in a car crash in 1973 robbed Bembeya of their most vital force. The band abandoned recording and live shows for three years following his death. During the 1960s and 1970s, Bembeya toured widely in Africa, making the occasional visit to Moscow to consolidate Soviet-Guinean ties. They are also one of the few African bands to have visited Cuba. By the late 1970s Bembeya had succeeded in establishing a distinctively Guinean sound and held a reputation throughout Africa. In 1985 the band visited Europe, recording several new albums and featuring on the Dutch video *African Roots*. The lead guitarist Sekou Diabate, 'Diamond Fingers', also recorded a solo album, supported by the rest of the band.

1970s	SLP 4	Djanf Amagni
1971	SLP 24	10 Ans De Success
	SLP 39	Parade Africain
	SLP 44	Special Recueil Souvenir
1978	SLP 59	Le Defi
1982	SLP 61	La Continuité
	SLP 64	Regard Sur Le Passé
	SLP 65	Memoire de Aboubacar Camara
	SLP 66	Discotheque '76
1985	F1014785	African Roots (Compilation)
1985	ESP 8418	Télégramme
	ESP 8419	Montagne
1986	ESP 8430	Bembeya Jazz National
	ESP 8431	Yekeke

Doumbia, Balla (b. Guinea, 1912). Balla Doumbia started learning balafon at the age of three. By the time he was 19, he was performing in public. Shortly afterwards he migrated to Mali where he established a national reputation as 'Le Parleur de Balafon'. He then left Mali for Senegal where he worked under the marabout Tiemoko Diawara. Later in his career he toured both the UK and the USA accompanied by the dancers from Mansour Gueye. He then took up an academic appointment as Professor of Balafon at the School of Arts in the University of Dakar. On the record listed below (his only available album) he is featured playing balafon accompanied by kora and a second balafon.

1981	SAF 50109	Balla Doumbia et Son Ensemble

Kante, Mory (b. Kissidougou, Guinea, early 1950s). Mory Kante was born into a family of famous musicians and griots. At the age of seven he was sent to the school of Oral Tradition to learn the first principles of the griot tradition and in time he joined the famous Rail Band of Bamako as a singer. This was the first time that his traditional heritage and training had come into contact with modern African urban pop and these early experiments in fusion music quickly made him a favourite with Bamako audiences. However, despite the band's popularity (and that of the rival Ambassadeurs), economic circumstances forced a move in 1977 to Abidjan. He subsequently left the Rail Band to pursue a solo career, forming an enormous group of 35 musicians and dancers. By the early 1980s he had established a reputation which stretched far beyond the confines of Mali, Guinea and Côte d'Ivoire and in 1981, having attracted the interest of Ebony Records, he recorded his first album with the assistance of Abdoulaye Soumare, an experienced sound engineer who had previously worked with Stevie Wonder. His first release proved to be an immediate success and Mory moved to Paris with a new group called Les Milieus Branches. The new band toured widely, playing over 100 shows in Europe and Africa. His music during this period can best be described as eclectic, with a conscious effort to prove that all modern dance styles, from salsa to breakdance, originated in Africa. He also tried to establish a new genre, where balafon and synthesiser met on equal terms. After a couple of years out of the limelight, Mory Kante resurfaced in 1984 with the classic album *A Paris*, mixing traditional and modern with the help of established session men like Jules Kamga, Doh Albert and Mobio Venance. His music is clear and simple, combining kora with brass and electric piano to produce a sound which fuses funk, soul and rock with the inspiration of traditional African music. In 1985 he collaborated with many other African musicians in the Tam Tam Pour L'Ethiopie project – Africa's answer to Band-Aid. By the mid-1980s he was performing regularly in Europe and Africa, with a group reinforced by the recruitment of the female horn section from the Afro-British group Orchestra Jazira.

1980s	LS 73	A Paris
1986	(Barclay)	10 Cola Nuts

Amazones, Les. All-female dance band, formed in Guinea in 1961. Les Amazones are today one of the outstanding bands to have emerged from Guinea. The band, usually comprising between 15 to 20 musicians, is sponsored by the Guinean Police Force and the women are all serving officers in the gendarmerie. Like Bembeya, the group has undergone numerous personnel changes over the last two decades, since it was set up by Keletigui Traore. Playing a mixture of traditional and Congo music, the band comprises electric guitarists, percussionists, vocalists and a full horn section. They have toured widely in Africa and have made several highly acclaimed visits to Europe. Sadly, they have only released one LP although several front-line members have released solo albums. While the band continues to enjoy massive popularity not only in Guinea but throughout Africa, they are in danger of being typecast as a 'feminist' band by western audiences. This charge is totally unjustified.

1983	SLP 76	Au Coeur de Paris

Diabate, Sona. Sona Diabate, guitarist, singer and balafon player with Les

Amazones was born into a family of traditional musicians. She speaks several languages and is the younger sister of Sekou Diabate, lead guitarist of Bembeya Jazz. She has worked with Miriam Makeba, who lived in Guinea for several years under the patronage of President Sekou Touré. She is now a full-time member of Les Amazones and recorded her first solo album in 1985 under the musical direction of Dembo Camara.

| 1985 | SLP 77 | Sons de la Savanne |

Sylla, M'Mah (b. Guinea, May 1958). An outstanding vocalist, Sylla started her career with Dirou Baab. As a solo singer with Les Amazones she recorded her first album in Paris in 1985 under the direction of Maître Mamadou. An acoustic album, featuring flutes, guitars and vocals, her first solo release is a landmark in contemporary African music.

| 1985 | SLP 78 | La Rossignol de Guinée |

African Virtuoses. Formed in 1979 by five of Guinea's most accomplished and experienced musicians, the African Virtuoses play a gentle paced acoustic style. Led by Honomou Jerome Claver (b. N'zerekore, 1951), ex-Nimba Jazz guitarist, the band comprises Sekou Diabate (b. Farranah, 1938), bass player and member of Balla and the Balladins for 18 years; Sekou Kouyate (b. Kindia, 1939), kora player and leader of Miriam Makeba's band for eight years; Abdoulaye Diabate (b. N'zerekore, 1953), solo guitarist and Fassou Habass (b. N'zerekore 1957), drummer with experience as percussionist and vocalist with Nimba Jazz.

| JBZ 002 | Nanibali |

Keletigui. Keletigui et Ses Tambourins are one of Guinea's most popular bands. Led by Keletigui Traore on sax, the band features a four-strong guitar attack, several percussionists and strong horn section and four front-line vocalists. They recorded two LPs towards the end of the 1970s, displaying their mastery of the cool and relaxed style which has become the hallmark of contemporary Guinean music.

| SLP 30 | Keletigui |
| SLP 55 | Le Retour |

Les Sofas. Known properly as Camayenne Sofa, 'Les Sofas' have proved to be one of the most influential of all Guinean bands, with a constant changeover in personnel as musicians move on to join other outfits. Currently led by François Koivogui, the band now comprises 13 members. Known in their early days as Camayenne Sextet, outstanding graduates would include Bossely Keita, Mamadou Camara and Salia Camara (now with Kaloum Star), Papa Kouyate (drummer with the Quintette Guinean de Myriam Makeba) and Ange Miguel, a vocalist currently with Les Tambourins.

SLP 52	Le Percée
SLP 56	A Grands Pas

Balladins. Formerly led by Pivvi and currently by Balla, Les Balladins have proved to be one of Guinea's most consistent bands. Comprising eight members, the band specialise in rumbas, boleros and a distinct Guinean style known as 'yankadi'.

	SLP 31	Yakhadi Gere (With Pivvi)
	SLP 47	Lumumba (With Balla)
1980	SLP 75	Objectif Perfection

22 Band. Formed in Kankan in the late 1970s.

1980	SLP 67	Venez Voir
	SLP 68	22 Band

Super Boiro. Formed in the early 1970s and currently led by the trumpeter Mamamdou Niaissa.

SLP 32	Mariama
SLP 46	Were Were
SLP 58	Super Boiro

Horoya. The Horoya Band National, led by Mitou Traore, was formed in 1965 as a 12-piece rumba band. They started playing in Kankan before moving to Conakry, the capital, where they established a permanent base.

SLP 41	Zoumana

Various

Guinea has produced many fine bands over the last two decades but sadly very little of their music has reached a wider market. Listed below are a few outstanding albums currently available outside Guinea.

SLP 1	Orc. Paillotte
SLP 2	Orc. du Jardin Du Guinea
SLP 57	Syli Authentic: Dans L'Arène
SLP 73	Le Palm Jazz de Magenta: Les Palmes du Success

SLP 70   Tropical Djoli Band: Style Savanne

Compilations. Many of the best songs by Guinea's leading bands are available on a series of excellent compilations. Featuring Bembeya, Super Boiro, Horoya, Les Sofas, Keletigui and many others, they represent a good introduction to the variety of contemporary Guinean music.

SLP 8	Guinea An 10
SLP 16	Guinea An 11
SLP 21	Guinea An 12
SLP 35	Discothèque 71
SLP 40	Discothèque 72
SLP 45	Discothèque 73

Jawara, Jali Musa (or Diawara). A Mandingo from northern Guinea, Jawara is today one of the most famous kora players both inside and outside Guinea. His fame was established in 1983 when he released one of the most outstanding albums to have emerged from Africa. A stunning blend of amplified kora, acoustic guitars, female vocals and the exquisite balafon playing of Jalimorijan Kuyateh, the recording has a mesmeric effect on listeners, which, in the words of one admirer 'haunt the memory for days'. The record was originally released in Paris in 1983 but such was its lasting quality and popular appeal that it was eventually licensed to the London based Oval label who re-released it in 1986 in an effort to maximise its distribution. It is perhaps worth quoting from the Oval sleeve notes. 'In contrast to many other forms of African music, the rhythm in this Manding music is not so much a beat as a pulse, evoking the sensation of being in a boat, rocking on the water. But despite its subtleties, the music is remarkably exhilarating. Played loud, it rouses spirits and inspires physical reactions. And once you have acquired a taste for the eerie, timeless sensuality of these women's voices, your perception of other kinds of music will be permanently altered.'

1983   TAN   Djeli Moussa Diawara (Released on Oval
                       OVLP 511 as Jali Musa Jawara)

10
Guinea-Bissau and Cape Verde

Although compelled to be a part of the lusophone (Portuguese-speaking) community, these small territories are closely related to their French speaking neighbours. Known as Portuguese Guinea until independence in 1975, Guinea-Bissau is a small coastal country nestling between the Cassamance region of southern Senegal and the much larger state of French-speaking Guinea. The original inhabitants were displaced several centuries ago by the Baga people who came from the east. The dominant culture is now Mandinka with Bissau marking the southern boundary of their territory. The Portuguese arrived in Bissau in 1446 and established slave-trading posts which became the main centres of that obnoxious trade. There were also British and French posts at various times. The boundaries between Bissau and the neighbouring states were drawn up in the nineteenth century and the country remained under Portuguese rule. During the 1960s a liberation movement, led by Amilcar Cabral, came to prominence and by 1975 independence was declared for Guinea-Bissau and the Cape Verde islands, whose people had struggled together under the colonialists. The Cape Verde islands, situated farther north off the Senegalese coast, have a more mixed Creole population and, due to ethnic differences and the poor communications between the territories, they have recently begun to drift apart economically and politically. The lusophone heritage and their common struggle in past decades remains as a tenuous link.

Musical styles in Bissau have more in common with the Gambian and Cassamance form than the Guinea/Mali sound of the closely-related Malinke people. The repertoire of the National Ensemble is very similar to that of the Gambian equivalent, with kora and balafon the most prominent instruments. The popular music, which is based on the Mandinka tradition, is often delivered in French or Portuguese. There is a handful of records available from Cobiana Jazz and Naka Ramiro. In 1986 Dulce Mario was nominated by Radio France International as a rising star to listen out for.

NCL001   Conselho Nacional de Cultura (Liberation songs in Balanta, Creole, Fula and

Mandinka.)

SMD 002	Super Mama Djombo: Festival Vol.2 (Pop music guitar band with, presumably, an earlier Vol.1.)
SEES12	Spontaneous Expression: Solidaridade
DYA81055	Naka Ramiro & l'Orchestre de la Guinea-Bissau; Je Viens d'ailleurs
SAF 50072	Jose Carlos Schwarz et le Cobina Jazz; Vol.2
SYL 8303	Tam Tam 2000
SYL 8304	Cabo Verde; Destino

11
Senegal

Until the late 1970s Senegalese music was to a great extent dominated by the imported music of Cuba and local versions of Cuban music sung in Wolof and other local languages. Traditional music, for example the kora music of the griots, remained popular and widespread but with regard to the development of modern urban styles, Senegal, like so many French colonies lagged behind anglophone Africa. The development of a distinct Senegalese style really only started with Independence and it was not until the 1970s that local idioms, instruments and traditions began to be incorporated into the popular urban styles. For the French colonisers, it was an obligation to bring metropolitan culture to the colonies, thus seriously inhibiting the development of local styles. For example, even as late as 1978, the major French recording company, Pathe-Marconi was able to release a sampler album entitled *L'Unité Africaine Vol.1*, which represented Senegal with two Johnny Halliday songs.

The first major Senegalese band to break out of the metropolitan mould was the Star Band de Dakar, which, over a period of two decades, was able to train dozens of musicians and establish a distinct Senegalese style. Others followed in their wake and by the 1970s Wolof was in wide use. The Cuban melodies became more dramatic and the rhythms more syncopated. The 'tama' (a small talking drum) was introduced and in time became a lead instrument. Indeed, the manner in which the tama was played helped define which generation listened to the music. The elder generation preferred the quiet and melodious music of bands like Orchestre Baobab while the on younger generation listened to the more frenetic rhythms of Youssou N'Dour or Super Diamono. Eventually, the music of Senegal was given the generic name 'Mbalax', a Wolof term denoting percussion-based music featuring an improvised solo on the sabar drum. Today, Senegalese pop music is a sophisticated blend of the old and the new. Essentially percussion based, it also includes electric guitars, horns and kit drums while utilising the full variety of traditional Senegalese instruments – kora, tama, sabar and balafon.

By the mid-1980s, mbalax had emerged as one of the most potent and popular styles in Africa. Thanks largely to the efforts of Youssou N'Dour and Toure Kunda, Senegalese pop found large and appreciative audiences in

SENEGAL/THE GAMBIA

the UK, France and the USA. Many other stars followed in their wake including Mory Kante, with his kora fusions, Idrissa Diop, Ismael Lo and Super Diamono. However, the appeal of Senegalese music was not limited to mbalax and the kora traditions of Senegambia found a growing market outside the country. What remains to be seen is whether the current popularity of mbalax will survive the fickle tastes of western audiences or whether, like juju, it will decline and revert to a strictly localised form.

Traditional Music

1970s	OCR 15	Senegal: La Musique des Griots
	SNG20 001/002	La Voix du Senegal
	ARN 33179	Senegal: La Kora Vol.1
	ARN 33313	Senegal: La Kora Vol.2

	LDX74596	Math Samba: Timbuyo
1976	OL6121	Senghor and his Troupe: African Tribal Music and Dance
	SAF 50104	Babou Diabate
1980s	SAF 50105	Abdoulaye Idi Seck: Folklore du Senegal
	SAF 50106	Pape Soly Drame
	ETH 4323	Music of the Diola-Fogny/Cassamance
	ETH 4462	Wolof Music: Senegal and Gambia
	ETH 8505	Ousmane M'Baye: Songs of Senegal

N'Dour, Youssou (b. Dakar, Senegal, 1959). African singer-composer and drummer, Youssou N'Dour is today the leading exponent of mbalax music and a true African superstar. The son of musician parents, Youssou was introduced to music at an early age, making his public debut at the age of 12. By the time he was 14, he was already performing before large audiences acquiring the nickname 'Le Petit Prince de Dakar'. By 1976 he was holding down a regular spot at the Miami nightclub in Dakar performing with the uncrowned kings of Senegalese pop – the Star Band de Dakar (formed in 1960). In 1978 he recorded for the first time, with the Star Band, and the following year parted company with several other musicians to create his own outfit – Etoile de Dakar. The same year they had their first hit with the single 'Xalis Money'. Youssou recorded three albums with Etoile before moving to Paris where the group was reorganised and renamed Super Etoile. Youssou then embarked on a new phase in his career which saw the release of several more albums including the classic *Immigrés*. By this time, Super Etoile was a 14-strong dance band comprising guitars, sax, vocals and percussion. Utilising traditional Wolof rhythms, and singing in Wolof, Youssou's brand of mbalax became widely popular in Senegal and France, with a reputation extending throughout West Africa. From a base in Paris, Youssou and the band made substantial inroads into the international market, touring in the UK, Holland and the USA. However Youssou did not forget his African fans and continued to appear regularly in Dakar, performing at his own nightclub, the Thiosanne. By the mid-1980s, Youssou N'Dour was on the verge of a major international breakthrough. His insistent dance rhythms and exciting live shows stimulated a ready and appreciative market for his music while his distinctive voice found its way on to LPs by western stars as diverse as Peter Gabriel and Herbie Hancock, and his drumming on to the Paul Simon album *Graceland*. At the moment, he is perhaps the hottest African singer in the world, with fans from Senegal to Japan and from Gabon to Los Angeles. At the beginning of 1987 he made an extensive tour of West Africa and another of the USA, where he supported Gabriel in concert.

1980	ET 001	Toulou Badou Ndiaye

	MAG 119	Xalis
	ED 008	Mouride
	ED 010	A Abidjan (live)
1983	MCA 302	Thiapathioly
	MCA 304	Ndiadiane Ndiaye
	PAM 02	Absa Gueye
1984		Diakarlo (with Etoile 2000)
1985	CEL 6709	Immigrés
1986	ERT 1009	Nelson Mandela

(The majority of Youssou's albums are bootlegs and appeared originally as cassettes in Senegal. Other cassettes, from which albums were not reproduced include *Ndakaru, Tabaski, Daby, Live in Paris, Yarou.*)

Xalam. Taking their name from a Senegalese stringed instrument, Xalam are an eight-piece group founded in 1969. They started as amateurs, playing salsa and Cuban rhythms on Sunday afternoons before turning professional in 1975 following a successful African tour in the company of Hugh Masekela and Miriam Makeba. For the next four years they toured the towns and villages of Senegal, researching local folk traditions and evolving a unique style. They made their first visit to Europe in 1979 when they performed at the prestigious Berlin Jazz Festival. They were quickly seized upon by the western press and on their return to Dakar represented their country at the annual Senegal Jazz Festival. During the festival they met and played with many of the world's greatest jazz musicians and followed up this success with an African tour, visiting Côte d'Ivoire, Liberia and Nigeria. In 1981 they made their way to the USA where they featured in a Walt Disney film about African music. On their return to Europe they continued to build their reputation with several highly acclaimed live shows including a memorable performance at the Paris Jazz Festival. They continued to tour Europe regularly and opened a show for Crosby, Stills and Nash before 20,000 fans at the Paris Hippodrome. Their reputation continued to grow and in 1984 they were invited to record the percussion tracks for the Rolling Stones' album *Undercover.* Since then, Xalam have played in most European countries, thrilling audiences everywhere with their fusion of jazz, rhythm and blues and African music.

1979	XPS 001	Ade-Festival Horizonte Berlin
1979	RCA 250	Marche à L'Ombre
1983	CEL 6656	Goree
1985	ENC 134	Apartheid

Super Diamono. Comprising 10 musicians, Super Diamono were formed in 1975 by singer and composer Omar Pene. They started out as a traditional band but when they played at weekends they turned their hands to pop and Cuban styles. In 1977 they decided to turn professional and develop a personal style utilising Senegalese traditions which they dubbed 'Afro-feeling music'. They brought in electric guitars, traditional percussion and started playing 'mbalax-blues'. As their style developed and their reputation grew, several founding members, including Ismael Lo and Aziz Seck, left the band to pursue solo careers. With lyrics written by Omar Pene, the band concentrated on the problems confronting the youth in Africa. Few of their albums have reached European markets and many of their most famous songs – 'Ma Beugue Yaye', 'Confederation', 'Rewu Taax' and 'Domi Gainde Ndiaye' – are only available on cassette in Senegal. In 1984 they travelled to Europe for several concerts and took advantage of the occasion to record their first album. They were joined by the Gambian vocalist Musa N'Gom and returned to Europe in 1986 when they made their British debut.

1984	8011	Mam (live)
	GR 7604	Geddy Bayam
		Ndakami
1986	ENC 193	People

Toure Kunda. A ten-piece fusion band from Senegal, formed in 1979 by Amadou Tilo, the eldest of four brothers. Toure Kunda are now firmly established as one the most popular African bands on the French and the international music scenes. The four brothers were born to Soninke parents in the Casamance region of Senegal. Named Amadou, Sixu, Ismaila and Ousmane, the brothers underwent a standard colonial Catholic education before establishing a local reputation as a singing/percussion troupe. They played a specifically Casamance rhythm/dance known as Djabadong – which to outsiders held strong reggae resonances. In 1979 the brothers moved to Paris and began to experiment with fusions of reggae and African music. They were inspired by traditional African idioms and tended towards the acoustic side in their live performances, grounding their music on vocals, kora, balafon and percussion. In time, several of these instruments were replaced by electric instruments (including electric guitar and synthesisers) while the basic line up was augmented by the addition of several more musicians from France, Cameroon and the Antilles. Ismaila and Sixu had already recorded in 1977 but it was the arrival of the elder brother, Amadou, in 1979 which really sparked off a period of extraordinary creativity. They began to play regularly in and around Paris, establishing a certain reputation. In 1980 they released their first LP and followed up this initial success with a second album in 1981. For the next two years the band played regularly to consolidate their growing reputation but it was the tragic death of bandleader Amadou in 1983 which seemed to concentrate the band's vision and maximise their commercial appeal. In 1983 they released the memorial album *Amadou Tilo*. In 1984 they embarked on a successful West African tour, visiting Senegal, Mali and Côte d'Ivoire before returning to Paris to record their fourth album. A film of their African tour was shown on French television and the band responded to the massive publicity with live shows throughout France, a tour of the UK and a live double album. By 1985 the band was established in the top echelon of commercial African bands with a reputation stretching from Majorca to Dakar and from London to New York.

1980	CEL 6549	Toure Kunda
1983	CEL 6599	Turu
	CEL 6646	Amadou Tilo
1984	CEL 6663	Casamance au Clair de Lune
	CEL 6710/11	Live (double)
1985	CEL 6740	Natalia

Konte, Lamine (b. Kolda, Senegal). A singer-composer, guitarist and kora player, Lamine Konte was born into a family of kora players in the Casamance region of Senegal. He first studied kora under his father, Dialy Keba Konte, before moving on to study with another great player – Souldiou Cissoko. He also studied at the School of Arts in Dakar, practising every day to develop his own style. By 1960 he had formed his own group with a number of friends and had established a national reputation as a contemporary artiste capable of introducing new influences into the kora tradition without compromising the basis of the music. In 1965 he represented his country at the Black Arts Festival in Dakar. In 1972 he moved to Paris, leaving his group to pursue a solo career. In 1972 he recorded two albums featuring solo kora tracks with traditional arrangements while introducing a few Afro-Cuban numbers. In 1977 he released the eclectic *Tinque Rinque* – a musical potpourri of kora, rock and folk music, demonstrating his mastery of both acoustic and electric instruments. He continued to record on a regular basis, linking up with Bozambo to record the sound track for the film *Bako L'Autre Rime*. He perhaps lacks the commercial appeal of fellow-Senegalese stars, but he remains a musician of outstanding technical ability, able to operate and command attention in both the traditional and modern settings.

1975	ARN 33179	Les Rythmes, les Percussion et la Voix de Lamine Konte Vol. 1
	ARN 33313	Les Rythmes, les Percussion et la Voix de Lamine Konte Vol. 2
	ARN 33701	Afrique, Mon Afrique
1977	SAF 50049	Tinque Rinque

1978	SAF 61002	Bako L'Autre Rime
1979	ESP 165530	Baara
	C20 000	Africa Africa, du Sénégal aux Amérique

Star Band de Dakar. The Star Band, Senegal's premier dance band was formed on 3 August 1960 to perform during the country's Independence celebrations. Most of the members came from the Guinea Band de Dakar and in time, the Star Band became the training ground for many of Senegal's future stars including Youssou N'Dour. In 1960 the line-up included musicians like Mady Konate (who later led the Tropical Jazz Band) and the Nigerian Dexter Johnson who later released many Cuban titles with Super Star de Dakar. Many bands hived off from the Star Band including Star Number One (later Orc. Number One and Number One De Senegal) featuring the singers Papa Seck, Doudou Sow and Magatte N'Diaye, Etoile 2000 and the most famous offshoot, Youssou N'Dour and Etoile de Dakar.

1960s	IK 3031	Sala Bigue
		Birame Penda Vagare
		N'Deye N'Dongo
		Kaele
		Alara Biriname
		Sim Bon Bon
		Mariama
		Bamos Pa'al Monte

Diop, Idrissa. Born in Senegal, Idrissa Diop began his musical career with the local band Rio Groupe at the tender age of 16. Of mixed descent (Serere, Wolof and Peul) he learned a variety of percussive styles from his grandfather. Between 1976 and 1980 he played with the celebrated Dakar band Sahel de Dakar, one of the first bands to modernise Senegalese traditions. In 1982 he moved to Paris, touring Europe and helping in the recording of the album Gorgui. This was followed by a tour of the USA where he again helped out a friend, Cheick Tidiane Fall, with his recording, Guedj. In 1983 he returned to Senegal where he was instrumental in establishing the group Tabala with ex-Sahel musicians Seydina Wadde and Oumar Sow. The following year he returned to Paris to accompany the Zairean keyboard player Ray Lema on his European tour. In 1985 he joined the band Jericho (formed to press for the release of Fela) and with whom he performed before 350,000 people at a memorable show in Paris organised by S.O.S. Racisme. In September 1985 Idrissa formed his own group Les Gaiendes (the Lions). Singing in Wolof and featuring percussion of all kinds, Idrissa established a reputation as a musician prepared to comment on the problems of Africa – apartheid, famine and immigration. In 1985 he recorded his first solo album.

Wade, Seydina Insa. Guitarist and singer, Insa Wade has been described as a troubadour of modern times. In 1985 he recorded an excellent album with his friends Idrissa Diop and Oumar Sow.

1985	ESP 8415	Yoff

Maal, Baaba. A popular young Peul musician breaking through the Wolof monopoly, singing in the Tuculeur language. A graduate of the Ecole des Beaux Arts, Dakar, Baaba had, by 1986, released at least six cassette albums with his first disc expected in 1987.

Various

1970s	SAF 50054	Orc. Diarama de Saint Louis: Folklore Senegal
	SAF 50056	Orc. Goram: Senegal Authentic
1977	SAF 50066	Conde Sekou et le Koten' Diming Jazz
	SON 8208	Mamadou Seck et Bouboucar Diabate
	SAF 50026	N'Diaga M'Baye: Soiree Senegalaise Vol. 1
	SAF 50028	Soleya Mama et le Waatoo Sita Vol. 1
	SAF 50029	Soleya Mama et le Waatoo Sita Vol. 2
1980s	CM 636	No. 1 du Senegal: Objectif 2000
	MCA 307	Orc. Baobab: Coumba
	MCA 306	Various: Panorama du Senegal Vol. 1 (An excellent introduction to the contemporary music of Senegal featuring Etoile 2000, Super Diamono, Orc. No. 1, Youssou N'Dour, Orc. Baobab, Orc. Canari.)
	VAL 001	Guelewar: Sama Yaye Demna N'Darr

Togo, sandwiched between Ghana and Benin, displays the expected variety of traditional musical styles, utilising xylophones, drums, flutes, shakers, musical bows, horns, whistles and even lithophones – an arrangement of four or five basalt stones arranged in a circle and struck like chimes. In the south of the country are the Ewe – a musical people with a heritage of poetry, drama and music. In the mountainous north live the Kabre, who by avoiding traders and slavers were able to retain a lively culture connected with the agricultural cycle and the organisation of age groups. Music was primarily functional and used to accompany both male and female labour.

Traditional music

OCR 16	Musique Kabre Du Nord Togo (A compilation of vocals, various instruments, funeral dirges, ritual music and age ceremonies.)
ROUND 5004	Togo: Music From West Africa. (A compilation of traditional Togolese music featuring a number of folk song various instrumental tracks and accompanied by a detailed booklet.)

Modern Music

The modern urban music of Togo was heavily influenced by the wave of Congo music which swept francophone Africa during the 1960s and 1970s. Few internationally known stars have emerged from the modern Togolese music scene, in part a reflection of the size of the country and in part a reflection of the dominance of the music scene by external musical styles. Congo music, Latin rhythms, highlife, disco, soul, reggae have all at one time or another tended to dominate the Togolese scene. However, occasional use has been made of traditional rhythms to give a distinctly Togolese feel to the music. Like neighbouring Benin, Togo has, with a few

TOGO/BENIN

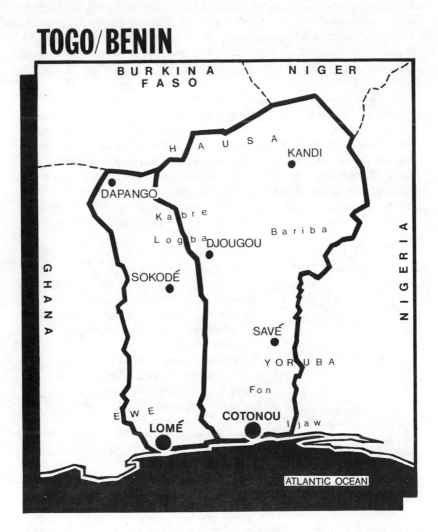

notable exceptions, failed to capitalise on the popularity and potential of specifically Togolese musical idioms.

Bellow, Bella. Born in 1956, Bella Bellow flourished during the late 1960s as a female vocalist with a truly African reputation. By the time of her premature death in a car accident in 1973 Bella Bellow had performed in several neighbouring African countries as well as in France, Belgium, Germany and the USA. Her only album, listed here, was recorded with the help of Manu Dibango.

1977	SAF 61001	Album Souvenir

Mala, Afia. Born in Lomé, the capital of Togo, Afia Mala won first prize in the 1980 Song Contest in Cotonou. She went on the road for the next three years touring Burkina Faso, Togo and Benin. She was encouraged by Jimmy Hyacinthe to record *Lonlon Viye* in 1984.

1984	MI 1101	Lonlon Viye
	TAN 7003	Maitre Gazonga: Les Jalous Saboteurs
	. SAF 48301	Koukou Mab Junior: Togo Africa
	SAF 50015	Akofa Akoussah: Tango
	SAF 50006	Yta Jourias: Metsa Volomiye
	SAF 50004	Amouze Hefoume: T'Aimer
	SYL 55	Nimon Toki Lala: Banind
	MBH 101	Mabah: Neerem (Female vocalist assisted by Manu Dibango)
1986	MBH 102	Mabah: Second album

13
Benin

Benin, formerly called Dahomey, is situated between Nigeria and Togo on the West African coast. With a glorious past, culminating in the establishment of the kingdom of Dahomey, Benin was finally conquered by the French towards the end of the nineteenth century. Like the majority of African countries, it today contains a multitude of cultures and languages with a diverse musical tradition. Leading styles include the music of the Nago region – a style very similar to the sakara music of neighbouring Nigerian Yorubas. Featuring drums, sanzas and the gode (a small single stringed fiddle), this music is played on every social occasion. For the Fon of southern Benin, music played an important ceremonial role at the court of the kings of Abomey. Their modern recreational music is characterised by the use of rattles and calabashes. The music of the Mahi, featuring zithers and clappers, has not stood the test of time and is seldom heard today. Somba music features male vocals accompanied by flutes and rattles while Taneka music utilises flutes, drums and bells. Other leading traditional styles include Dompago, Yowabu, Dendi and Bamba.

To a great extent, the modern urban music of Benin followed the same path as other West African francophone countries, modernising traditional rhythms and themes while borrowing heavily from the all-embracing Congo sound. One of the leading Benin musicians is the horn player Ignace De Souza, whose career not only demonstrates the role of the individual in the development of music but can be taken as representative of the general evolution of the modern Benin sound.

Born in 1937, Ignace grew up in the capital city, Cotonou. As a child he learned the traditional music of the Fon before being invited by a local entrepreneur to form a band called Alfa Jazz. The instruments were owned by the manager and Ignace started on the saxophone. The band developed slowly but in time were joined by two more experienced musicians from Nigeria, Zeal Onyia and Babyface Paul. They followed current trends in their music, playing a mixture of highlifes, boleros and quicksteps. Influenced by the sound of E.T. Mensah, the band would occasionally copy his hits. During the 1950s there were few other professional bands in Benin but Ignace remembers the Police and Army bands in particular. The French colonialists did not encourage the development of local dance bands, although brass bands existed in many villages.

In 1955 Alfa Jazz collapsed and Ignace made his way to Ghana – a haven for musicians – to join the Rhythm Aces. But he had a eye on the future and steadily saved his money to buy his own set of instruments which would make him independent of promoters and managers. De Souza remained in Ghana for almost ten years, introducing the Congo sound to Ghanaians and training a new generation of musicians in both the practical and the theoretical aspects of music. One of his earliest students was Nana Ampadu of African Brothers fame. In 1964, Ignace formed his own band – the Black Santiagos – and the following year rented the Ringway Hotel as a performing base. He invited other stars to come and perform at his club and by the late 1960s big names like Fela and Geraldo Pino were frequent visitors. The band also toured regularly, not only in Ghana but in neighbouring countries like Togo, Benin and Nigeria. Sadly, in 1970, Ignace de Souza and several of his musicians were expelled from Ghana by the Aliens Order and Ignace was obliged to return to Cotonou. But even by the early 1970s, music had not really developed much in Benin; the public were reluctant to patronise musicians while the musicians themselves had not yet developed a distinctive Benin sound and continued to play Latin and Congo music. A few bands were able to record (mainly for Pathe-Marconi) including François Aquessy, Lemiel et les Super Stars, G.G. Vickey and Gnonass Pedro, who was to resurface in the mid-1980s with the dance floor hit *Les Femmes D'Abord*.

By the 1970s a few more bands had appeared but in comparison with musical developments in Ghana, Nigeria and Zaire, Benin remained something of a musical backwater. Gnonass Pedro and his Dance Band, Elrigo and Los Commandos continued to entertain with Latin rhythms while a few bands from neighbouring Togo, including Erico Jazz, Los Muchachos and the Melo Togos occasionally brought in more specifically Congo rhythms. During the 1970s many Ghanaian musicians also performed in Benin, playing the popular soul music, but all bands in the country were forced to abide by the government's curfew regulations which seriously impeded the development of a Benin urban music scene. None the less, several influential bands did remain operative, including Ignace De Souza's own outfit along with Orchestre Poly-Rythmo, Les Astronauts and Disc Afrique.

By the 1980s Benin music and musicians had largely failed to make an impact on either the African or the international music scene, with the exception of Wally Badarou, a fusion musician and arranger who has worked in Jamaica and the Bahamas for Island records. He has worked with British group Level 42 and with Herbie Hancock, Manu Dibango and Fela. It remains to be seen whether a country with such a rich musical heritage can now catch up with its neighbours to produce an authentic Benin sound.

Traditional Music

	OCR 17	Musique Dahomeennes. (A compilation of various indigenous musical styles, ritual and recreational.)
	MC 20 141	Pondo Kakou (Dahomean Yoruba drum music)
	MC 20 159	Ogoun Dieu Du Feu (Ogun, God of Iron)

Modern Music

	2BE 13	Les Imbattables Leopards: O Idy Idrissa
	TAN 7007	Orc. Poly-Rythmo: Zero + Zero
	ANS 8415	Nel Oliver
	SYL 8311	Gnonnas Pedro et Ses Dadjes: Les Femmes D'Abord
1986	ILPS 9822	Wally Badarou: Echoes

14
Burkina Faso

Burkina Faso, formerly known as Upper Volta/Haute Volta, is a landlocked country situated in the centre of West Africa. Bordered by Ghana, Togo, Côte D'Ivoire, Niger, Mali and Guinea, Burkina Faso displays the cultural diversity typical of African countries. Yet like several other countries in Africa, Burkina has yet to establish a national music industry capable of highlighting either the talent of musicians or the variety of traditional music which exists and is widely enjoyed.

Very little music of the Burkinaba has reached either a wider African or an international market. The country, like so many francophone states came under the influence of metropolitan French culture, the compelling Latin/Cuban music and modern Congo rumba. Burkina has produced several regional stars, like Bozambo and Hamidou Ouedraogo, but their success seems to owe more to intrinsically African idioms (appreciated by neighbouring states) than to any determined attempt to exploit the cultural richness and diversity of Burkina Faso. This is in spite of the regular international film festival held in Ouagadougou which attracts African artists of international repute. One recent innovation is the formation of a 12-piece women's group, Colombes de la Révolution, inaugurated by the guitar-playing President, the late Thomas Sankara. Several albums of Burkinaba music are currently available including some traditional selections and a number of more urban sounding albums.

Traditional Music

SOR 10	Haute Volta (A compilation of Mossi, Bambara, Peul, Lobi and Gan music.)
2CO62 11568	Les Griots de Ouagadougou
OCR 51	Musiques du Pays Lobi
OCR 58	Musiques du Bisa du Haute Volta

BURKINA FASO

Modern Music .

Ouedraogo, Hamidou. (Born in Upper Volta, in the village of Dori, Hamidou moved to the city of Ouahigouya in 1954 with his elder brother. They eventually settled in the capital, Ouagadougou, working as garage mechanics. Hamidou, a Peul by birth, started his musical career slowly, teaching himself the harmonica before moving on to the accordion. By this time he was singing and composing in Peul, Mori and French and had become a master of the 'Gumbe' dance. Hamidou then formed his first band, L'Orchestre Super Volta, with his friend, the guitarist Moise. He released several albums during the 1970s, while often singing on stage with another top Burkina band – L'Orchestre Rythmo Del Yalinga.

SON 8204	Hamidou Ouedraogo: Le Vedette Voltaique
SON 8207	Hamidou Ouedraogo: Le Chanteur Voltaique
DPX 806	Georges Ouedraogo: Ganfou-Gnafou
	Georges Ouedraogo with Bozambo: Special Haute Volta
SAF 50035	Echo Del Africa National
SAF 50050	Orchestre Volta Jazz (led by Kone Idrissa)
SAF 61003	Quatre Black Brothers (led by Charles Malonga)
BZ 2222	Litende Byee: Feu Tropicale

15
Mauritania

Little research has been done on either traditional or modern Mauritanian music. Situated on the Atlantic coast of West Africa, and bordered by Senegal, Mali and Morocco, the desert republic has a mixed musical heritage with elements derived from sub-Saharan black African culture and from North African Arab culture. Very few records have been released of Mauritanian music, the bulk of which portray 'traditional' idioms. The leading exponents of music in Mauritania remain the griots, a hereditary caste of professional musicians who pass their techniques and repertoire from one generation to the next. This is the 'classical' music of the country – a style where music and poetry are often closely linked. Two main instruments are used by the griots – the tidinit (reserved exclusively for men, it is a four-stringed lute and sound box incorporating tiny metal bells) and the ardin (played by women, it is a ten-stringed harp with a calabash resonator). Mauritanian traditional music also encompasses a variety of drums and calabashes which, although popular, are not usually considered to be part of 'classical' music.

With regard to modern urban sounds, it is a sad fact that either insufficient research has been conducted or Mauritania has no business structure for recording, releasing and marketing LPs. Mauritania can thus be considered to be atypical of modern African countries where indigenous music has by and large proved to be a mainstay of contemporary society.

OCR 28	Musique Maure (with excellent sleeve notes)
SAF 50010	Musique de la République Islamique du Mauritainie (1)
SAF 50023	Musique de la République Islamique du Mauritainie (2)
SAF 50062	Musique de la République Islamique du Mauritainie (3) (This selection of three albums features the words and music of Saidou Ba – a musician who performs on the hadou (African guitar).)
SAF 50067	Bacar Cheike Drame: Music de la République Islamique du Mauritanie

16
Niger

Niger, a large, landlocked country in the Sahel region of West Africa, remains one of the least developed of all African countries. Bordered by Mali, Algeria, Libya, Chad and Nigeria, Niger is at the cross roads of Africa, combining black African and Arab culture. With a total population of just over three million, Niger displays a diversity of ethnic groups, languages and musical traditions. Among the major ethnic groups are the Sonrai, the Djerma, the Maouri, the Ader, the Haoussa, the Beri Beri and the Tuaregs. Instrumentation displays a similar diversity including a variety of drums, calabashes, trumpets, fiddles (goje) and the zari – a circular iron ring struck like a triangle.

As throughout much of West Africa, the leading musicians are the professional griots, who tend to satisfy the musical demands of the sedentary population. The griots attach themselves to a patron and illustrate his exploits through songs. They also perform at various social ceremonies like baptisms and weddings. However, in a country where animism has not been completely eliminated by Islam, some griots specialise in the invocation of jinns and other supernatural forces. The nomadic Tuareg are of Berber (North African) origin. They number about half a million, divided into separate tribes and families all sharing the same hierarchical social structure. Traditionally they have no professional musicians but the marabouts (priests) provide the music necessary for social and ritual occasions. Both men and women perform in different styles and in terms of instrumentation favour drums, harps, flutes and choral arrangements.

Niger is still a country in transition from pre-capitalist social and economic structures. Many of the population still follow the nomadic way of life while in the major cities and towns, infrastructure and other urban developments are far from complete. In terms of music, this situation has produced little in the way of commercially available Nigerois music. Like the rest of francophone Africa, Niger came under the musical dominance of the Congo sound which even today remains the key influence on the growth of an indigenous music industry. Niger has produced no great regional stars and records from Niger are few and far between. It is to be hoped that in the future, greater interest will be taken in the music of Niger

NIGER

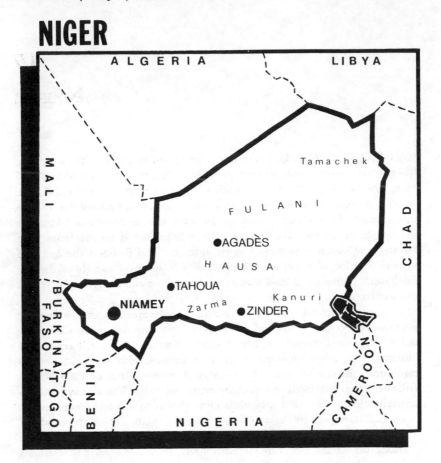

and that at least part of the country's rich musical heritage will be preserved on disc.

SOR 4	Rythmes et Chants du Niger (Featuring music from the Sonrai, Haoussa and Tuareg and the Griots.)
OCR 20	Niger: La Musique Des Griots (Presented in all the major languages of Niger, this excellent introduction is accompanied by extensive sleeve notes.)
OCR 29	Nomades Du Niger (A compilation of songs and music to accompany dances.)
ETH 4470	Tuareg Music of the Southern Sahara

17
Cameroon

Situated between Nigeria and Gabon, Cameroon is today at the centre of the contemporary African music explosion. Cameroon is comprised of a huge number of ethnic groups, each with its own traditions and culture which perhaps helps explain the enormous range and vitality of the modern music scene. Among the major ethnic groups are the Beti (noted for their xylophone and rattle ensembles); the Bamileke (noted for tambours and vocals); the Bamoun (drums and xylophones); the Bakweri (drums and vocals); the Fali, from the north of the country, as well as the Fang, the Ewonde, the Duala and the Fulani. As in most African countries, traditional music served a variety of religious, social, recreational, ritual and spiritual functions, including, for example, the utilisation of music by the Fali to help attract termites which were then used as food. Cameroon is also noted for the mvet, a type of zither, and the use of stone chimes (lithophones). Religion also played an important role in social life, whether it was traditional religion, or Islam penetrating from the north, or Christianity, Catholic and Protestant, encroaching from the coast. The country is also officially bi-lingual, reflecting both the French and British colonial heritage.

Traditional Music

SOR 3	Danse et Chants Bamoun
SOR 9	Musique Fali
OCR 25	Musiques Du Cameroun: Bakweri, Bamoun, Beti
6803 031	Music of the Bafia of Cameroon (Belgian Museum label)
ETH 4372	Music of the Cameroons
ETH 4451	Bulu Songs of the Cameroons
NDY 4027	Chant Du Monde: Vol. 1 - Cameroon
SAF 50057	Musique Traditionelle du Cameroun
AA 1001	Le Cameroun Danse (featuring Orc. Cercul Jazz)

CAMEROON

Religious Music

EX 33 177	Psalmodies Camerounaises
CALIG 17751	Missa Bassou
BAR 920 120	Lydia Ewande
SAF 50011	Chorale St. Kisito
SAF 50018	Chorale Oyenga Bele

Modern Music

Cameroon is today one of the main epicentres of commercial African music. The music was led to the marketplace by Manu Dibango with his first big hit 'Soul Makossa' which created a new wave of interest in the urban popular music of the country. But Cameroon had a much longer history of urban music, much of it recreational rather then professional. The songs composed by Lobe Lobe and Lobe Rameau were considered more of a diversion from work than the basis for a professional living. But, as in other African countries, the Second World War proved a catalyst for the development of a modern urban sound. Foreign influences from Cuba and Zaire were grafted on to indigenous growths like the makossa beat and the rhythms of bikutsi, mangambe and assiko. Cameroon had a long tradition of guitar playing but after the war the instrumental base was enlarged with the importation of other western instruments. Another source of inspiration was Cameroon's well developed tradition of religious music. Finally, the music industry itself arrived in the form of an expanded radio network, the opening of new recording studios and the dissemination of records.

During the 1940s and 1950s all the music was released on fragile shellac 78 rpms, very few of which can now be located. Early stars included Mama Ohandja, Charles Lembe, Jean Bikoko, Anne Marie Nzie and Oncle Medjo. Mama Ohandja was born in 1942 in Ebanga into a family of respected traditional singers. He made his debut as a singer in 1961 and by 1964 had established his own band which toured all parts of the country. In 1967 he formed another outfit known as Mandoline Jazz which adapted traditional bikutsi rhythms to modern instruments. By this time he had established a national reputation with many major hits such as 'Me Tsim', 'Eko Mot' and 'Eyim be Ngon'. He also adapted the Ekomot folkloric tradition to modern arrangements. By the 1980s he was appearing regularly on television with his new band, Le Confiance Jazz.

Another star of the 1950s and 1960s was Oncle Medjo, born in 1914 at Afane. Growing up in the village environment in the Bulu country, he developed a sound knowledge of assiko folkloric traditions. By 1942 he had mastered the guitar and was performing semi-professionally on traditional village evenings. He made his first recording in 1963 on the Samson label –

one of the most popular of the Cameroonian recording companies. He recorded several hits before making the transition to the urban environment. He is now an established star directing his own 40-strong dance troupe and performing all over the country.

Pierre Didy Tchakounte was born in Douala in 1950 and is now well known as the inventor of 'mangambe' – a dance inspired by Bamileke folklore. Well-versed in both traditional and western music, he made his first recordings in 1975, although he had been composing songs for at least a decade before. Early hits included 'Tonta', 'Monde Moderne' and 'Mequela' but his biggest breakthrough came in 1979 with the release of the LP *Mangambe Mythology*, followed up by *Sophisticated Mangambe*.

Finally, we should mention L'Orchestre National, which was formed in 1978 to mark President Ahidjo's twentieth year in power. The band was launched to inject new life into the country's musical heritage with the composers consciously researching Cameroonian folklore for traditions adaptable to modern orchestration. Led by Francis Kinque, the orchestra comprises 34 musicians who play both modern and traditional instruments.

Another important aspect of modern Cameroonian music has been the Christian musical tradition. Claude Ngumu for example, was trained in the western classical tradition at the seminary in Yaounde. He then moved to the Catholic University in Rome and later to the department of musicology at the University of Vienna. However, despite his professional expertise in the classical music world, he has not cut himself off from traditional music. In fact he was born into a family of well-known balafon and mbe musicians. Combining these two traditions, he now uses Cameroonian traditions in Catholic church services. His recordings like *Cameroon Psalmody*, *Ewondo Mass* and *Ebony Cross Oratorio* represent authentic African religious masterpieces. Another musician working in the same area is Messondo born Jean Bikoko. The son of a Catholic lay preacher, he was born in 1939. As a child he sang in church but every evening would participate in traditional assiko dances and songs. He soon learned to play the guitar and would perform in a small ensemble comprising guitar, maraccas and bottle. In 1960 he recorded his first hit song for the radio which established his reputation as one the leading modernisers of assiko. Further release followed on the Samson label before he moved to AfricAmbiance, with whom he recorded his biggest hits. During the 1970s he returned to his native Bassa region to recruit a traditional dance troupe. Now 40-strong, the troupe tours Cameroon regularly, further publicising and developing the assiko tradition. Finally, Pierre Tchana should be noted. He, like Bikoko, received his early training in a church choir. At the age of 12 he won first prize in a Radio Douala music competition for his performance on the flute. In 1959 he moved to Yaounde to complete his education but continued with his musical activities with some radio work before releasing his first single in 1965. Over the next decade he recorded many songs for Gilles Sala and

Maxicam Records. In 1975 he took up a position with a recording company in Benin (Dahomey) before releasing his first LP in 1976.

None the less, despite this impressive level of musical activity, the industry only really took off in Cameroon in the wake of Dibango's 'Soul Makossa'. Out of the varied traditions and the inspirational work of Dibango, Francis Bebey, Eboa Lotin and the various early stars, there suddenly emerged an eruption of new talent, utilising both indigenous traditions and hi-tech recording facilities to produce a wave of new dance music of exceptional quality. Bebe Manga burst on the scene as a nightclub singer; Vicky Edimo, the talented bass player, began to support the major stars; guitarist Toto Guillaume and the Black Styles marked out their territory, while dozens of others appeared in period of enormous musical creativity. Names like the Tulipes Noires, College Vogt, Ekambi Brilliant, Tim and Foty, Elvis Kemayo, Tala, Mike Kounou, Mbida Douglas, Dikalo, Ngalle Jojo, Joe Mboule, Dina Bell, Ebeny Wesley and Jacky Doumbe began to appear regularly in the Cameroonian charts. There was a brief downturn in the popularity of these new wave musicians towards the end of the 1970s, but by the early 1980s Cameroonian music had found its second wind to produce a truly international generation of new stars. Many moved to Paris for their recordings, where musical creativity combined with new influences (particularly from the Antilles) to produce truly international dance music. Musicians like Moni Bile, Alhadji Toure, Sam Fan Thomas, Lapiro de M'Banga, Misse Ngoh, Pierre De Moussy, Bony Mballa and Johny Tezano spread their hard makossa rhythms around the world. Manu Dibango also maintained his international appeal with new, hard-edged fusions. Today, the music of Cameroon is among the most popular in Africa, influencing other styles like highlife and soukous, with its irresistible rhythms and sophisticated production.

Dibango, Manu (b. Emmanuel Dibango, Douala, Cameroon, 1933). Singer, composer, sax-player, pianist and arranger, Dibango is one of Africa's true international superstars. Born in Douala to Protestant parents, he was sent to Paris at the age of 15 to prepare for a professional career. But despite the disapproval of his parents he persevered with music, studying classical piano before taking up the saxophone in 1954. Two years later he moved to Brussels, playing sax and vibes with a number of jazz bands. However jazz was not his sole inspiration and in 1961 he travelled to Zaire, newly independent and the source of some of the hottest sounds south of the Sahara. He only intended to stay a short time but remained for over five years, playing with Kalle and African Jazz on over 100 singles and running his own nightclub. In 1965 he returned to Paris with Kalle and Gonzales and together they recorded several outstanding albums. However, despite this success and invaluable experience, Dibango was determined to pursue his own musical direction. He released several more singles over the next five

years including the raunchy 'Tribute to King Curtis' in 1970. In 1972 he
released his first solo album but it was his third release, *Soul Makossa*,
which established his international reputation. The song became a
world-wide dance floor hit and gave Dibango the opportunity to expand his
band to 14 members. He was now in a much better financial position which
provided him with the means to live in New York for a couple of years,
playing with other giants of the jazz world. Now known everywhere as the
'Makossa Man', Dibango experimented with all styles of music although his
main inspiration remained Africa. It was therefore no surprise that in 1975
Dibango gave up the USA and returned to Côte d'Ivoire where he was
appointed musical director of Orchestre RTI – the house band of Ivorian
television. He continued to release records throughout the 1970s, becoming
a household name in both Africa and Europe with frequent tours and a
string of outstanding albums. He was in Jamaica in 1979 where he recorded
a couple of albums with the legendary reggae rhythm section, Sly and
Robbie. Dibango retained his following into the 1980s, recording frequently,
touring the world and still finding time to help other musicians with their
material. Musically, Dibango never stands still, as his career so amply
illustrates. He started with classical music, moved on through jazz and
congolese music before perfecting makossa and moving on again to reggae
and electric-pop. He is also active in the cinema, having written the score
for several films including *L'Herbe Sauvage, Ceddo* and *The Price of
Freedom*. In 1974 he won two oscars for best instrumentalist and best
composer. Now at the peak of his career, he is guaranteed to fill concert
halls anywhere in the world. While his position as Africa's best known
musician is unchallenged, we should never forget his immense contribution
to the music of Cameroon.

1960s	424 826	Répondez
	424 827	Affaires du Quarier
	424 828	Grand Success (These EPs were recorded by Dibango et Son Orchestre in Zaire and released on the Philips-Fontana label.)
1968		First LP
1971	360 045	Soma Loba (Third LP)
1973	360 047	Soul Makossa (Also CRLP 503)
	360 048	Makossa Man (Also DL3007)
1974		Super Kumba
1975	46507	Africadelic (Soundtracks for movie backgrounds)
1976		African Rhythm Machine
		Manu '76
		Afrovision Big Blow
	PSI 3036	African Voodoo

1977		Afro Music
1978	362 002	Scores for 'Ceddo' and 'L'Herbe Sauvage'
1979		Disque D'Or (double album of greatest hits)
	362 009	Anniversaire du Pays
1980	AF 1980	Gone Clear
	ESP 7512/3	Rasta Souvenir (double reggae album)
	DWAPS2104	Doctor Bird
1982	ESP 7515	Waka Juju
	ZL 37829	Surtension
1983	ZL 37815	Sweet and Soft
	AF 1985	Melodies Africaines Vol. 1 (piano solo)
	AF 1986	Melodies Africaines Vol. 2 (piano solo)
	ALB 365	Soul Makossa (double compilation of hits)
	ALB 381	Makossa Man (double compilation of hits)
	AF 1983	Mboa
1984	362 018	Ah Freak Sans Fric/Home Made
	AF 1984	Deliverance
1985	CEL 6114	Electric Africa (Also 824 745)
1986	5900	Afrijazzy (With Hugh Masekela guesting. The UK Polygram release features a new version of 'Soul Makossa' subtitled 'Big Blow'.)

Bebey, Francis (b. Douala, Cameroon, 1929). Dubbed the African renaissance man, Bebey has established a unique reputation as singer, composer, guitarist, poet, author, musicologist and film-maker. Born the son of a Christian minister, Bebey attended a French school where he acquired a familiarity with both the religious and the French musical traditions. He took a degree in mathematics at Douala before proceeding to France in the 1950s to study modern languages at the Sorbonne. During this period he began experimenting on the guitar and was strongly influenced by the playing of Segovia. He returned to Africa to work briefly as a radio journalist in Nkrumah's Ghana before moving to the USA in 1961 to study broadcasting in New York. In 1964 he decided to devote his full-time energies to African music and made frequent trips to various parts of Africa, both performing and researching the continent's vast musical heritage. He also continued to write and, in 1968, published his first novel, *Agatha Moudiou's Son* which later won the prestigious Grand Prix du Litérature de l' Afrique Noir. Since then he has published a total of nine volumes, including *Ashanti Doll*, *King Albert* and his best-selling analysis of African music, *African Music: A People's Art*. His first LP was released on the Philips label in 1969 and since then he has released another 17 albums on the Ozileka label. He has won many international awards for his music, which is sung in French, English and Douala. He is also the master of a variety of styles playing anything from classical guitar to rumba, makossa and pop. As one of Africa's most knowledgeable and accomplished musicians, he has done much to establish the place of African music in the contemporary music scene.

1969	P70 468L	Concert Pour Un Vieux Masque
1971	OZIL 3301	Guitare d'Une Autre Rime (African folk selection)
1972	OZIL 3302	La Condition Masculin
1973	OZIL 3303	Fleurs Tropical
1975	OZIL 3304	Je Vous Aime Zaime Zaime
1976	OZIL 3305	Une Guitare Pour Venice (guitar and poetry)
1978	OZIL 3306	Ballades Africaine
1979	OZIL 3307	Un Petit Ivorien
1980	OZIL 3308	Prière Aux Masques
1981	OZIL 3309	Bia So Nika (makossa/rumba)
	OZIL 3310	Rire Africaine
	OZIL 3311	Haiti (guitar trio)
1982	OZIL 3312	African Sanza (also ADSC 86015 - sanza solo)
	OZIL 3313	New Track
1984	OZIL 3314/5	Super Bebey (double album)
1985	OZIL 3316	Heavy Ghetto: Anti-Apartheid Makossa
	OZIL 3317	Le Solo de Bruxelles (guitar solo)
	EM 2334	Pygmy Love Song
	OCR 27	Pièces pour Guitare Solo

Thomas, Sam Fan (b. Bafoussam, Cameroon, 1952). Singer, composer and guitarist, Sam Fan Thomas burst on the international scene in 1984 with the mega-hit 'African Typic Collection'. His career started in 1968 when he joined the Black Tigers led by the blind guitarist, André Marie Tala. He stayed with Tala for the next eight years, recording several singles and featuring on the soundtrack of the film *Pousse Pousse*. The band also recorded in Paris and toured Senegal. It was during this period that Tala developed his unique Tchamassi rhythm. Then in 1976, Sam left to pursue a solo career releasing his first solo LP *Funky New Bell*, on the Satel label in 1976. A second LP followed in 1977 but it was his third release, with the hit song 'Rikiatou' which finally established his reputation in western Cameroon. In 1983 he travelled to Paris to record *Makassi*, with its hit song 'African Typic Collection'. The song not only established Sam's national reputation but became a massive international dance floor hit, with amazing sales in Sierre Leone, Paris and the West Indies where it was eventually released as a 12" single. He maintained his commercial momentum with his fifth album, *Neng Makassi*, in 1985. On the Tamwo label and featuring many of Cameroon's top session musicians, it retained the sophisticated production of *Makassi*, without scaling the heights of his greatest hit. In 1986 he released his sixth LP but much of the originality of his earlier releases had been more than matched by other Cameroonian stars.

1977	SAT	Funky New Bell
1984	TAM 4	Makassi
1985	TAM 11	Neng Makassi
1986	MS 5004	Makassi Plus

Manga, Bebe (b. Elizabeth Prudence Manga Bessem, Mante, Cameroon, 1948). Singer, composer and pianist, Bebe Manga taught herself music before starting a professional career in 1973 in various Douala nightclubs. She then moved to Gabon for a period, performing a mixture of European ballads and Douala folk-songs. She moved briefly to Abidjan before arriving in Paris in 1980 to record her first LP – the outstanding *Amie*. This album featured a variety of congolese, European and makossa tracks but it was the western pop number 'Amie' which rocketed Bebe to international fame in 1982. Written by Ebanda Alfred and backed by Nelle Ayoum (both formerly of Los Camaroes), 'Amie' went on to sell over a million copies, in the process spawning dozens of cover versions, including the 1985 disco hit by Nayanka Bell. In 1982 Bebe toured both the Caribbean and Japan to promote her song. In 1983 she was awarded the French 'Maracas D'Or'. The same year she moved to New York in an effort to break out of her 'African' pigeon-hole. However she failed to make the transition to mainstream commercial success and now performs only occasionally with the Haitian outfit Tabou Combo. Other recordings by Bebe Manga are however available on the excellent compilation *Fleurs Musicales du Cameroun*.

| 1982 | SIIS 10 | Amie (also SMP 6022) |

Ngoh, Misse (b. Francois Misse Ngoh, Mbonjo, Cameroon, 1949). A gifted guitarist who has sold in excess of 100,000 records in Cameroon, Misse Ngoh joined the band Los Calvinos as a youngster. They specialised in makossa but tried to introduce their own ideas into the standard format. Regarded as a perfectionist when it comes to production, he is also a talented lyricist. He succeeded in establishing his own following by introducing the essewe, a traditional rhythm from the coastal province.

| 1978 | ESP 165517 | Ea Nde Longe (with Bozambo) |
| 1979 | ESP 165 529 | Tata Ngoh |

	ESP 165 536	Nasi Ma Sunga
1980	ESP 165 542	Muembolo
1981	ESP 165 550	Wanba
	ESP 165 555	Na Mea
1983	IBM 003	Na Mende Kusa
	SAF 50051	Cameroun'am
1985	EP 004	Kossy

Tala, Andre Marie (b. Western Province, Cameroon, 1951). Singer and guitarist. Tala went blind at the age of 13, a setback which encouraged him to turn to music. He was eventually 'discovered' by Manu Dibango who joined together with some friends to enable the young guitarist to travel to France for a recording session. In 1973 he released 'Sikati' and 'Potaksima' which proved to be very popular amongst Cameroonians. He was awarded various prizes during the 1970s and scored several films. He likes to mix traditional and modern and is responsible for developing the tchamassi rhythm. He sings in both English and French as well as several local languages.

1976	F 360084	Black Woman
1982	AND 33833	Binam
	AND 33834	Mother Africa
1984	AND 33855	Je Vais A Yaounde

Guillaume, Toto (b. Douala, Cameroon, 1955). One of Africa's most gifted guitarists, Toto is widely acknowledged as the best session guitarist in Cameroon. He made his debut with a school band in Douala before moving to BonaBeri where he carved out a reputation with the Black Styles. In 1974, inspired by his girlfriend he released the hit single 'Françoise'. In 1975 he scored again with 'Mba Ne Wae'. Working under the stage name Toguy, Toto is now accepted as Cameroon's 'Makossa Master' and he can be heard on dozens of the best makossa albums. He also plays in Miriam Makeba's touring group, while pursuing his solo career.

1980	ESP 165 521	Toguy
1981	ESP 165 538	Isokolo
1982	ESP 165 551	Dibena
1983	ESP 8404	Makossa Digital
1985	TN 591	Elimbi Na Ngomo

Roosevelt, Eko (b. Louis Roosevelt Eko, Lobe-Kribi, Cameroon, 1946). Keyboard wizard, singer, arranger and guitarist, Eko can be considered Cameroon's most talented all round musician. As a child it was his ambition to become a church organist and when he moved to Douala Technical

School, he gained an informal musical training by organising musical evenings for his friends. In time he became a great pianist, excellent organist and accomplished guitarist. He takes pleasure in arranging traditional music for a full orchestra. He can fill concert halls anywhere in Cameroon and has made frequent overseas tours. In 1980 he was appointed conductor of the National Orchestra. He has another side to his music, however, and has demonstrated his ability to play popular dance styles on a number of LPs.

1976	CL 503	Kilimandjaro – My Home
	DPX 811	Funky Disco Music
1980s	DPX 817	Osi Bakele Mba
	DPX 828	Nalandji

Jojo, Ngalle (b. Francis Ngalle Ekollo, Douala, Cameroon, 1956). Jojo started his musical career in secondary school, singing and composing before he was 'discovered' by Nelle Eyoum – the father of modern makossa. In 1975 he moved to Paris to continue his studies and recorded his first solo album in 1977. The popularity of this disc turned him into a star in Cameroon and he maintained his rapid rise to fame with *Madila* in 1979 and the chart-topper *Petit Madam* in 1980. In 1981 he established his own recording company, producing records for other top Cameroonian artists like Ebanda Manfred, Villa Viene and Milla.

1979	ESP 165 520	Madila
1980	ESP 165 535	Petit Madam
1981	ESP 165 541	Papa Est Jaloux

Bell, Dina (b. Charles, Dina Ebongue, Douala, Cameroon, 1953). Dina Bell was born into a musical family; both his father and grandfather were musicians, and as a child he learned to sing and play guitar. His teachers at school and the local minister were quick to recognise his talent but by the mid-1970s Dina had more or less abandoned religious music to concentrate on makossa. In 1979 he recorded his first album, *Yoma Yoma*, his second *Mbem A'Iyo* in 1980 with two more in 1981, *Longe* and *Epoupa*, confirming his precocious talent. He is currently the star singer on the Eri label and one of the country's most popular musicians.

1979		Yoma Yoma
1980		Mbem A'Iyo
1981		Longe
		Epoupa
1983	BAZ 020	Etom Am
1984	BAZ 030	Mboa

Nzie, Anne-Marie (b. Anne Marie Nvounga, Bibia Lolodorf, 1932). Known as 'The Queen Mother of Cameroonian song', Anne Marie Nzie started her musical career at the age of eight, singing in her village. She owed much of her later success to her brother Cromwell, one of the greatest musicians in the country. During the 1950s many of her most popular songs were released on the French label Pathe-Marconi – including 'Nguiamba', 'Mah Banze' and 'Ma Belle Na Mur'. She started her career in the era of 78 rpms, few of which are still available, and by the 1960s was the most popular and influential female singer in the country.

1970s	062 15807	Sara
	NUM 48014	
1984	TC 0003	Liberté

Zambo, Marthe (b. Ebolowa, Central-South Province, 1947). One of Cameroon's favourite singers, Marthe Zambo started her career singing informally at school functions. In 1970, at the age of 23 she was spotted singing at a nightclub in Njadmena in Chad and was contracted to the club for the next two years. In 1972 she moved south to Douala where she met up with Ekambi Brilliant and became a sophisticated cabaret star. She recorded her first LP for Decca before moving on to Fiesta, with whom she recorded her first national hits 'Ndedi' and 'Sili Ma Mongo'. By 1978 she had moved over to the Safari Ambiance label for whom she still records. On her most recent releases she has made maximum use of Cameroon's many talented session musicians, including Alhadji Toure.

DPX 818	Bikola
DPX 826	Patricia
SAS 046	Sili Ma Mongo

Lottin, Eboa (b. Emmanuel Eboa Lottin, Banamouti-Douala, 1942). Eboa Lottin was born into a famous family. His father, a Cameroonian national hero, was a martyr of the coastal 'Native Church' and a founder of the African 'Godspiel'. Consequently, Eboa's early life was surrounded by a religious and musical atmosphere. In 1962 he recorded his first single 'Mulema Mwam, Elimba Dikalo' which was released by Philips. By 1982 Eboa Lottin was acknowledged as a makossa master. Playing harmonica and guitar, his interests extend beyond music to encompass literature, theatre and cinema. He has stabilised his musical career and releases an LP every two years.

1975	Bessombe
1977	Muyenge Ma Ngando
1979	Tete Youngo

1981		Tata Coco
1983	TG 587	Les Trois Visages
1985	TSI 002	Disque d'Or (double album)

Kemayo, Elvis (b. Cameroon, 1949). Singer, composer, guitarist, arranger and producer. Elvis Kemayo is a true pan-African musician, travelling the continent in search of good music to record, arrange or produce. He joined his first band, Negro Fiesta, as an 18-year-old singer and guitarist. From there, he moved on to Les Mutins in Gabon before leaving for Paris in 1972. He remained in France for five years, studying music and touring Europe. In 1977 he performed with Manu Dibango at the Paris Olympia. During these years he released a couple of LPs on the Fiesta label before producing his first LP, also on the Fiesta label. Towards the end of the 1970s Kemayo moved on to Gabon where he settled and was eventually appointed the artistic director of Gabonese television. In 1981 he released his own second LP *Paradis Noir*. A distinguished session performer and arranger, Kemayo became closely involved with the leading Gabonese outfit, Les Diablotins, producing an outstanding series of seven LPs for them during the early 1980s. However, Kemayo did not entirely neglect his own career and in 1984 made an immense impact with his tenth anniversary album featuring a medley of many of the years best makossa dance tracks with the help of top session men Alhadji Toure and Toto Guillaume. In 1985 he reunited with Les Diablotins to produce two more albums. He is much sought after as a producer but, with his own musical talents, he is now on the verge of a major international breakthrough.

1978		Africa L'An 2000
1981	KSP 005	Paradis Noir
1984	SAS 054	10ème Anniversaire

Baba, Ali (b. Amadou Baba Ali, Garoua, Northern Cameroon, 1956). Artist, acrobat, painter and singer. Ali Baba made his breakthrough in 1980 as a dancer with the National Ballet of Cameroon. He remained with the troupe for the next four years, acquiring a sound knowledge of the great variety of Cameroonian traditional culture. His extraordinary dynamism earned him the title of 'Le Demon de la Danse Africaine'. In 1984 he moved to Paris where he enriched his repertoire by learning the dances of the various African nationalities to be found in the cosmopolitan centre. In 1985 he returned to Africa, touring Nigeria, Chad and Cameroon. His undoubted musical abilities encouraged Safari Ambience torecord his songs and in 1985 he released his first LP. With an exciting stage show, combining music, dance and theatre, Ali Baba remains one of Africa's most versatile performers.

1985   SAS 056   Le Demon de la Danse Africaine.

Bile, Moni. Moni Bile is today the most popular makossa singer in both Cameroon and Paris. With five LPs released to date, he has established a reputation for sophisticated production, incessant dance rhythms and sweet vocals. He makes use of only the very best session men and has replaced Sam Fan Thomas as the dance floor sound.

1983	AT 0058	Bijou
	AT 0061	O Si Tapa Lambo Lam
1984	AT 0064	Chagrin D'Amour
1985	MB 0111	Tout Ca C'est La Vie
1986	MB 0113	African Melody

Ewanje, Charles. Guitarist and singer, Charles Ewanje has marked out his own musical territory, somewhere between Francis Bebey and hot makossa. A trained classical guitarist, he specialises in sophisticated arrangements using some of Cameroon's finest session men, including Valery Lobe on drums and Vicky Edimo on bass.

1983   EW 001   Longe Lasu

Veterans, Les. One of Cameroon's finest big bands. Originally a ten-piece outfit, they made their commercial breakthrough in 1983 with two albums, one of which became record of the year. Specialising in the bikutsi rhythm, they also proved themselves adept at soukous and have never been slow to utilise both traditional instruments and extra musicians to produce the required sound. Their music features the accordion to produce a rootsy, traditional feel.

1983	TC 0001	Nle Ne Ngon
	TC 0002	Wa Dug Ma
1985	TC 0007	Au Village

Ekwalla, Hoigen. One of the stars of the 1980s, Ekwalla is a talented vocalist and guitarist who, like many of his countrymen, makes full use of the best Cameroonian session musicians. Playing an up-tempo, full-blooded makossa, he has recently been utilising the hi-tech skills of Antillean musicians.

1983	BENY 001	Makossa Party
1984	NJJ 002	Ebol'a Ngosso
1985	NM 660	Bila O Diba

| 1986 | NM 661 | Minya |
| | MH 0102 | Quand La Femme se Fache |

Mbida, Douglas. Another outstanding singer-guitarist who, like Ekwalla, has recently been experimenting with the best of the Antillean stars, including Jacob Desvarieux and George Decimus. He made his first recording in 1981 and consolidated his success with several more albums including the outstanding *Mot Mfob*, which won the coveted Maracas d'Or in 1982.

1981	ESP 165552	Adzo Ane Mezik
1982	OY 1238	Mot Mfob
	OY 1250	Ma Vie A Moi

Tamwo, Isadore. Chart-topping singer and producer of Sam Fan Thomas's big hits. He too uses the very best session men – Toto Guillaume, Denis Hekiman and the omnipresent bassist and arranger Alhadji Toure.

1983	TAM 002	Mme Sans Calecon
	TAM 003	Mossia Jacky
1984	TAM 005	Tchouanou
1985	TAM 010	Emancipee Mariama
1986	TAM 020	Toi et Moi

Makossa

There are literally hundreds of modern makossa stars in Cameroon. It is by far the most popular urban style while the international successes of Moni Bile, Sam Fan Thomas and Manu Dibango have created a new standard for musicians and record buyers alike.

Mboule, Joe.

| DPX 815 | Esselemo |
| DPX 824 | Pjombwe-Aiyo |

Ekambi, Brilliant.

| JMA 17714 | Mongele |

Penda, Dalle.

| AOLP 004 | Tadi |
| DR 784 | Langwe Yo Te Mbo |

Yamson, Peter. A makossa 'crooner', based in Germany for several years.

YAM 1224	N'dola Mulema
YAM 1125	Bebwadi Mba Kwedi
YP 1227	Julie Partir

Tjahe, Marcel.

| AT 063 | Misso Ma Julietta |
| NJJ 003 | Mon Mari N'Est Pas Serieux |

Decca, Ben.

| HER 3401 | Pour Vous |
| AT 0062 | Mbango Muam |

Soleil, Nya.

| 1984 | N 5822 | La Vie Est Un Roman |

Jimmy & Fredo. Cameroon's hottest horn section, appearing on many Paris recordings by artistes of all nations.

| 1983 | 79428 | Nae Nae |
| 1986 | | Second album |

Tim & Foty

| ESP 165509 | Eda |
| ESP 165519 | Ddo Lam |

Doumbe, Jacky. Nicknamed 'Kape', Doumbe is one of Cameroon's foremost vocalists.

TRC 005	Muman Nya Ndolo
JDR 010	Tonton a Meya
JDR 011	Ne Nde Yeno
JDR 013	Monoki

Salle, John. Veteran Cameroonian vocalist.

| TRC 007 | Loleka |
| MSK 5002 | Special John Co |

Moussy, Pierre de. The master of smooth and lyrical makossa.

AOLP 006	Ka Lonka
TRC 009	Ndolo L'Amour (Also MOU 060)
MOU 010	Deuxieme Bureau

Mbala, Bonny. Vocalist and guitarist.

	BM 003	My Lady B
	BM 004	One Sapak
	BM 005	M'Akam

Kangue, Emile.

	AOLP001	Dikom Lam La Moto
	AOLP 010	Tube N'e Bobe
	AOLP 201	Emebe

Nkoti, François.

	AOLP 008	Retrait a Mbamba
	AOLP 014	Mbamba E Boi
	IBM 003	Na Mende Kusa Nu Popo
	IBM 006	Nkouanga

Ngosso, Ebeny. Up tempo makossa singer.

| 1983 | AT 0059 | Miango |
| 1985 | BT 1269 | Nya Mulema |

Black, Bebey. Singer-composer.

1984	GME 002	Aimez Aimez
1985	GME 004	Desir, Plessir, Souffrire
1986	GME 1239	Osi Bolone Dipita.

M'banga, Lapiro de. One of the outstanding artists of 1986 with the hit album *No Make Erreur*, featuring Naimro from Kassav, Toto Guillaume and Jimmy Cliff. A master of many styles from makossa to soukous.

| 1985 | MB 0101 | Pas Argent No Love |
| 1986 | | No Make Erreur |

Edima, Tity. One of the new crop of talented female vocalists.

| | DPX 823 | Medim Me Yom |

Bella, Uta. A new female vocalist supported by usual session stars.

| 1985 | BMCA 8401 | Afrikaan Music |

King, Biram. Singer-composer.

| | AT 0060 | Ye Mba Bobe |

BKR 1263   Mouana Moukala

Javis, Aloa, et Les Idoles.

SAF 50063   Operateur
AOLP 015   Ma Yem Ya

Various

ZK 004	Dapley Stone: Anou
DBLP 2001	Anina: Kolomou
TRC 008	Fefe Bekombo; Mon Amie est Jaloux
79432	Ebelle Bill; Welissane
SYL 55	Eugene Gbah: Issa Lebbet
ADC 1105521	Georges Happi: Blue Mind
IN 0079	J.P. Eyoumm Mbodi: Bonne Annee Cherie
TRC 011	Tokoto Ashanty: M'Boa
	Tokoto in Europe
AOLP 019	Jean-Paul Mondo: Sona Papa
TRC 014	Tchaya Daniel: Nabagna
BM 3101	Selisa: Boula Ane Animbok
EED 00283	Bella Njoh: Dina Lam Di
TRC 013	Frank Ndjemb: Nabenete Moni
79417	Georges Seba: M'Aye Bo Aya
K 4241	Dave Sakou: Coco Partout
PPN 81002	Pat Ndoye: Funky Revolution
ESP 165527	Peter Mukoko: Mboa
KEL 002	Gapitcha: Allumeuse
TAM 13	Tamis d'Or Samuel Tchamagni Vol. 1
GN 551981	Mack Anto: Koukou-Mama
TRC 008	Kamwa Papa Doro: Woukoup
RA 05821	Ondob'so: Africa
AOLP 0012	N'Kumbe: Ndutu Adongele
BIS 001	Super A Bis'n: Moto For Gabon
LEM 1250	Georges Lembomba: Longani
SAS 050	Daba Groupe: Long Way
L 8402	Koffi: Do'nku Djigne
JR 003	Francoise Milla: Timba Mbusa
OO1 E	Victoriano Bibang (Efamba): Mama Ane Mot Duma
EED 001	Ebanda and Villa Vienne: Mbua Madale
TCR 001	Jieupautha: Marie Marie
GME 003	Ntone Smith: Makossa Eclectique
NNM 184	Ange Ebogo Emerent: Experience
SAD 01	Egide Sadey: Soony

TRC012	Tonye Jackson: Ngo Mbondo La Lionne
SAF 18301	Ideku Dynasty: Zenguele Dance
TRC 010	Lobe Lobe Emile: Le Sharka et Le Makossa
SYL 55	Lolo: Reservation
BIS 002	Nden a Biscene: Go and Stay Before.
FUM 001	Francis Manga: Elinge Tir
TRC 006	Kamwa Barthelemy: Woukop
KAG 010	Mira: Issi
JMA 17710	Bertrand Mialet: Essomo
AT 068	Guy Lobe: Mon Amie A Moi
27254	Hilaire Penda: Jungle People
ENJA 4064	Voodoo Gang: Return of the Turtle
KULU 1001	Voodoo Gang: Elephants Wedding

Compilations. The most outstanding compilation of Cameroonian music, featuring the best of the past and present is the three-volume set on the Afro-Vision label. The selection features material from Tala, Nzie, Bikoko, Orchestre National, Dibango, Jojo, Guillaume, Manga, Roosevelt, Bebey and Lottin.

1983	FMC 001/2/3	Fleurs Musicales du Cameroun

Bobby Benson and his band in 1957 (Nigeria)

Hukwe Zawose (Tanzania)

Mahlathini (South Africa)

TREVOR HERMAN

Philip Tabane of Malombo, live at the Town & Country Club, London, 1987 (South Africa)

Manu Dibango and the 'Makossa Gang' (Cameroon)

Abdullah Ibrahim (Dollar Brand) (South Africa)

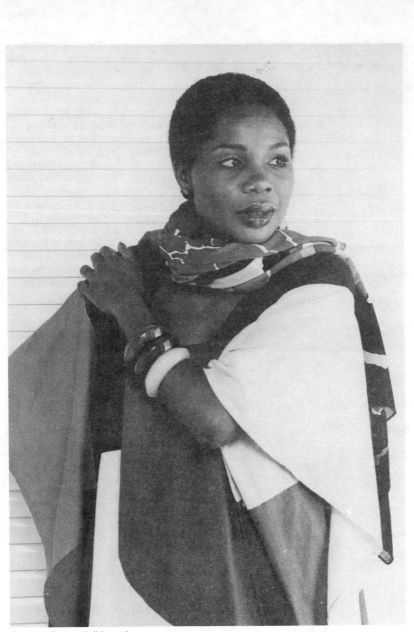

Onyeka (Onwenu) (Nigeria)

Hi-Life (Ghana)

Youssou N'Dour (Senegal)

Thomas Mapfumo (Zimbabwe)

Franco (on right) and OK Jazz, 1987 (Zaire) ▶

Miriam Makeba (South Africa)

Chief Commander Ebenezer Obey (Nigeria)

JAK KILBY

Above: Orchestra Super Mazembe (Kenya). *Below:* Fan Fan of Somo Somo (Zaire)

Part IV
Central Africa

CONGO/ZAIRE (A) RWANDA (B) BURUNDI

18
Congo–Zaire

There can be little doubt that over the last three decades the music of Congo-Zaire has exercised a profound influence over the musical development of the rest of Black Africa. Yet the story of the origin and growth of the modern Congo sound is far from simple either in geographical or chronological terms. We have to consider the various peregrinations of African music across the Atlantic and back, the cross-fertilisation with other African idioms and finally the idiosyncracies of the leading innovators – Wendo, Kalle, Franco and Dr Nico. Yet despite these various elements in the musical mix we must not lose sight of the common thread running through the last 50 years of congolese music – 'Le Folklore', the indigenous musical traditions of the Congo basin which have, in the long run, provided Congo music with its abiding strength and infinite variety. It is against this tradition that we must consider the arrival and incorporation of a variety of black styles into the modern music of Zaire.

The story begins in the 1920s, the age of the phonograph, with the growing importance of Leopoldville and Brazzaville as centres of detribalisation and acculturation. While the new urban elite tended to look towards Europe for cultural inspiration, 'folklore' managed to survive and flourish both in the rural areas and in the towns. Immigrant 'Hausas' (a catch-all for Nigerians, Ivorians and Cameroonians) helped with the diffusion of new rhythms and styles and, in particular, of guitar techniques.

By the time of the Second World War, with radio increasingly popularising the early Cuban rumba stars (particularly those appearing on the 'GV' series), new 'Congo-bars' were being established offering the customers both refreshment and indigenous dance music. In these bars, the new class of 'évolues' rubbed shoulders with the new underclass of the cities and by the early 1950s hundreds of ensembles were entertaining patrons with a variety of styles and sounds. Originally performed on likembe (sanza), guitar and bottle, the music was given a more modern feel by early innovators like Wendo Kollosai and Djhimmy. Early influences included rumba and highlife, but it was the 'folklore' which remained the heart of the music.

By the late 1940s several studios had been established in Leopoldville (later changed to Kinshasa) and within a decade nearly 4,000 titles had been released on shellac 78 rpms. Then in the early 1950s electric instruments and amplification were introduced and the Congo sound began to take on its modern form. Several stars stand out as central to the evolution of the modern Congo sound among them Bosco, the Katangan guitarist, Wendo, Paul Kamba, Nino Malapet, Essous but above all Joseph Kabaselle. In 1953 he formed the first of the modern orchestras, African Jazz, featuring guitars, double bass, congas, clips and male vocals. Increasingly Lingala, the language of the military and Congo river traders became the vernacular of the recording industry. During the 1950s, 'Congo music' flourished; Franco set up OK Jazz in 1956 with the Bantous appearing three years later across the river in Brazzaville. Out of this proliferation of bands, two distinct styles soon emerged. The first, owing more to tradition, was inspired by Franco while the second, more open to external influences was identified with Dr Nico. The introduction of the 'mi-solo' in the early 1960s (a secondary guitar solo between lead and rhythm) spurred on the two master guitarists to outdo each other. Brass and woodwind sections were also introduced, augmenting the sound and adding a new feeling of swing to the big orchestras. Kazadi (1973) has identified eight stages in the evolution of soukous and can be consulted for further details.

During the 1960s, Zaire was in political and social turmoil following the assassination of Lumumba and several years of Civil War. Many musicians took the opportunity to leave Zaire for the calmer waters of East and Central Africa, carrying with them the mature sound of modern Congo music. The sound also filtered further afield, influencing the musical development of countries as far away as Senegal, Mali and Madagascar. Then, towards the end of the decade, Zaire witnessed its youth revolt which served to intensify the antagonisms thrown up by a fairly rapid process of class formation. While the new bourgeoisie enjoyed their new-found status in the numerous clubs and dance halls, the urban poor stood outside, listening. The musicians did not create this tension but they were frequently guilty of exacerbating social divisions with their provocative lyrics. Increasingly, in both Kinshasa and Brazzaville, the youth condemned these new classes which they believed were perpetuating neocolonialism and cultural alienation. President Mobutu sensed their anger and sought to co-opt it in the famous campaign of 'Authenticité'. Musicians indigenised their names and a new sense of direction was found. One key turning point in this process was the successful showcasing of Tabu Ley at the prestigious Paris Olympia. On his return to Zaire he was feted as a national hero and taken on a national tour to celebrate his new international status. He became the first hero of the youth and opened up congolese music to a variety of new North American rhythms. In his wake dozens of new bands emerged, challenging the more established acts and generally remaining more faithful to indigenous traditions. A veritable cultural reconquest was now underway in which a number of young bands – Zaiko Langa Langa, Stukas and Viva La Musica – were able to establish national reputations.

Throughout the 1970s Congo music continued to expand into other parts of Africa with dozens of orchestras (Kiam, Kamale, Lipua Lipua, Bella Bella, Veve) rubbing shoulders with the smaller tighter soukous outfits like Stukas, Zaiko and Empire Bakuba. At the same time, both Tabu Ley and Franco continued to lay the foundations for their current legendary status with regular tours of Africa and a prolific output of records. A crop of talented female singers also emerged to challenge the men, and the basic sound was further augmented by the almost universal addition of the trap drum kit. By the 1980s congolese music was ready to erupt on a world stage with hundreds of talented musicians waiting in the wings. Many musicians took up permanent residence in Paris, Brussels and London, ready to meet the demand for soukous. By the mid-1980s a third generation of stars had emerged including Kanda Bongo Man, Souzy Kasseya, Fidele Zizi, Victoria, Pierre Moutouari and Orchestra Virunga.

There can be no doubt that today, the music of Congo–Zaire is the most potent musical form in the entire continent. It is a truly pan-African sound equally at home in anglophone and francophone Africa. Its appeal stretches from Senegal to Zimbabwe and it is now extending its grip to include a growing number of fans in the west. For the purpose of this book, I have combined the music of Congo and Zaire into a single chapter. The musicians themselves mix freely and it would be difficult to distinguish a specific congolese or Zairean style.

Traditional Music

The area of the Congo basin is occupied by different ethnic groups with a variety of languages and cultures. The area has also produced a wide variety of instruments, from bows and lutes to trumpets, fiddles, drums and zithers. Not much of this music has been recorded and there seems to be a disproportionate emphasis on the music of the pygmies of the tropical rain forest. The arrival of western culture and the implantation and expansion of Christianity since the end of the nineteenth century have had a marked influence on the region, producing a weakening of various musical traditions and considerable cultural collapse. The special circumstances of performance were no longer observed while traditional ensembles were no longer complete. The arrival of European instruments further ruptured traditional music. Christianity also played a significant role in the evolution of Zairean music. Not only were many musicians trained in church choirs but various religious pieces were rewritten to incorporate traditional instruments and idioms.

OCR 35   Musique Kongo Ba
                Bembe/Congo/Nseke/Lari

OCR 53	Polyphonies Mongo: Batwa Ekonda
OCR 61	Musique de l'Ancien Royaume Kuba
BM 2303	Ba Benzele Pygmies
6803054	Lunda-Zaire (variety of traditional music)
DL 11635	Vocal Music: Luba Shankadi (Belgian Museum)
6803073	Tshokwe Music of Zaire
LL 157	Music of the Rain Forest Pygmies
6803017	Musique Mpangu: West Kongo

Popular Music

Franco (b. L'Okanga La Ndju Pene Luambo Makiadi, Sona-Bata, Zaire, 1938). Singer, composer, guitarist and bandleader, Franco is beyond doubt Africa's most popular and influential musician. A legend in his own lifetime, he has led TPOK Jazz for over 30 years releasing hundreds of 45 rpms and well over 100 LPs. His career started at the age of 12 when he joined his first 'master', Ebengo Dewayon, as solo guitarist in the group Watam. In 1953 he recorded for the first time with Watam making his first solo record 'Bolingo Na Ngai Na Beatrice' on the Loningisa label. This recording made him a celebrity in Kinshasa and he was persuaded by his growing popularity to perform at live shows. Two years later, on 6 June 1956, OK Jazz was born – a ten-piece rumba outfit led by Franco, De La Lune and Essous. In 1957 the band moved temporarily to Brazzaville, returning to Kinshasa the following year. However, on his return, Franco fell foul of the law and was sentenced to jail for a motoring offence. On his release, Franco quickly re-established his reputation as 'The Sorcerer of the Guitar'. Indeed, so influential was his guitar playing that by the end of the decade two distinct schools of guitar playing had emerged, one led by Franco and the other by Dr Nico of African Jazz. Many early works by Franco are still available on the series of compilations entitled *Authenticité*.

Throughout the 1960s Franco and OK Jazz toured regularly and recorded prolifically, maintaining a clear musical direction despite numerous changes in personnel. Indeed, a list of OK Jazz graduates reads like a Who's Who of Zairean music and would include Vicky, Sam Mangwana, Youlou Mabiala, Wuta May, Mose Se Sengo (Fan Fan) Josky, Michelino, Dalienst, Essous, Papa Noel, Mayaula and so on. In 1976 Franco celebrated two decades at the top with the double album *20th Anniversaire*. By this time, the band could fill dance halls anywhere in Africa and proved the point with a 1978 African tour. By this time OK Jazz had grown to a 23-piece orchestra featuring four horns, four guitars, bass, percussion and a bevy of frontline vocalists. The sound of this magnificent orchestra in full flight can perhaps best be appreciated on the 1980 double album *24th Anniversaire*.

As a social satirist and commentator of the highest order, Franco has occasionally run into trouble with his lyrics, most notably in 1978 when he was imprisoned for two months for his songs 'Helene' and 'Jackie'. However, later the same year he was decorated by President Mobutu for his contribution to the development of Zaire's musical heritage. Two years later, he received the highest accolade of all when he was dubbed 'Le Grand Maître' of Zairean music, only the second musician to be so honoured. Franco entered the 1980s at the peak of his powers, astounding new fans with his power and eloquence while retaining the fanatical following built up during the previous quarter of a century. In 1980 he established his own record labels – Edipop, CHOC and Le Passeport – under the umbrella of his holding company, African Sun Music. He also began to spend more time in Brussels, although rumours of his exile from Zaire were exaggerated. In 1983 he made an attempt to crack the international market with tours of Europe and the USA. He also established a second band to support him on his international travels. Now on the verge of a major international breakthrough, a multimillionaire and owner of a hotel-nightclub in Kinshasa, Franco is the epitome of a successful African musician. He has been described as 'The Balzac of African music' and intends to continue playing beyond the year 2,000. The full story of his career is told by G. Ewens in *Luambo Makiadi and 30 Years of OK Jazz*.

1960s	DS 7950	Le Bon Vieuz Bon Temps de l'OK Jazz
	360 070	Authenticité Vol. 1
	360 071	Authenticité Vol. 2
	360 072	Authenticité Vol. 3
	360 078	Authenticité Vol. 4
	360 124	Authenticité 1962-1964
	360 125	Authenticité 1960-1962
	360 006	L'Afrique Danse Vol. 6
	STX 229	A Paris
	360 144	Les Merveilles Du Passé
	2C15015973/74	OK Jazz Vol. 1 & 2
	360 156	Les Merveilles Du Passé 1963
1972	062 15574	Les Grands Success Africaines Vol. 4
1973	360 053	Editions Populaire – Azda
1974	360 056	Editions Populaire – Mabele
1975	360 081	10th Anniversaire 1965-1975
	360 103	Grand Success
1976	360 082/3	20ème Anniversaire
1977	360 104	Na Loba Loba Panda
	360 105	Ba Beaux Frères
	360 096	African Party
	360 116	Live Chez 1-2-3 a Kinshasa

	360 108	Mbongo
1978	360 114/5	Live Recording of Afro-European Tour
1979	360 132	Africain Dances
1980	FRAN 004/5	Le 24ème Anniversaire
	FRAN 009	A Bruxelles
1981	POP 01	Respect
	POP 02	Bimansha
	POP 03	Tailleur
	POP 04	Mandola
	M 2376	En Colère
	M 2377	A Paris
1982	POP 17	Coopération (with Sam Mangwana)
	POP 18	Se Dechaînement
	POP 12	Special Mix 83
	POP 21/22	Disque D'or et Maracas D'or
1983	POP 20	A 0 Heure Chex 1-2-3
	POP 23	Franco Presents Simarro Massiya
	POP 25	Franco Presents Josky
1983	POP 26	Chez Safari Club de Bruxelles
	POP 27	Chez Fabrice a Bruxelles
	GEN 103	L'Evénement (with Rochereau)
	JJLP 008	Greatest Hits
	CHOC 0001	Choc Choc Choc (with Rochereau)
	CHOC 002/3	Choc Choc Choc (with Josky)
1984	POP 28	Très Impoli
	POP 30	Candidat Na Biso Mobutu
	POP 31	A L'Ancienne Belgique
	POP 32	Chez Rythmes et Musique
	ASLP 999	10 Years Ago
	MD 9091	US Tour Vol. 2
1985	POP 29	Le FC 105 de Libreville
	CHOC 004	Mario
	CHOC 005	Mario
	ASLP 1001	Fifteen Years Ago
	ASLP 996	Camarade Nini Akobomba
1986	CHOC 006	La Vie Des Hommes
	ESP 8427	Massu (with Jolie Detta)
	POP 33	A Nairobi
	REM 570	Bois Noir
	CHOC 007	Special 30 Ans (with Simarro)
1987	ASM 001	Attention Na SIDA
	RETRO2	Originalité (the original 1956 recordings)

Dr Nico (b. Nicholas Kasanda Wa Mikalay, Tuluaborg, Zaire, 1939). Guitarist and composer, Dr Nico was born into a musical family and graduated from the Leopold III Institute as a technical teacher in 1957. However, he was inspired by his father, a gifted amateur accordionist, and by his elder brother, Mwamba Dechaud, a rhythm guitarist, and in time Nico became a guitar soloist of outstanding virtuosity. As a founder member of the seminal African Jazz in 1953, Dr Nico became one of the most popular and influential guitarists of his generation, contributing as much as Franco to the development of the modern Congo sound. Kasanda acquired the nickname Dr Nico following his outstanding performance at the Zairean Independence celebrations in 1960. He recorded many hundreds of singles with African Jazz, the best of which have since been released on the compilations *Joseph Kabaselle et L'African Jazz*. Led by Kabaselle (aka Le Grand Kalle), African Jazz toured West Africa and Europe during the early 1960s, influencing a new generation of African musicians. However in 1963 Nico left the band with Rochereau to form a new outfit known as African Fiesta. During the 1960s African Fiesta set the standard for Congo music, spawning hundreds of imitators and releasing hundreds of singles in the process. Then, in the 1970s, following the collapse of his Belgian record company, Dr Nico withdrew from the music scene, feeling that he had been cheated financially. He made a few more singles, available only in Zaire, and played the odd show, but was generally prepared to wait until he could secure a better financial arrangement. The opportunity came in 1983 in the form of a deal with a new company – Africa New Sound based in Lomé, Togo. Accompanied by his brother, he recorded several LPs backed by Les Redoubtables de Abeti including *Mikalay, Dieu de La Guitare*. Altogether, these sessions produced enough material for ten LPs, although only five were finally released. In 1984-5 Dr Nico recorded a further two LPs in Paris and arranged for his first American releases on the label of the African Music Gallery in Washington. His sudden death in 1985 robbed African music of perhaps its most entertaining, influential and inventive guitarist. Since his death Dr Nico has been the subject of numerous studies, all stressing his central role in the development of modern Congo music. The God of the Guitar, Professor of Music, it has been rumoured that the bottle played a central role in his early death. Whatever the truth of this, there can be no doubt that Africa lost one of its greatest creative talents in his premature demise. Interviewed early in 1985 Dr Nico had this to say: 'I am back on stage now, waiting in the centre to challenge all of them.'

1962	360 107	Authenticité Vol.5
1963	360 150	Eternal Dr Nico Vol. 1 1963-65
	360 151	Eternal Dr Nico Vol. 2 1963-65 (Both released by Sonodisc in 1985.)

1969	360 005	L'Afrique Danse No. 5
	360 011	L'Afrique Danse No. 8
1970	360 024	L'Afrique Danse No. 10
1974	SAF 50003	Toute L'Afrique Danse
1975	SAF 50007	Sanza Zomi Na Mibale
1980	SAF 61008	Dr Nico et L'African Fiesta – Bunga
1981	SAF 61009	Afrique Tayokana
1984	LPKR 1003	Kassanda Wa Mikalaya
1985	ANS 8404	Dieu De La Guitare
	ANS 8412	Aux USA (Both also available on Tabansi Nigeria.)

Kalle, Le Grand (b. Joseph Kabaselle Tshamala, Matadi, Zaire, 1930). Singer and composer, Joseph Kabaselle, aka Le Grand Kalle, has been acknowledged as the father of the modern Congo sound, with an influence on both Tabu Ley and Franco, while leading African Jazz for over a decade. He gained his earliest musical education as a chorister in a Catholic school, making his debut at the age of 19 with L'Orchestre de Tendence Congolais. His earliest recordings were released on the first of the Congo labels – Editions Ngoma and Editions Essengo.

In the early 1950s he joined a new ensemble in Kinshasa, Surboum Jazz, playing a fusion of folklore, jazz and Afro-Cuban, before establishing his own outfit, the legendary African Jazz, in 1953. Against the fashion of the times, African Jazz abandoned the more popular polkas and mazurkas and switched to rumbas and sambas. With an acoustic line-up and a new fusion of black music, Kalle and African Jazz flourished during the years leading up to Independence in 1960, marking the transition from traditional to modern in the development of modern Congo music. During the 1950s members of African Jazz included such luminaries as Manu Dibango, Essous, Malapet, Rossignol, Dechaud, Dr Nico and Rochereau. The majority of records they released were of course 78 rpms but the best of African Jazz can still be found on two excellent compilations entitled *Joseph Kabaselle and L'African Jazz Vols 1 & 2*. This set includes the classic cut 'Independence Cha Cha'. Shortly afterwards Kalle recorded 'Okuka Lokole' to commemorate the visit of Louis Armstrong to Zaire in 1960.

In 1961 Kalle and the band embarked on an extensive West African tour, influencing the overall development of music in a number of francophone West African states. Bembeya Jazz from Guinea have acknowledged the influence of Congo music on their development. The fame of African Jazz also spread across the Atlantic with their songs 'Para Fifi' and 'Kale Kato' becoming early cross-over hits of the late 1950s. By 1960 Kalle and African Jazz had established a reputation as the pre-eminent Congo orchestra, releasing hundreds of singles (mainly on Decca) and dominating Kinshasa audiences with their unique blend of vocals, percussion and guitars. Sounds from the mid-1960s can still be found on *Authenticité Vol 5*

But things were not well within the band and in 1963 Dr Nico and Rochereau left to form African Fiesta. Kabaselle continued with African Jazz for two more years but in the aftermath of a successful African tour in 1965 he stepped down to consider his future. Yet the band remained popular and in 1966 Kalle returned with a grand comeback show in Brazzaville. In 1970 Kalle travelled to Paris to record some albums with the help of various Cuban musicians and Manu Dibango, collectively known as the African Team. The mature sound of Kabaselle can still be found on *L'African Team*. Kalle's career dipped in the 1970s but such was his abiding influence on a younger generation that in 1980 Kalle was consecrated as the first 'Grand Maître' of Zairean music by the national union of Zairean musicians. Kalle's death in 1982 stunned the musical fraternity. Many notable songs were composed in his memory including the beautiful 'Hommage à Grand Kalle' on the Franco/Tabu Ley collaboration album *L'Evénement*.

1984	360 142	Joseph Kabaselle et L'African Jazz Vol. 1
	360 143	Joseph Kabaselle et L'African Jazz Vol. 2
	360 104	Kalle and the African Team
	360 105	Kalle and the African Team

Ley , Tabu (b. Tabu Pascal, aka Rochereau, Bundundu, Zaire, 1940). Singer, composer and arranger, Tabu Ley is without doubt Africa's most popular and influential singer. In a career spanning 25 years he has composed more than 2,000 songs and released in excess of 100 albums. A man of exceptional artistic ability, he has led the way in developing the Congo sound from the early era of 78 rpms to the very latest in hi-tech recording equipment. He came to music at an early age, assimilating both indigenous traditions and the music of the Catholic Church. It was as a composer that he first came to public attention when, at the age of 14, he penned the song 'Bésame Muchacha' which became a hit when recorded by Kalle. Five years later, in 1959, he joined Kalle and African Jazz on a full time basis confirming his precocious talent with the 1959 hit 'Kelia'. Rochereau, as he was now known, remained with African Jazz until 1963 when he split to form his own outfit with Dr Nico, a new orchestra called African Fiesta. The band released singles at a prolific rate, many of which can still be found on various early compilations. Throughout the 1960s Rochereau's talent flowered. However in 1965 he split from Dr Nico and formed his own orchestra – African Fiesta National. He constantly encouraged innovation within the basic rumba framework, introducing new instrumentation, elements from other styles like salsa, soul and disco while adding French and English to his repertoire in Lingala and Spanish. He also consolidated his African reputation with frequent tours of the continent and a prolific recording schedule. In 1970 he renamed the band Afrisa International and travelled with them to Paris to perform at the prestigious Paris Olympia. The shows were a resounding success, with the two LPs from the same time reflecting the relaxed and lilting sound of classic Congo music. On his return to Zaire, Rochereau was feted as a national hero and taken on a national tour to celebrate his international status. During the 1970s he continued to invigorate his music, augmenting the size of the orchestra and embarking on ambitious African tours. Afrisa also proved to be a fertile training ground for a younger generation of musicians including Sam Mangwana and Mbilia Bel. In 1975 Tabu Ley retired temporarily from the music scene to look after his business affairs only to make a triumphant return to centre stage with an outstanding show at FESTAC, captured on a double live LP. By the 1980s, Tabu Ley was on the verge of an major international breakthrough. He established his own production company, Genidia, and released an outstanding series of LPs, featuring the mature sound of Afrisa International – a driving forceful dance beat interspersed with slower haunting ballads. Recently he embarked on an ambitious series of international tours, including visits to the USA, Europe and Japan. His repertoire is enormous while his artistic talent remains undiminished. He remains one of Africa's true superstars.

In an interview with the author in 1985, Tabu Ley talked openly of his career, at the same time shedding light on the development of Zairean music and the constraints under which it is made.

Tabu is my father's name. Ley is my father's father's first name. I adopted this name following a party edict proclaiming a new ideology of 'authenticité'. Previously I was called Tabu Pascal. Rochereau is my artistic name although it has been my name since 1954. I got it when I was 14 during a French history lesson. When the teacher asked us the name of one of Napoleon's generals only I knew the answer and the other kids were punished. They weren't too happy about it and called me Rochereau to tease me. I liked the name and kept it as my artistic name. I came from a musical background and my musical life is part of my heritage. My grandmother, Ina Gori, was a well-known griot, and I inherited her gifts. In 1954 I began to sing solo at the end of year school celebrations. I did not sing religious songs but a popular hit by Kabaselle. People advised me to contact Kabaselle and work in his band. I met Kabaselle in 1956 and wrote songs for him to which he put his name since I was still studying with the priests. Then, in 1959, I wrote 'Kelia' my first song in my own name, Tabu Pascal Rochereau. This song made me very well known.

I finished studying in 1959 and immediately joined African Jazz. However, after two months the band went to Belgium to play at the Independence celebrations and I was not allowed to travel. When they returned in 1960 my musical career really started. Then the line-up included Manu Dibango, Dr Nico and Kabaselle, but in 1963 the band split up.

The history of Zairean music starts with the formation of Lingala. This came about when the Belgians wanted to build the railroad. The people they recruited came from everywhere and spoke many languages. A common language was needed – Lingala. The base for recruitment was Kinshasa, this was where the people rested and amused themselves, mainly by making music. The people were from all over Africa. However, it was the wives of the railway workers who helped develop Zairean music as they were left back in Kinshasa. They used to get together and play what is known as 'kebo', without instruments, but with handclapping. When the men came back they added drums, the West Africans added accordions and guitars. Also each missionary school had its theme (fanfare) played on trumpets and saxophones and these were then added to the music. At one time, Zairean music was all horns but the guitar was easier. Often the kids of marriages between West African men and Zairean women learnt the guitar.

Now, my style is always changing in time with technical changes, new recording developments and the public's taste as well as current musical developments. It is important to play African music but to use the best sound techniques available in order to convince the public.

1960	360 140	Belle Epoque Vol. 1
	360 141	Belle Epoque Vol. 2
1962	360 070	Authenticité Vol. 1
	360 071	Authenticité Vol. 2
1963	SAF 50002	Rochereau/Kalle/Ndombe Pepe
	SAF 50003	Rochereau/Kalle/Ndombe Pepe
	SAF 50004	Mokrano
	360 127	Lisaso
	360 128	Tabu Ley
1964	360 051	Succès d'Hier
1965	360 145	Les Merveilles du Passé
	360 149	Rochereau/Sam Mangwana Vol.3
	360 150	Rochereau/Sam Mangwana Vol.4
1969	360 004	L'Afrique Danse No. 4
	360 008	Les Merveilles du Passe No. 4
	360 009	Tango Ya Ba...
	360 012	Seigneur Rochereau Presentent
1970	360 028	La Musique Congolais
	360 019	La Musique Congolais
1971	360 028	A L'Olympia Vol.1
	360 029	A L'Olympia Vol.2

1973	360 040	Pitie
	360 046	Afrisa International
	360 074	Afrisa International
1977	360 97/98	FESTAC 77
1978	360 119/20	On Tour
1979	360 127	Dernières Nouveautés
1982	EVVI 12	Maze
	DS 7912	A Abidjan Vol. 1
	DS 7913	A Abidjan Vol. 2
	DS 7914	A Abidjan Vol. 3
	DS 7925	A Abidjan Vol. 4
	SMP 6005	Special An '82 Vol.5
	SMP 6006	Special An '82 Vol.6
1983	GEN 101	En Amour Y Pas De Calcul
	GEN 104	Femmes D'Autrui
1984	GEN107/18	Loyenghe
	GEN 109	In America
	EVVI 13	Mpeve Ya Longo
	SHAN43017	Tabu Ley et Mbilia Bel
1985	GEN 111	Mobutu
	GEN 113	Sarah
	ST 1010	Afrisa Selection
1986	GEN 117	Maracas d'Or 85-86
	GEN 118	FC 105
	GAETA 01	La Beauté d'une Savage
	GEN 119	Sacramento (with Bel and Nyboma)
1987	GEN 121	Ley, Bel and Faya Tess (a new female vocalist)

Bel, Mbilia (b. Mbilia Mboyo, Kinshasa, Zaire, 1959). Female singer and dancer who started her career as a dancer in the chorus of Abeti Masekini – another leading female singer from Zaire. While performing with Abeti, Mbilia was spotted by Tabu Ley who invited her to join his own chorus – the Rocherettes. After several years in training, during which period she made several tours with Tabu Ley, Mbilia Bel eventually emerged as a solo singer, taking turns with Tabu Ley in fronting Afrisa. In 1983 she released her first solo album and also shared the honours with Tabu Ley on *Loyenghe*. Her reputation as one of Zaire's leading vocalists was confirmed by the success of her 1984 recordings and successful tours of the USA and Australia. In 1985, despite the birth of her first child, she maintained her commercial momentum with the excellent *Keyna* and her first British release on the Stern's label. With a string of hit albums to her credit, Mbilia Bel continues to perform and record with Afrisa. In 1985 she was voted Africa's best female singer in a Radio France International radio poll.

1983	GEN 102	Eswi Yo Wapi
	GEN 105	Faux Pas
1984	GEN 107/8	Loyenghe
	GEN 110	Ba Gerants Ya Mabala
1985	GEN 114	Keyna
	ST 1011	Boya Ye
	SHAN4305	Mbilia Bel
1986	GAETA 01	La Beauté d'une Savage
	GEN 120	Beyanga

Mangwana, Sam (b. Kinshasa, Zaire, 1945). Singer and composer, Sam was born in Zaire of Angolan extraction and is today considered to be one of Africa's most experienced and popular singers. His professional career started at 18 when he joined Tabu Ley and African Fiesta as singer and musical arranger. He stayed with them for many years, although he occasionally left them to perform with a number of other bands including Los Batitchas, Negro Band and L'Orchestre Tembo. To each of these groups, Sam brought his distinctive singing and arranging abilities. In 1972 he was invited to join forces with Franco, the other giant of Zairean music, with whom he spent a very fruitful three years, before returning to Rochereau briefly in 1975. This vast experience at the very top level of Zairean music not only enhanced Mangwana's reputation as a vocalist but enabled him to meet and perform with the cream of Zairean musicians. So when Sam decided to pursue a solo career in 1976 he was able to turn to these musicians for assistance. Between 1976 and 1982 Sam Mangwana and the African All Stars toured widely, visiting almost every country in Africa as well as the West Indies and Europe. During these years, the band established a truly pan-African appeal. Working from a base in Abidjan, Sam eventually established his own SAM label in 1979. However he continued to license his records to other companies, including Star Musique and Celluloid. Sam's biggest breakthrough came in 1982 with the highly acclaimed recording of the Congo classic 'Maria Tebbo'. The same year he was invited to record again with Franco, eventually releasing the all-time classic *Cooperation*. Further success came with the haunting *Canta Mozambique* in 1984 and the 1985 smash hit 'Furaha Ya Bibi'. As a compulsive wanderer across the African continent, Sam Mangwana is established as one of the most exciting and versatile performers to have emerged from Africa.

1965	360 149	Belle Epoque Vol.1 (with Rochereau)
	360 150	Belle Epoque Vol.2 (with Rochereau)
1977	360 031	Sam Mangwana with Festival Maquisards
1979	79390	Georgette Eckins
	79391	Matinda

1981	SMP 6000	Affaire Disco
	SMP 6008	Est Ce Que Tu Moyens
	ASLPS027	A la Camerounaise
1982	CEL 6638	Affaire Video
	CEL 6639	Nsimba Eli
	SAM 02	Maria Tebbo
1984	CEL 6729	Georgette Eckins (also ALP 1)
	CEL 6730	Les Champions
	SAM 04	Canta Mozambique
1985	ASLP 409	In Nairobi
	ASLP 943	Cherie Magy (Kenya)
	BIR 02	Sam (Kenya)
	EFA 021	Les Champions Pt 2

Bantous (Les Bantous de la Capitale), one of Africa's most famous rumba bands was formed in Brazzaville in 1959, quickly making a name as leading interpreters of Cuban rumba. Co-led by the two sax players, Dieudonne (Nino) Malapet and Jean-Serge Essous, who had both helped found OK Jazz with Franco, the Bantous made their presence felt in Brazza before embarking on an ambitious West African tour in 1960. The band continued to experience nonstop success despite frequent changes in personnel and like the other great congolese orchestras acted as a training school for younger musicians. In 1965 the band launched a new sound, and a new dance – Le Boucher – which was regarded by many as a renewal and revitalisation of rumba. This was followed in 1966 by the introduction of 'soukous' – a dance style which proved so popular that it later became a generic name for most Congo music. However the mid-1960s also proved to be a period of rapid changes in the composition of the band. First Essous departed for France after visiting Paris for a recording session. Malapet then took over as sole leader. Then, in 1967, following the proclamation of 'authenticité' the band underwent more personnel changes and a number of new recruits, including the singer Kosmos (Come Moutouari), made their presence felt. Popular hits of the late 1960s included 'Makambe' and 'Mibale'. The band continued to thrill audiences throughout the 1970s, both with their tight rumba rhythms and the virtuosity of their leading solo performers – the vocalists Tchico, Kosmos and Pamelo Mounka, the guitarists Nedule Papa Noel (also ex-OK Jazz) and Samba Mascott, and of course the distinctive sax sounds of Nino Malapet and Essous. In 1974 the wheel turned full circle when the band made a highly successful tour of Cuba. The Bantous continued to record on a regular basis, celebrating 20 years at the top with their 1980 double LP *Special 20th Anniversaire*. In the last few years several leading members of the band have branched out to pursue successful solo careers, often backed by the rest of the band. In 1987 Pamelo Mounka was appointed 'Chef d'Orchestre' and composer.

1960s	AFR360154	Les Merveilles du Passé
1963	360 146	Les Merveilles du Passé 1962-64 Vol.1
	360 147	Les Merveilles du Passé 1962-64 Vol.2
	360 148	Les Merveilles du Passé 1962-64 Vol.3 (All released in 1985 by Sonodisc.)
	SP 2089	El Manicero (The best African version of 'Peanut Vendor'.)
1976	SAF 50022	Marie Jeanne
	SAF 50045	Tcheka
	SAF 50046	Bandoki Na Boyi
1980	BAE 4005	Special 20ème Anniversaire
1984	AP 052	Bakolo M'Boka Vol. 1
1987	VME001	Pamelo Mounka et Les Bantous; L'Amour et la Danse

Papa Noel

1984	AP 048	Selia Zozo
1986	PV 015	Allegria

Nino Malapet

1984	MP 33004	Mokilimbembe

Mascott, Samba

1968		Sammy Ozwi Ya Sika (Decca)
		Zwana (Decca)
1969		Tara Me (Tropicana)
		Bouzitou (Pathe Marconi)
1970		Bolingo Ti Be Oko (Voix Bantous)
		Sammy Na Cathy (Voix Bantous)
1974		Anaba Sammy Na Cathy No. 3 (FRESAM)
		Femme Nouvelle (FRESAM)
1981	VAU 004	Mayanguila (with the Bantous)

Essous, Jean-Serge

1984	19759	Lily Germaine
1985	PS 003	Philosophie

Kosmos, Moutouari

DPX 827	Kamani Modo
SAS 044	Naleli Congo

Tchico (b. Pambou Tchicaya Tchico). One of Africa's most creative and prolific recording stars. He has led a chequered career; from early successes as a singer with the Bantous he moved on to pursue a solo career in Nigeria with his Waka Waka Band with whom he recorded many albums. During this period he also made several albums with fellow vocalist Lolo Lolita and L'Orchestra Les Evades de Ponton La Belle, including the all-time classic – *Jeannot*. By the mid-1980s Tchico had moved to a base in Paris where he linked up with a new congolese supergroup called Les Officiers of African Music, featuring the combined talents of guitarist Denis La Cloche, singer Passi-Jo and Tchico. They made several memorable appearances including an outstanding show in Amsterdam, captured live on one of the few African videos commercially available.

Year	Catalogue	Title
1978	SAF 50093	Josintha
1979	SAF 50094	Afro-Festival (Also M2354)
	ENLPS 42	Fantastic Tchico
	SAF 50095	Musique Congo-Star
1980	SAF 50999	Meditation
1981	M 2362	Brothers and Sisters
1979	SAF 50091	In Nigeria (with Lolo Lolita)
1983	SAF 50112	Les Evades de Ponton La Belle (with Lolo): Jeannot
1984	AR 0990	Nostalgie D'Afrique (with Les Officiers)
1985	MCL 217	Les Officiers Attaquent (with Les Officiers)
	ORB 007	Full Steam Ahead (UK version of above)
1986	AR 1000	Kilimanjaro

Passi Jo

79424	Les Hommes Voltigeurs

Verckys (b. Kiamuangana Matesa, Zaire, 1944). By the 1980s, Verckys had established a reputation both as one of Zaire's best sax players and as the controller of a vast music empire. He started his musical career as a sax player with Franco in OK Jazz before leaving towards the end of the 1960s to establish his own outfit, L'Orchestre Veve. The band continued to feature Verckys' raucous horn arrangements and he composed many hits during the 1970s. But while Veve became one of Zaire's favourite bands, Verckys was paying as much if not more attention to his business affairs. He started as a sponsor for younger bands when he left Franco and began to buy equipment for hire. In 1976 he formed his own production company and over the next few years released a series of compilations featuring many of the best Congo orchestras. Entitled *Les Grands Success Des Editions Veve* *(Vols 1 - 9)*, these compilations included material by Veve, Kiam, Kamale, Lipua-Lipua and Zaiko. In the meantime he had reorganised his own band and continued to release albums of the highest quality. By the 1980s Verckys was established as a major musical force in Zaire. He produced albums by many top stars including Bakuba, Langa Langa Stars and Victoria and built one of the best studio complexes in the country. He then purchased a pressing plant and added rehearsal rooms and nightclub to the Veve Complex in Kinshasa. By 1985 he had broken the monopoly of Franco and Tabu Ley, thus earning their lasting enmity. He continued to release dozens of albums on his EVVI label and is today a force to be reckoned with on the Zairean music scene.

1969	360 041	Veve/Maquisards
1970	360 106	Baluti
	360 016	Dynamite
1970s	SAF 50008	Isabo
	SAF 50009	Vebaka Serment
1978	SAF 50073	Les Grands Success Vol. 3
1980s	EVVI 01	Nalobaka Na Tina
	EVVI 02	Seliba
1985	REM 650	L'Immortelle Veve (with Josky)
	EVVI 11D	L'Immortelle Veve; Dribling Ya Somo
	EVVI 63D	Est Ce Que

Lipua Lipua. Orchestre Lipua Lipua were one of the most popular bands of the 1970s. Featuring at one time or another such luminaries as Nyboma, Vata Mombassa and Mulembu, they established a reputation for sweet and inventive soukous.

1974	360 063	Mombassa
1983	VVLP 83	Pasi Ya Mosapi Vol. 1
1984	AR 0988	Vata Mombassa; En Colère

Bokelo, Johny (b. Bokelo Isenge, Zaire). One of Zaire's most influential guitarists, Johny Bokelo started his career in the 1950s with Orchestre Congo Success, a band formed by his brother Dewayon (Paul Ebengo). Honours were shared on the early albums but the guitar virtuosity of Bokelo soon overshadowed his brother's contribution and by the mid-1960s top billing had gone to Bokelo. He continued to sing about love and its problems but also recorded several advertising songs for Skol beer and Toyota. The majority of his material was released on singles, many of which appear on the various compilations of Congo music. In 1967 Bokelo enhanced his reputation for stylish innovation by introducing a new dance – the Kirikiri – to Kinshasa audiences. The following year he established his own band under the name Johny Bokelo and the Congo 68 and continued to record prolifically. In 1970 he renamed it Orchestre Congo de Bokelo but faced with a rising generation of new musicians his appeal faded. He continued to play occasionally and record sporadically until his career, along with those of Mayaula and Dr Nico, was revived by the opening of a new 24-track recording studio in Lomé. Backed by Les Redoubtables D'Abeti, Bokelo recorded several outstanding albums which introduced him to a new generation of fans, most notably *Isabelle*, his 1984 hit album.

1966	360 014	L'Afrique Danse
1967	360 007	L'Afrique Danse No. 7
1981	AFMS 008	1981
1984	ANS 8403	Isabelle (also WNL 401)
1985	ESP 8420	Mwan'Ansel (with Orc. Mbondo Africa Music)

Maquisards, Les Grands. One of Zaire's most influential orchestras, Les Grands Maquisards (Warriors) were formed towards the end of the 1960s in the Shaba region in the south of the country. Unfortunately, however, memories of the Katanga secession remained strong and several members of the band were imprisoned by Mobutu who suspected them of supporting the secessionists. The band held together for several more years and proved to be a fertile training ground for musicians who later went on to establish significant solo careers. Early members included the vocalists Josky, Dalienst and Kiesse Diambu (each of whom later starred with OK Jazz), the guitarist Jobs and Diana.

1985	360 155	Les Merveilles du Passé 1968-69
1976	360 086	Rosa
1973	360 041	Veve/Les Grands Maquisards

Mounka, Pamelo (b. Bemba Pamelo Mounk'a, Congo). Singer and composer and now acknowledged as the finest singer to emerge from Congo-Brazzaville. Pamelo made his debut as a singer in 1963 at the side of his first 'master' and friend, Tabu Ley. He moved on to the Bantous for several years, singing alongside Kosmos and Samba Mascott, establishing a national reputation as a gifted and soulful singer. During this early part of his career, Pamelo released more than 70 singles, recorded in a makeshift Brazza studio. By the 1970s he had carved out a niche in the competitive Congo music scene, singing about love and its victims and steadfastly refusing to be influenced by newer sounds from abroad. His fast maturing talent can be heard to best advantage on *Les Grandes Succes Africains*

Vol. 9. His biggest breakthrough came in 1981 when he was invited by Eddyson Records to record in Paris. He complied with the smash hit of 1981 – the LP *L'Argent Appelle L'Argent.* Playing with the best of Congolese musicians, Master Mwana Congo, Pablo, Salsero and the ubiquitous Eddie Gustave, Pamelo followed up his first major commercial success with a series of recordings which confirmed his talent both as singer and arranger. In 1983 he reunited with his old 'master', Tabu Ley, to celebrate his 20 years in the music business with the immediately forgettable album *20 Ans De Carrière.* In 1985, he found his touch again with the majestic album *En Plein Maturité.* Today Pamelo Mounka stands at the threshold of a major international breakthrough. With a softer paced rhythm and a sophisticated backing arrangement, his voice has reached a new peak of maturity which fellow musicians rate as one of the best in Africa.

1975	064 15968	Les Grands Succes Africains Vol.9
1981	SON 79406	L'Argent Appelle L'Argent
	SON 79413	Samantha
1982	MAY 014	Selimandja
	SON 79422	Propulsion
1983	RC 2001	Ca Ne Se Prete Pas (Africain No.1)
	GEN 106	20 Ans De Carrière
1984	SON 79430	Camitana
1985	ANS 8407	Metamorphose
	AP 049	Assetou Diarabi
1986	BM 002	L'Amour et La Danse (with the Bantous/Malapet)
	IS 001	Cynthia

Zaiko Langa Langa. A guitar band, formed in Kinshasa in 1969 and still in the forefront of Zairean 'new wave'. Over the last 17 years, Zaiko have led the way in the development of the Congo sound with a much rougher and simpler type of soukous. Founded by the drummer Bakunde Ilo Pablo, Zaiko acted as a catalyst for a younger generation of bands which emerged in the 1970s including Empire Bakuba, Viva La Musica and Stukas. The band features three guitarists, bass and drums in support of a strong front line of four, sometimes more, vocalists – originally Likinga, Lengi-Lenga, Bimi Ombale and N'yoka Longo. The band proved to be extremely popular with the youth and established their reputation with a succession of frenzied soukous hits. The vast majority appeared originally as 45 rpms but a few have been compiled on the excellent *Oldies and Goodies* album. By the 1980s, Zaiko had become one of the most prolific bands in Zaire, releasing dozens of albums on a bewildering variety of labels. The band also experienced a fairly vigorous turnover in personnel with ex-members going on to form their own outfits including Viva La Musica in 1974 (and thus indirectly Victoria in 1982), Grand Zaiko Wa Wa, Choc Stars, Langa Langa Stars and Historia. Taken together, these groups comprise the very heart of Zairean new sound – a music which has been described as 'exploring the cultural space of Zairean music, to the very frontiers of imagination'. Zaiko toured West Africa in the mid-1970s and now often appear in Paris and Brussels. The original line-up included N'yoka Longo, Bimi Ombale, Efonge, Likinga, Lengi-Lenga, Bozi Boziana and Mavuela on vocals, Pepe Manuaku and Matima on solo guitar, Sukami and Zamuangana on rhythm guitars, Moanda on tumba and Pablo on drums. Eight original members remain.

1970s	MGL 003	Oldies and Goodies 1974-1978 (released 1985)
	SAF 50076	Editions Veve Vol. 6
1981	FCZ 001	Sarah Djenni
1983	FCZ 002	La Tout Neige
	IADS 007	Tout Choc-Anti Choc
	19757	Zekete Zekete
	PZL 3368	Zekete Zekete 2eme
	MGL 001	Zekete Zekete 3eme
1984	EVVI 03	Crois-Moi
	PZL 84001	On Gagne Le Process
	REM 100	Mere Tity
	CM 635	Wina
	EQ 4001	De Paris A Brazzaville
1985	KKM 001	En Europe
	PZL 8586	Pusa Kuna
	PZL 85002	Ziko Eyi Nkisi
	PZL 85003	Tala Modela Echanger
1986	REM 20	Muvaro
	REM 540	Kay Kay
	PZL 199	Eh Ngoss, Eh Ngoss
	MA	Thy Thy Na (J-P Buse, Popolipo and some of the Zaiko line-up.)
	PZL 86/87	Au Japon, Nippon Banzai

Langa Langa Stars. Formed in 1981, Langa Langa Stars represent one of the most productive of all the Zaiko offshoots. Led by Bozi, the band play in the hard rough style perfected by Zaiko. However, the entire Zaiko school remain close companions and while they perform as solo units they also collaborate on projects. For example, Langa Langa Stars have recorded with the both the Choc Stars and Zaiko. By the mid-1980s many of these outfits had already split to form new bands, each with a distinctive studio sound. Lately the singer Evoloko Jocker has assumed a leading role.

1983	FVVI 16	Requiem
	EVVI 17	Avenir Mbeya
1984	JPM 30384	Rencontre (Pablo/Zaiko; Bozi/Langa)
1985	EVVI 22	Likombe
	EVVI 24	Moyeko (with Choc Stars)
	REM 330	Bouquet Des Flores
	REM 340	Soleil
	REM 350	Eliyo
1986	EVVI 47	Evoloko Jocker; La Carte qui Gagne
1987	EVVI 71	Evoloko Jocker; Done Bis

Clan Langa Langa. An informal recording group comprising members of the Zaiko family.

| 1982 | CLL 011 | Majolina |

Choc Stars. Formed in 1983, as an offshoot from Langa Langa Stars, Les Choc Stars feature Bozi Boziana and Ben Nyambe on vocals and Tshimpaka Roxy on lead guitar. In 1984 they released two singles and two LPs to introduce their new dance rhythm – Roboti Robota.

1985	CHOC 055	A Paris
1986	ORB 009	D.V.
	ORB 010	Awa Et Ben (Also available on Rythmes Et Musiques.)

Victoria (Victoria Eleison). Led by Emenya, Victoria emerged from the ranks of Viva La Musica in 1982. The band had a big hit with 'Sans Preavis' in 1983 and followed up in 1984 with hit songs entitled 'Dallas' and 'Dynasty'. The band was led by Emenya and Cartouche, both vocalists. The group split in 1984 with Cartouche striking out on his own with Historia, establishing a new hard, soukous sound.

1984	REM 370	Sango Mabala Commission
	EVVI 20	Okosi Ngai Mfumu
1986	ESP 8423	Cartouche; Double Jeu
	EVVI 46	Kimpiatu
	REM 610	Emenaya Emerite
1987	EVVI 70	Manhattan

Grand Zaiko Wa-Wa. Formed in 1980 by Manuaku, lead guitarist from Zaiko. Manuaku had redefined the role of the lead guitar as the lead instrument in modern Congo music producing a harder rhythm – the

Cavacha – accompanied by much rougher vocals. He likes to take traditional folk dances and modernise them to contemporary idioms.

1980s	EVVI10D	Le Grand Maître Waku Manuaku
1986	425.003	Shimita et Le Grand Zaiko Wa Wa

Wemba, Papa (b. Shungu Wembadia, Kasai, Zaire). As a singer and composer, Papa Wemba first came to notice in the early 1970s as a singer with the 'new wave' outfit, Zaiko Langa Langa. He left the group in 1974 and set up Isifi Lokole, followed in 1976 by Viva La Musica. Early recordings can be heard on the compilation album *L'Afrique Danse*, alongside other new bands like Zaiko and Les Trois Frères. As one of the strongest guardians of Zaire's musical tradition, Papa Wemba, despite his eccentric appearance, became a champion of the 'Authenticité' movement. By the 1980s his reputation was established and Papa Wemba left Viva and recorded several LPs in Paris with the cream of Zaire's musical community. In 1984 he made an excellent LP with Lita Bembo, Bozi Boziana and Esperant in a new super group called La Guerre des Stars.

1970s	360 117	L'Afrique Danse
	IDD 2536	Papa Wemba et L'Orchestra Viva La Musica
1980s	PASS 01	Papa Wemba et Les Djamuskets à Paris
1984	REM 140	Firenze
1985	TCHIKA 07	La Guerre Des Stars
1986	AR 00862	Mavuela
	BMP 001	Siku Ya Mungu
	REM 10	Mwana Molokai
	REM 560	Ma Bijoux

Trio Madjesi. An excellent trio of vocalists who appeared on the scene in 1972. Backed by Orchestra Sosoliso, they were originally heavily influenced by James Brown, who had toured Zaire in 1969. Comprising Loko Massengo, Saakul and Matadidi, the band toured widely in Africa, including visits to Togo, Congo, Ivory Coast and Gabon. They released many singles including their most famous song 'Sex Madjesi'. Towards the end of the decade the band split up; Matadidi returned to Angola, Loko Massengo moved to Congo while Saakul remained in Zaire. In 1983 they reunited in Paris where they are now based.

1973	360 043	Sex Madjesi Vol.1
	360 044	Trio Madjesi Vol.2
	360 053	Trio Madjesi Vol.3
1984	SDI 114	Le Retour De Trio Madjesi

BAE 4004	Loko Massengo; L'International Rumbaya
SAS 041	Loko Massengo; Non Stop Tchiabuala
BAE 4001	Loko Massengo & Michael Boyibanda
SAS 049	Loko Massengo – Bloque Zinque

Muana, Tshala (b. Lubumbashi, Zaire). Female singer, composer and dancer, Tshala Muana was born into a family of singers and dancers and was active from an early age in a number of cultural troupes. She first made her mark as a dancer, adapting the traditional Mutuashi dance to a more modern idiom. She then turned to singing and performed with several of Kinshasa's leading bands. During the mid-1970s she recorded several singles but left the country in 1979 to pursue an international career. She settled in Côte d'Ivoire and converted the notoriously discerning Ivorian public with several hits. Between 1981 and 1984 she toured extensively throughout West and Central Africa prior to her arrival in Paris where, in 1984, she recorded her first LP. She had been voted one of Africa's best female singers in various opinion polls, but with the success of her first LP she was voted top female artist in 1984. In 1985 she visited the USA and with the help of Alhadji Toure and Prosper Nkouri she recorded her second album which became a firm favourite with the record-buying public. Today, along with Abeti, Mpongo Love and Mbilia Bel, she stands at the forefront of Zairean music.

	ARCS 3690	Amina
1984	TM 058	Kami
1985	SAS 051	Mbanda Matiere
	SAS 057	M'Pokolo

Love, Mpongo (b. M'pongo Landu, Kinshasa, Zaire, 1956). Known as 'La Voix du Zaire', M'pongo Love has been crippled with polio since the age of four. Despite this setback, she was determined to pursue a career in music and after graduating from high school and a spell working as a secretary she was given the opportunity to turn professional. In 1977 she toured East Africa and on her return to Zaire was invited to perform with OK Jazz at the 1977 FESTAC in Lagos. She released her first LP the same year. On her second album she recruited the help of some Africa's best session musicians, including Eko Roosevelt, Jules Kamga, Vicky Edimo and the omnipresent Alhadji Toure. In 1983 she maintained her tradition of utilising experienced session men and with the help of Dino Vangu and Sammy Massamba released the outstanding *Femme Commerçante*. In 1984, with the assistance of Bopol and Wuta May from Les Quatres Etoiles, she released another successful album entitled *Basongeur*. She continued to tour widely, including a tour of Scandinavia in 1984 to mark the International Year of the Handicapped. In 1986 she toured the UK and confirmed her international status with three new releases.

1977	360 102	L'Afrique Danse
1980	DPX 821	La Voix Du Zaire
1983	SAS 036	Femme Commerçante
1984	SAS 047	Basongeur
1985	INV 001	Chante Alexandre Sambat
	INV 003	Exclusivité Ya L'Amour
	NK 5113	Une Seule Femme
1986	REM 440	Mokili Complique

Abeti. Born Abeti Masikini, Abeti is today one of the foremost Zairean female vocalists. Her career stretches back to the early 1970s although it was only towards the end of the decade that she began to issue LPs and from there establish a truly pan-African reputation. Backed by her band Les Redoubtables and supplemented by her troupe of male dancers (Les Tigres) and female dancers (Les Explosives) she is capable of presenting one of the most exciting live shows on the African continent. Many famous musicians have graduated through the ranks including the most well known, Mbilia Bel.

1971	SONICS	
	79398	Masikini
1970s	SAF 95301	Abeti (Also AME 9101)
1980s	ZIKA 001	Jalousie
1981	DPX 829	10th Anniversaire
1984	ANS 8402	Ba Mauvais Copistes
	ANS 8406	Tourda Nini (Les Redoubtables)

Pablo (b. Pablo Lubadika Porthos, Zaire, early 1950s). Singer-composer, and guitar virtuoso, Pablo first made his mark with a succession of Zairean bands during the 1970s. These included the Kin Bantous, Lovy du Zaire, Groupe Celibithou and Orchestre Kara. Towards the end of the decade he moved to Paris, like so many other Zairean musicians, before linking up with Sam Mangwana and the African All Stars to help record the classic song 'Georgette Eckins'. He then concentrated on a career as a session musician, helping a number of other celebrities to record their solo albums – including Pamelo Mounka, Master Mwana Congo and Assi Kapela. But Pablo was not content to pursue a successful session career and maintained his distinctive personal guitar style with a series of outstanding solo albums of fast and sweet soukous. However, it was his contributions to the excellent Island compilation, *Sound d'Afrique*, which made him a houshold name to a new market of international music lovers. Two songs in particular, 'Bo Mbanda' and 'Madeleina', marked him out for stardom. He performed irregularly with Les Quatre Etoiles but declined to join them on a permanent basis. In 1985 he released his first British LP on the Globestyle label. As perhaps the leading exponent of contemporary soukous, Pablo remains much sought after as a session guitarist while continuing to thrill audiences everywhere with his solo albums.

1980s	SYL 8308	Concentration
	AMR 109	Idie
	COSIC 1001	Revient En Force
	DARL 019	En Action
1985	ORB	Pablo Pablo Pablo
1986	BR 013	Safula (with Tutu)

Kanda Bongo Man (b. Kanda Bongo, Inongo, Zaire, 1955.) Singer composer, Kanda represents the third generation of modern Zairean music. He left school at the age of 18 to play in a local Kinshasa band before moving on to the well-known Orchestre Bella Mambo in 1976. He stayed with them for several years as the lead vocalist, scoring several hits and establishing a national reputation. Even today, he considers Bella Mambo to have been one of the best congolese bands. In 1979 he made his way to Paris and for the next few years worked hard to perfect his own brand of high-speed soukous, jumping straight into the sebene without the slower introduction favoured by the older generation. He also abandoned the horn section, so typical of the congolese sound, preferring to run a small band comprising 5-6 musicians. In 1981 he released his first solo album on the Afro-Rythmes label and followed up this initial success with two more outstanding recordings and a serious and professional approach to touring and live performances. Now based in Paris, Kanda is the subject of intense press coverage, including a stunning performance at the 1983 WOMAD Festival in the UK. He made several return visits to the UK, enhancing his reputation with every show, and in 1985 made a highly successful tour of Canada. He occasionally guests on other albums and is widely considered to be one of the brightest stars in the Zairean musical firmament.

1981	AR 00181	Iyole
1982	AR 00981	Djessy
1984	BM 0055	Amour Fou
1985	ORB 005	Non Stop Non Stop
1986		Malinga
1987	BM 0057	Lela Lela

Kasseya, Souzy (b. Kasseya, Shaba Province, Zaire, 1949). Singer-guitarist Souzy Kasseya is today one of Zaire's brightest and most inventive guitarists. He started playing at an early age with several well-known bands including Vox Afrique, where he temporarily teamed up with Sam Mangwana. He also established a career as a talented producer working with many major stars including Bebe Manga, Tshala Muana and François Lougah. In 1977 he made the move to Paris and became one of the most sought-after session guitarists. In 1984 he released his first solo album featuring the pick of the Paris-based session musicians, including Rigo (Ringo) Star on guitar and Salsero on drums. However, it was one song from the album which made an immediate breakthrough, 'Le Téléphone Sonne', which, when remixed for international consumption became an enormous cross-over hit. Released in the UK on the Earthworks label, the single helped Souzy establish an international reputation as a purveyor of the modern soukous sound. A master of production and studio sophistication, Souzy remained in demand as a record producer while his rare live shows guaranteed dance floor satisfaction. In 1984 Souzy performed live in London with Sam Mangwana and returned later to fufil a solo engagement. Further releases (both LPs and 12" dance singles) confirmed Souzy's fast maturing talents.

| 1984 | SAK 001 | Le Retour de L'As |
| 1985 | ELP 2008 | Le Phenomenal Souzy Kasseya (also SK84003) |

Quatre Etoiles. Les Quatres Etoiles, one of the few African supergroups, were formed in Paris in 1983 by four of Zaire's most accomplished musicians. Featuring Bopol on bass, Nyboma and Wuta May on vocals and Syran on lead guitar, the band is supplemented on stage by two or three supporting musicians. However, while the four stars constitute the core of the group there is a pool of other Paris based musicians who are only too happy to join in for an evening when one of the leaders misses a show. Others in the same circle include the vocalists Jean Papy and Passi Joe, Boffi on drums and the guitarist Ringo Star. To date they have released only three LPs, which have topped charts in Paris, London and Zaire. The band performs frequently in both Paris and London, selling out wherever they go and forcing fans to their feet with irresistibly simple soukous. However all the musicians involved in the group also pursue successful solo careers, releasing outstanding albums and helping each other and a younger generation of musicians to recreate the distinctive sound of Les Quatres Etoiles.

1984	SYL 8307	Enfant Balileke
1985	TAN 7009	Dance
1986		Zunkuluke

Bopol. Bopol Mansiamuia, a graduate from Afrisa and Orchestre Mode Success, is equally at home on lead, rhythm or bass guitar. He has fronted several other ensembles working with musicians like Assaka and Baba Ley. He moved to Paris in the early 1980s releasing several solo albums and featuring of dozens of others. A founding member of Les Quatre Etoiles, he continues to record his own distinctive material – a thumping dance beat supported by simple sing-a-long melodies.

1970s	INLP 001	Innovation Vol. 1 (also SMP 6026)
	INLP 002	Innovation Vol. 2
	INLP 003	Innovation Vol. 3
1980s	SMP 6011	Deception Motema
	LDS 001	Marriage Force
	SYL 8301	Manuela
	SYL 8305	Samedi Soir
	SYL 5310	Helena
1985	CEL 6749	Ca C'est Quoi
1987	SYL 8320	Serrez Ceinture

Syran. An exceptionally gifted guitarist, much sought after as a session musician, Syran Mbenza started his career with Orchestre Super Lovy. He then moved on to the African All Stars playing lead guitar on the Sam Mangwana classic 'Marie Tebbo' before joining Les Quatres Etoiles in 1983.

1980s	79416	Ilanga
	SOUL 001	Kouame
1986	ST 1018	Kass Kass (with Passi Jo and Jean Pappy)
1987	SYL 8328	Sisika

Nyboma. One of Africa's most popular tenor singers, Nyboma started his career with Orchestre Baby National in 1969. He then joined Bella Bella and Lipua Lipua for short spells before establishing his own outfit, Les Kamales, in 1973. The band went on to become one of Zaire's favourite rumba orchestras during the 1970s with several hit singles including their most popular song 'Kamale'. In 1979 he moved to Togo joining forces with Sam Mangwana and the African All Stars. Two years later he moved on to Abidjan where he recorded his classic hit 'Doublé Doublé', which was later released in Paris on an album of the same title. In 1982 he moved to Paris where he helped establish Les Quatres Etoiles. He has released several solo albums including a recent collaboration with the Empire Bakuba vocalist Pepe Kalle. Although several early albums are now unavailable, Les Kamales are heavily featured on both the Veve and L'Afrique Danse compilations.

1970s	VOZ 1003	Baya Boya
	SAF 50087	Les Kamales

	360 109	Ayindjo
1983	CEL 6624	Doublé Doublé
1985	SYL 8313	Bandona
1986	SYL 8324	Empire Bakuba (with Pepe Kalle)

Wuta May. The fourth and final member of Les Quatre Etoiles, Wuta May is an experienced and gifted vocalist who started his career in the late 1960s with Orchestre Continentale. He then moved on to join Franco and OK Jazz for a productive eight-year spell during which time he composed much of the band's best material. He has produced a series of excellent solo albums while maintaining his commitment to Les Quatre Etoiles.

1980s	79419	Le Beach
	79427	Ole La Vie
	LPKR 1004	Tshitsha
	LPKR 1013	Cheque Sans Provision (With Dino Vangu)
	SOW 002	Tout Mal Se Paie Ici Pas

Mabiala. Le Prince. Youlou Mabiala, like Wuta May, learned his craft during a long apprenticeship with OK Jazz. He often duetted with Franco and composed several of the band's most popular songs. He left the band in 1980 to establish a solo career backed by his own band Orchestre Kamikaze-Loningisa. Since then he has released a clutch of albums, each featuring his distinctive voice and well-orchestred material. Loningisa are capable of several gear changes in the course of a single song, making their music eminently danceable. A darling of the women, Youlou is one of Congo's biggest stars.

1980s	K 4224	100 Per Cent
	POP 05	Keba Na Mantraque
1983	IADS 001	Judoka
	150 175	Carte Postale
1984	POP 022	Motema Na Ngai Television
1985	AP 050	1 x 2 = Mabe
	TCHIKA01	Beyouna
	PS 002	Couper-Soucis
1986		5th Anniversaire

Somo Somo. Formed in Zambia in 1974, Somo Somo remains the brainchild of guitarist Mose Se Sengo, known universally as Fan Fan. A master guitarist, Fan Fan graduated through the ranks of OK Jazz, joining them in 1968 and playing lead guitar on several outstanding tracks. In 1974 he split from Franco, for whom he still has enormous respect, and established the first incarnation of Somo Somo with the help of his friends,

Prince Youlou, Celi Bichou and Kwamy. However the venture was short-lived and Youlou soon rejoined Franco, with Kwamy changing sides to join Afrisa. Fan Fan was however determined to go it alone and over the next ten years travelled widely establishing new groups in Zambia, Kenya and Tanzania. All were called Somo Somo. He released several albums in Kenya, few of which are still available. In 1984 he arrived in London to establish a new group and spread the gospel of soukous in the UK. He soon formed a 'London' group of enthusiastic and experienced musicians (ex-Ivory Coasters, Ipi Tombi, Jazira, etc.) whose first release became the critical success of 1985. The band toured widely both in Britain and Europe, making several television appearances to consolidate their growing reputation. Somo Somo proved to be something of a training school for British musicians and the band underwent a fairly rapid turnover in personnel. In 1986 Fan Fan travelled to Paris to record his second LP for Stern's, this time featuring the combined talents of fellow Zaireans like Passi Joe, Jean Pappy, Jimmy and Fredo on horns and Herman Asafo-Agyei on bass.

1970s	EFA 05	Amba
	EFA 019	Shikamoo
1984	ST 1007	Somo Somo
1986	ST 1014	Paris

Lema, Ray. Zairean guitarist, keyboardist and composer, Lema modernises folklore material in a style completely different from the soukous school. He began playing in 1965 mixing traditional rhythms with a classical keyboard style. Heavily influenced by the rock style of Jimmy Hendrix, he abandoned his studies in 1972 to form his first group. He later backed Tabu Ley and was organiser of the Zairean National Ballet. In 1979 he travelled to the USA on a Rockefeller Foundation award, and returned with a new musical mix using reggae, funk and soul elements. He is now based in Europe.

1979	CEL 6631	Koteja-Koluto
1980s	CEL 6658	Paris-Kinshasa-Washington D.C.
	CEL 6756	Medecine

Taxi Pata Pata. Led by Nsimba Foguis, the first Zairean vocalist in London, Taxi follow on from Somo Somo as a hot club favourite. Their first record was released in 1987.

1987	TAXI	Mbote – Happy People

Stukas. Backing group of Lita Bembo, one of the longest serving 'new wave' artistes. Bembo, who is of CAR origin, has a distinctively wild vocal style but the Stukas have not made the commercial penetration of some groups which have copied them.

1980s		Conflit
	ST 005	Valalim
	REM 130	Dadou

Empire Bakuba. Led by the giant-sized Pepe Kalle, with his deep, throaty vocal style, Bakuba are yet another example of the high-energy Kinshasa style of soukous, which utilises voices and guitars without the horn sections of the 'classic' stylists.

1980s	REM 70	Amour Propre
	8730	Obosini Kisonde
	EVVI 45	Cherie Ondi
1985	PF 770	Bonana 85
	REM 360	La Belle Etoile
	REM 410	Trop C'est Trop
	REM 490	Muana Bangui
1986	SYL 8324	Bakuba (with Nyboma)
	8040	Adieu Dr Nico

Star, Rigo (or Ringo). A Paris-based guitarist who is one of the finest individual talents working in the European studios, where he also arranges material in collaboration with star vocal performers.

1980s	EDYson	Rigo Star
1986	MA 4005	Rigo and Josky: Jotongo
	MA 4017	Rigo and Koffi: Ai,Ai

Various

There are countless bands and individual artistes from Zaire who have released albums, and to attempt to list them all would be an impossible task. These are just a few of the many musicians from Congo and Zaire who have released their own albums: Master Mwana Congo, Jerry Melekani, Mayaula, Shaba, Dalienst Ntessa, Josky Kiambukuta, Matalanza Sax, Fidel Zizi, Simarro Massiya, Dindo Yogo, Lengi Lenga, Zao, Kosmos, Pierre and Michel Moutouari, Geo Bolingo, Carlito, Bozi Boziana, Kofi Olomide, D'Jenga Ka, Mimi Ley, Mav Cacharel, Maika Munan, Bovic, Ya Mauro, Bibi Dens, Ndombe Opetum, Theo Blaise, Diblo Dibala, Michelino, Aurlus Mabele.

With a total population of under two million, Gabon contains over 40 ethnic groups, displaying a linguistic, religious and artistic diversity unusual even in Africa. Music plays a central role in ritual and religious observation, while similar to the griots of West Africa, the mvet players accompany epic narratives of the past. Gabon also displays a great variety of instruments, including the mouth bows and harps of the Masengo, the mvet (harp-zither), xylophone and rattles of the Fang, the vocals and handclapping of the Okamba, the bow-lutes of the Pounou, the drums of the Kota and the unforgettable polyphonic yodelling of the pygmies. Contemporary Fang music emerged from two distinct cults; the older mbiri religious style and the twentieth-century Bwiti music, associated with the use of the psychotropic 'eboga' plant. Bwiti developed as a kind of urban religion as the Fang came together in the major trading centres. Other Gabonese styles to be found on record include the music of the Gbaya, one of the largest ethnic groups who spread into neighbouring Cameroon and whose main instrument is the sanza; the Bateke of the south-east, many of whom live in Congo and whose music is based on sanza, zither and drums and the Mitsogho of central Gabon who are famous for their harps and musical bows. Finally we should mention the distinctive pygmy music, well represented on vinyl due perhaps more to their exotic connotations than the significance of their music. This is not to underrate the unique qualities of their vocals. But the fact remains that while much of African music is as yet unrecorded, the pygmies have been singled out for the attention of mainly western anthropologists and ethno-musicologists. In Gabon, the pygmies are divided by region into the Babongo, the Akoa, the Bakola and the Bibayak. The Bibayak live in a close symbiotic relationship with the Fang. Their music is essentially vocal, with voices entering the musical cycle at intervals to construct a complex polyphony. The pygmies have no musical instruments of their own, although they have adopted the mbeny drum of the Fang.

Traditional Music

ETH 4457   The Pygmies of the Ituri Forest

GABON

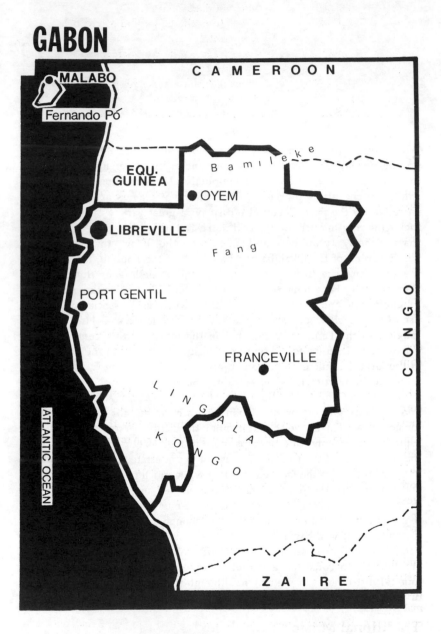

ETH 4402	Music of Equatorial Africa
FF 4214	Music from the Equatorial Microcosm: Fang Bwiti
VPA 8232	Gabon: Musica de un Microcosm Equatorial
OCR558504	Gabon: Musiques des Pygmies Bibayak
OCR 41	Musiques du Gabon
OCR 84	Gabon: Musiques des Mitsogho et de Bateke

Popular Music

The popular music of Gabon came to prominence in Europe during the 1980s through the efforts of the Paris-based singer and poet Pierre Akendengue whose creative talents almost rival those of Cameroonian Francis Bebey. Akendengue, however, is a true individualist and for a more representative measure of popular taste one must look to the powerful musical exports of the neighbouring countries Cameroon and Congo, which dominate the Gabonese scene. Since the inauguration of the powerful radio station Africa No 1, the voice of Libreville and the sounds of Africa can be heard across the continent (and even in Europe with a sensitive SW receiver). In 1985 the 24-track studio Mademba was opened in Libreville and with several production companies in action, the future for music in this commercial centre seems assured.

Akendengue, Pierre (b. Port Gentil, Gabon, 1944). Akendengue, singer, composer, poet, guitarist and dramatist, is without doubt Gabon's most musical son. He was born into a musical family and by the age of 14 had composed several songs which had been played on the radio. In 1964 he left Gabon to finish his studies in Paris, acquiring his baccalaureat from Orléans, and a degree in literature from Caen before proceeding to the Sorbonne to study pyschology. It was during this period that Akendengue went blind and eventually returned to Gabon. However he soon began to speak out against the government and was forced to leave the country in 1972. But he had not neglected his music and in 1974 he released his first LP – *Nandipo*. On this classic album, Akendengue established his distinctive and unique style, making use of a wide variety of techniques, styles and instruments. By combining music and poetry, modern and traditional instruments, politics and parables, Akendengue presented a thoughtful, mature new sound. In 1976 he was awarded the annual MIDEM prize for composing the year's best francophone songs. In 1977 he was the beneficiary of a presidential pardon and was invited back to Gabon to represent his country at FESTAC in Nigeria. In 1978 he released his third album *Eserengila*, which picked up the 1979 Maracas d'Or. By the 1980s

Akendengue had established a reputation throughout Africa with his innovative and imaginative music. In 1983 he released *Awana W'Afrika*, displaying a more modern, electric, dance-orientated side to his music. In 1985, due to popular demand his first two albums were re-released. By this time Akendengue was touring regularly, in America, Europe and Africa and had established his own record label.

1978	LDX 74677	Oppression
		Eserengila
1983	CBS 25355	Mando
	NTAKN 13003	Awana W'Afrika
1984	NTAKN 13004	Reveil de L'Afrika
1985	SH 10045	Nandipo
	SH 10063	Obota
1987	AKN 13005	Pirogier

Massako. Orchestre Massako are one of Gabon's most popular dance bands who have over the years released many albums and singles, while supporting many of the country's top solo stars in the Libreville studio. Sponsored by the Police, their line-up has over the years read like a who's who of Gabonese pop. Currently led by vocalists Mack Joss, Chakara and Menghe, with Sec Bidens and and Sita Mbele, the band was formed in 1978 by Mack Joss Nono Mishima. They started as a rumba-Afro-Cuban band but have over the years added elements of makossa to their style. Early hits included 'Yvette', 'Bonne Annee', 'Operation Aluti', 'La Vie', 'Commandement Supplementaire' and 'Tata Batu'.

1983	SAF 50107	Amara Toure et Massako
1985	PRO 008	Super Forme (also MAS 008)
	PRO 009	En Verve (also MAS 009)

Diablotins, Les. A 15-piece big band from Gabon, Les Diablotins are one of the finest soukous outfits in Africa. Much underrated and seldom heard outside Gabon, they emerged in the early 1980s with a string of albums, all recorded in Paris and all directed by Elvis Kemayo, then Director of Music for Gabonese TV. The most outstanding songs include 'Weekend à Libreville' from Vol. 4 and 'Changement de Mentalité' and 'Africa No. 1', both from Vol. 7. The last of these songs is used as the theme song for the powerful Gabonese radio station, 'Africa No. 1', which promotes 18-hours of non-stop African music daily to most of Central and West Africa. More recently Les Diablotins have been providing musical backing for other Gabonese stars.

1981	DB 1760	Les Diablotins a Paris Vol. 1

1982	DB 1761	A Paris Vol. 2
	DB 1762	A Paris Vol. 3
1983	DB 1763	A Paris Vol. 4
	DB 1764	A Paris Vol. 5
	DB 1765	A Paris Vol. 6
	DB 1766	A Paris Vol. 7
1985	MD 1769	Diablotins '85
	MD 1770	Diablotins '85
1985	MD 1771	Santa Backita et Les Diablotins
1985	MD 1768	Angele Assele et Les Diablotins

Missema. Missema are one of Gabon's most popular female choral groups. Backed by a full electric band, the 30 or more singers produce a powerful sound which is only now beginning to be appreciated outside Gabon.

1985	MI 2002	Avec Missema en Vacances
1986	MI 2003	Missema au Centenaire

Various. Today Gabon has a lively music scene with a well-developed infrastructure of clubs, studios and pressing plant. Current pop bands include Noukogha, Ignonga, Boemame, Mademba, Pierre Clavier Zeng and Cooperative.

1978	SAF 55101	Orc. Afro-Success
1979	DPX 814	Martin Rompavet: Air Gabon
	SB 009	Sec Bidens: Top Nuveaux No. 2
	J 5129	Hilarion Nguema: Espoir
1985	MH 0102	Hilarion Nguema: Le Retour de Veteran
	REM 380	Ange Linaud: Lady
	GM1936	Cooperative. Super Ngo Ngo (Hot soukous with Sec Bidens and others)
1985	ESP 7516	Douema Domingue: Fatal
1985	MD 1767	Angele Assele: Esperancia
1985	EV 1266	Vyckos-Ekondo: Le Cable du Tandima
	AZ 20003	Aziz Inanga: N'Kala (Female vocalist, folk arrangements.)
	SAS 037	Julien Nzengui (with Sammy Massamba)
1986	MPHB 1244	Marie Philomena Battosougha: Phi Pepe

Compilations. There are three excellent Gabonese compilations currently available, featuring the best of Gabonese pop. Published by the Agence Nationale de Promotion Artistiques et Culturelle (ANPAC), these records represent a conscious attempt by the government to introduce Gabonese musicians to a wider public.

1984	AN 4001	L'ANPAC presente Vol. 1 (Hilarion Nguema, Marcel Djabioh, Jean Assele, Itsiembu-Y-Mbin, Jo-Man Anquilet)
1984	AN 4002	L'ANPAC Presente Vol. 2 (Pierre Clavier Zeng, Angete Revignet, Santo Backito, Julien Nzengui, Norbert Epandja)
1984	AN 4403	L'ANPAC Presente Vol. 3 (Mack Joss, Pierre Emboni, Yvon Dawensi, Obiang Okane)
1986	CIC8401/2	Bantu. (CICIBA was founded in 1983 on the initiative of President Bongo of Gabon by ten different central African countries – Gabon, Angola, Central African Republic, Comoros Islands, Congo, Equatorial Guinea Rwanda, São Tomé, Zaire and Zambia – as a centre for research and documentation into the region's common musical culture. On this double album, each country is represented with two songs. The album progresses from the more traditional music to more modern urban sounds. An excellent compilation which no one interested in the musical traditions of Central Africa should be without.)

20
Angola/São Tomé and Príncipe

Angola and the small off-shore islands of São Tomé and Príncipe are generally considered to be part of the Congo basin musical world. Little traditional music is available, although attention must be drawn to the Bantu compilation (see under Gabon).

With centuries of exploitation following the demise of the Kongo kingdom, Angola even today is confronted by the combined forces of internal subversion, foreign invasion and external economic exploitation. Under these circumstances it would be all too easy to assume that the life of the average Angolan contained little that was uplifting, enjoyable or pleasing. However, without minimising the very real hardships endured daily by the mass of the Angolan people, it would be impossible to discuss the country without making reference to the various ways in which people enjoy their leisure time and how music in particular helps ease the strain and stress of daily life.

There is a second reason for considering music in something other than its purely recreational context, for in Angola, as in many African countries, the development of a music industry closely reflected the development of other social and economic forces – a correspondence seen most clearly in the development of music in Zimbabwe in the years immediately following Independence. The same general interpretation can be generally applied throughout lusophone Africa where a vicious Portuguese colonialism inhibited the growth of modern, urban pop music. The industry, small as it was, remained under the direction of the Portuguese authorities who controlled access to recording equipment, access to the radio and even the organisation of major social and cultural events. Under such restrictive conditions, many leading musicians decided either to quit music or leave the country for more hospitable climes. In the countryside, where Portuguese cultural hegemony proved far less effective, 'traditional music' continued to flourish as perhaps the most potent cultural expression of the spirit of resistance.

When Angola finally won independence in 1974, many of the 'immigrés' returned home to enrich indigenous musical traditions with styles and rhythms picked up abroad. These will be described in greater detail later in this section.

ANGOLA

Among the main Angolan musical traditions we should mention the 'likembe' (a sanza-mbira) which finds a home from Cameroon to Sudan and from Mozambique to Angola. As a favourite instrument of traders, porters and workers during the first decades of colonial imposition the 'likembe' spread throughout Central Africa . As Kubik has noted, 'Often the likembe was the only companion of the solitary traveller to the mines and industrial urban centres.' By the mid-1960s, the likembe was still finding new converts throughout Angola. One of the most respected likembe musicians is Kafuna Mwozi Kandonga. Performing during the 1960s, Kandonga noted the recent introduction of likembe, describing it as an instrument of the younger generation. Those who are more interested in the likembe traditions of Angola should consult G. Kubik.

Very little 'traditional' Angolan music is currently available on vinyl.

6803 044	Humbi – Handa – Angola
6810 955	A Victoria e Certa
FW 5442	Angolan Freedom Songs
LDS 4308	Lieder Des Freiheitskampfes Angolas
MC11	Mukanda na Makisi
LLST 7311	Music of the Tshowke People of the Angolan Border
LLST 7313	Sanza and Guitar. Music of the Bena Luluwa. Angola / Zaire

Popular Music

The contemporary music of Angola is similar in style and form to the more familiar sounds of Zaire – a neighbouring country with whom Angola shares a long and close musical affinity. However, Zaire is not the only external influence on contemporary Angolan music; Brazilian troops were used by the Portuguese colonialists to suppress rebellions in Angola over a century ago, Brazilian radio can be heard in Luanda, while more recently Angola has played host to several thousand Cuban troops. It should therefore not be surprising to find identifiable Latin elements in modern Angolan pop. More recently, the music industry in Angola has produced several well known bands like Semba Tropical and Sensacional Maringa. They have made several overseas tours including visits to Zaire, the UK and Holland. However, it still remains the case that foreign invasion and internal subversion have taken their toll on the development of music in Angola.

Orquestra Caravela.

CCD 115	Amour Sans Frontières (Their first LP; Caravela are a ten-piece big band playing in the Congo style.)

Diana et Les Bobongo Stars (Led by Diana aka N'Simba Simon. Diana left Angola during the 1960s, making his debut as a singer with Tabu Ley in 1968. He remained in Zaire for the next eight years, performing with a number of top bands before forming his own outfit – Olympia. In 1976, following Independence, he returned to Angola. His music is identical to the Congo sound.)

MAN 001	Marguerida

Sensacional Maringa de Angola. (A big 15-piece band, featuring a distinctive horn section, Sensacional Maringa play a light, well-balanced type of merengue with definite Latin influences in the percussion and keyboard playing.)

IEFE 056	Lelu'eze

Dimba Dya Ngola. (Led by Boano Da Silva, Dimba are a 12-strong dance band which draw on a number of sources including Cuban, Zairean and highlife. With a full, round sound, they play an up-tempo dance style most reminiscent of Ibo highlife.)

IEFE 059	Luanda Cidade Linda

Os Jovens Do Prenda.

IEFE 042	Musica de Angola (A delightful album, featuring a basic Congo line-up.)

Manuel Francisco Gomes.

SG 113	Viva Coladera (Sounding like one of the poorer entries for the Eurovision song contest, this album is not typical of the current Angolan sound.)

Mito Nacurranza. A three man group.

IEFE 013	Nita Ti Sunga (this album is saved from almost total obscurity by the excellent guitar work of Jaimito. The sound owes more to South African jazz than to the Congo influence.)

Mario Ray Silva.

      CCD 123   Sungaly

Mura (An outstanding female singer. Strong Congo-highlife sound.)

      IEFE 064   Musica de Angola/Zaire

São Tomé/Príncipe

Until recently, the exciting music of São Tomé and the smaller island of Príncipe was almost impossible to find outside the islands themselves. One of Africa's smallest states, with a combined population of less than 80,000, the islands are situated in the Eastern Atlantic, almost equidistant from Nigeria, Gabon, Zaire and Angola. These ex-Portuguese colonies remain economically underdeveloped, politically unstable yet strategically important. Their music reflects a mixture of influences from the larger mainland neighbours which can be best be appreciated in the recent work of Conjunto Africa Negra – an eleven-piece guitar band who play a light and spacey music with stunning guitar solos which are reminiscent of the guitar work of Nico Mbarga. Three albums are currently available on the Portuguese Intercontinental Fonografica label.

1983	IEFE 043	Africa Negra '83
	IEFE 046	Angelica
	IEFE 052	Alice

Similar in sound, but capable of a greater variety of mood and tempo are Conjunto Os Leononses. Led by singer-composer Pedro Lima, they are an up-tempo guitar band.

    1983   IEFE 066   Conjunto Os Leononses: Maquidala

Finally there is the Portuguese-speaking singer Sum Alvarinho who combines fast Congo-style guitar breaks with distinctively Latin percussion.

    1983   IEFE 030   Sum Alvarinho: Musicas e Letras Alvarinho

21
Equatorial Guinea

The smallest one of the three West African Guineas, Equatorial Guinea is a republic made up of the mainland territory of Rio Muni between Gabon and Cameroon, and the island state of Bioko (Fernando Po) off the Cameroon coast. The Fang are the dominant ethnic group. Until gaining independence in 1968 it was a Spanish colony, but during the 1970s the internal politics turned very nasty, and those who could fled the country until the tyrannical regime of President Nguemo was overthrown in 1979. By all accounts, the mainland has been bypassed by the twentieth century(although recent travellers talk of dancing to Beatles' records in the villages). Since independence, the island of Bioko has emerged as the most economically important region and this is where the capital Malabo is situated. Communications with Cameroon and Gabon are good, better even than those between Rio Muni and Malabo, so not surprisingly, talented young musicians from Equatorial Guinea have emerged in these countries, among whom several have recorded in Paris. The predominant style is the makossa, as exemplified in the early 1980s albums recorded by Maele, Baltasa Baltasar Nsue (Le Grand Bessoso) and Victoriano Bibang (Efamba) which feature the studio talents of Cameroonians Toto Guillaume, Ebeny Wesley, Alhadji Toure, JC Naimro and several of Manu Dibango's band, including drummer Valerie Lobe and vocalists Sissy Dipoko and Florence Titty.

M5656	Maele: Evom Nguan
001B	Le Grand Bessoso: Tan Solo Si, Tan Solo No
001E	Efamba; Mama Ane Mot Duma

22
Chad

Chad, a conflict-ridden state in the centre of Africa, is a vast country, stretching from tropical rain forest in the south to desert in the north. Comprising a variety of ethnic groups pursuing different economic activities, Chad has been at the centre of centuries of human migrations. Yet despite its central role in the history and geography of the Sahel (the Bornu empire lasted almost 1,000 years), the music of Chad is hardly known at all.

The Sara utilise a variety of instruments including drums, harps, whistles and the 'koundou' – a portable xylophone. In the south-west of the country, in a region called Mayo-Kebbi, are a number of ethnic groups including the Massa, the Moundang and the Toupouri. This region came under the influence of Islam, although a great many non-Islamic traits remain. Using whistles, harps and vocals, the people of this region have perfected their own wind orchestras featuring a selection of indigenous wind instruments like flutes, horns and megaphones.

Yet Chad remains basically an Islamic country, where a caste of professional musicians has developed. Many of the leading professionals, narrators as well as singers, are now to be found in the capital Ndjamena. They perform at all the major festivities and occasionally record in the Radio Chad studios. In the south of the country are the Kanembu, an ancient people who have also developed their own caste of professional musicians – an outgrowth from the artisanal class. They use a wide variety of instruments including the hourglass drum, oboes, reed clarinets, the one-stringed fiddle (goje) and a selection of rattles, lutes and long, single-toned trumpets.

Very little commercial music has emerged from Chad; the country's recent past of almost continuous civil war has taken its toll on the creative and business initiative. Prior to the war, Chad had come under the spell of Congo rumba and during the war itself, the Zairean group Zaiko Langa Langa were playing in Ndjamena although it must be made clear that the popularity of modern pop music did not extend far beyond the bars and nightclubs of the capital and other major towns. For the vast majority of the population, traditional music remained the staple fare.

CHAD/CENTRAL AFRICAN REPUBLIC

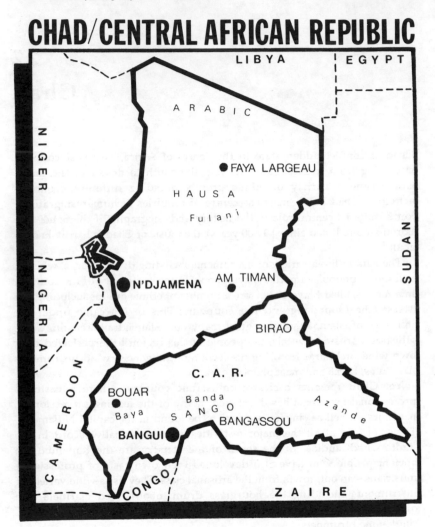

OCR 36		Les Sara
OCR 37		Le Mayo-Kebbi Occidental
OCR 38		Populations Islamisees
OCR 39		Percussions – Afrique No. 1; Tchad
BM 30L2309		Chad-Kanem; Anthology of African Music
ETH 4337		Music of Chad

23

Central African Republic

The CAR lies right in the heart of Africa between Cameroon, Chad and Sudan to the north and Congo and Zaire to the south. The capital Bangui, on the Zairean border, is a focus for travellers from throughout the region, as well as being an important international airport and gateway to the heart of the continent. The main ethnic groups are the Baya in the heavily-populated western areas, the Banda in the central savannah region and the Azende in the east. There are numerous other peoples in the north and south, including pygmies. Sango is the national language. The traditional music varies across the country with heavy influences from Hausa and Sudanic cultures in the north and Bantu styles in the south. In the forest areas a variety of horns made from wood, bamboo and antelope horn are used, while a wide selection of drums, percussion, xylophones, sanzas and zithers are also employed. The music of the pygmies is mostly vocal, with rattles and whistles their only accompaniment. Other than the OCORA discs there is little recorded music available from a country with so much variety, but an introduction can be found on the compilation album *Bantu*, which includes Mandja initiation music and the Zairean-influenced pop from the Aime Jazz Band.

OCR11-EP	Republique Centrafrique
OCR13	Musique Centrafricaine
BM 3012310	Central African Republic
OCR 43	Musique Centrafricaine

24
Burundi

Burundi, which is bounded by Zaire, Rwanda and Tanzania, is one of the most densely-populated countries in Africa. It is a mountainous, forested land, where most people lead traditional village lives, based on a subsistence farming economy. The only industrial centre is the capital Bujumbura. Pygmies, the original inhabitants of the area, are now very much a minority. The Hutus are the largest ethnic group and until recently their rivals the Tutsi have been the dominant social class. The main language is Rundi (Kirundi) which is rich in oral tradition. The most important collection of Burundi music is the OCORA collection, *Musique du Burundi*, originally released in 1967 and repackaged in 1982. This contains a wide variety of musical flavours and instruments including sanza (thumb piano), single string bows, flute and the extraordinary inanga, a trough zither with eight strings stretched over a dug-out softwood sounding board. The music for which Burundi has become internationally famous, however, is the ensemble playing of the ngoma drum, a large resonant instrument which symbolises the power of the royal court of Tutsi (disbanded in the 1960s) and is now preserved for ceremonial use. Up to 25 drummers participate in this group. The sequence heard on the OCORA disc has featured in numerous film sequences and had an important effect on British new wave pop groups during the late 1970s. That influence helped to generate interest in African music in the west, underlined by overseas tours for the Burundi drummers in 1983 and 1986. For all the huge variety of African music available, this is the closest to the stereotyped western image of 'jungle drums'. To hear the massive sound of this ensemble is an unforgettable experience. What the music lacks in subtlety or variety it more than makes up for with power and energy.

OCR 40	Musique du Burundi
ARN33682	Les Maitres Tambours du Burundi
VPA 8137	Musica del Burundi

25
Rwanda

Like its close neighbour Burundi, Rwanda is a small mountainous, densely-populated country which relies on subsistence agriculture and therefore preserves a traditional way of life which is only now being exposed to the outside world. The main ethnic groups are the Hutu and Tutsi, and the culture is virtually identical with that of its neighbour. In common with many African countries, Rwanda has formed a national orchestra which maintains and displays the music traditions of the region.They can be heard on the Bantu collection, along with John Beebwa, a contemporary musician who plays acoustic guitar in the style of the inanga zither and sings a haunting melody in praise of his master.

BM 30L2302   Music from Rwanda

Part V
East Africa

KENYA

SUDAN ETHIOPIA

UGANDA

Turkana

Gabra

Somali

Pokot

Ogaden

Boran

Samburu

Luhya

●ELDORET

KIpsigis

Luo

●KISUMU

Kikuyu

Orma
Sanyu

●NAIROBI

Maasai

Kamba

Taita

●LAMU

●MALINDI

●MOMBASA

SOMALIA

SWAHILI

INDIAN OCEAN

TANZANIA

26
Kenya

The popular music of Kenya, indeed of East Africa as a whole, presents particular problems for those interested in buying records and keeping up to date with new releases. Yet, paradoxically, there is no shortage of information about the music of East Africa and in contrast to other regions it can be regarded as an area where musicologists have made great headway with regard to both traditional and modern urban music. Thus while we have a great deal of information about the origins and development of music, about the organisation of the industry and about the social context of music-making, actual recordings from East Africa are seldom available outside the region while very few East African bands have succeeded in touring either in other parts of Africa or outside the continent. To this extent then, the music of East Africa is still to assume a significant position in the international market.

The traditional music of Kenya exhibits all the variety in style and instrumentation that one could expect from a country comprised of numerous ethnic groups. These include Kikuyu, Kamba, Luo, Luhya, Somali, Maasai, Turkana, Gabra, Pokot, Sambaru, Boran, Ogaden, Kipsigis and Taita. There are dozens of smaller communities whose music has been well described in a number of publications. Amongst the bewildering variety of instruments to be found in Kenya can be listed the following using the standard musical classification. Idiophones – leg bells, leg rattles, and tambourines. Aerophones - whistles, cow horns, wooden trumpets, flutes and pan pipes. Chordophones – fiddles, mouth bows, lyres and thumb pianos. Membraphones – military drums, clay drums, single and double membraphone drums. The music itself is usually performed by amateur musicians although professional musicians do exist. The social context of music-making embraces all the events and occasions with which we usually associate music in Africa – from ritual ceremonies to work songs, praise songs, recreation, lullabies, children's games, love songs and popular entertainment. Anyone more interested in traditional music and society can consult the relevant publications listed in the bibliography while I have tried to present below those titles of traditional music currently available.

Traditional Music

FW 8716	Songs From Kenya: David Nzomo Trio
AIT 3	Nyanaza: Songs From the Lakeside
LDX 74475	Kenia: Chants Des Guerrieres Massais
H 72063	Africa. Ceremonial and Folk Music of Kenya
ETH 4428	Songs of the Watutsi
ETH 7852	Children's Songs From Kenya
ETH 8502	African Politics. Songs from Kenya in Swahili and Kamba
ETH 8503	Kenyan Folk Songs
ETH 8715	Work and Dance Songs From Kenya
ETH 8911	Gospel Hymns from Kenya
ZAIT 511	The Bomas of Kenya
AIT 503	Muziki Wa Ki-asili (Folk Music of Kenya)
POLP 315	Various Original Musical Instruments of Kenya
PKLP 102	Folk Music of East Africa
SSLP 001	Safari Souvenir
TR 139	Kikuyu Dance Songs with Accordion
TR 168	Town Dance Songs With Guitar and Rattle

Religious Music

Kenya, despite significant Islamic influence, particularly along the coast, can be regarded basically as a Christian country. As such it has generated a substantial corpus of religious music. Particularly favoured are the large gospel choirs.

DMA 01	St Stephens Church Choir: Heri Maziwa Uliyonyongo
DMA 02	St Stephens Church Choir: Nzabibu Wa Kweli
MT 001	St Stephens Church Choir: Tribute to Mzee Kenyatta
WLP 4 MTC	Machakos Town Choir: 25th December Kazaliwa
WLP 5 MTC	Machakos Town Choir: Malaika Wawili
WLP 15	Machakos Town Choir: Sauti Yake Bwana
KAYA 01	Muungano National Choir: Imbeni Halleluya
MZB 1004	Moi Tawala Kenya

Tarabu

Tarabu music, stemming from the late nineteenth century, is a style confined to the Swahili-speaking East African coastal region. Originating on the island of Zanzibar, tarabu sounds like a mixture of local traditions with strong Indian and Arabic influences. However, with a style which stretches from Somali to Mozambique there must be strong, localised musical distinctions. For example, Malindi tarabu is said to be 'purer', while the Zanzibari style is said to be more 'Arab'. With a pedigree almost a century old, tarabu cannot be considered to be a static or dying musical tradition. Despite drawing its inspiration from traditional Swahili culture (a form that goes back as far as the twelfth century), tarabu is today a lively and popular style, benefiting from both the old and the new in Swahili culture.

During the 1930s, the instrumentation was basically Arabic, utilising the lute, the pottery drum, the gambuz (a guitar-like instrument), the zither, the fiddle, tambourine and rattle. In time, the music benefited from the introduction of new instruments including the violin, guitar, accordion and tabla, while electric amplification also contributed to a change in style. Of course tarabu was not immune to the external influences which swept Africa during the 1950s and 1960s and elements of Latin music, often mediated through Zaire, started to effect the sound of post-war tarabu. To date, there is only one available record of tarabu selections over the last few decades. Perhaps in the future more will be heard of this vibrant and historic style.

OMA 103   Songs the Swahili Sing

Modern Kenyan Music

A great deal has been written about post-war Kenyan guitar music. I have made particular use of articles by Low, Roberts and Kubik and anyone interested in reading more about the subject is advised to consult these sources. The most comprehensive article is that by Low in which he attempts a periodisation of Kenyan guitar music. He suggests the following typology.

1. Late 1940s – early 1950s. Guitars had been played in Kenya before the Second World War but the earliest recordings and broadcasts of guitar music date to 1945. During the late 1940s several musicians established national reputations with their 'dry' acoustic guitar playing, singing in Swahili for predominantly urban audiences. Early pioneers included Fundi Konde (who was the first to switch to electric guitar), Paul Machupa, Jumbe and Kabaka. Particularly prominent were Luo and Luhya guitarists, who drew on both urban and western styles as well as making use of traditional

idioms. The basic style which emerged was that of vamping.

2. Early 1950s – early 1960s. During this period many guitarists switched to the finger-picking style, performing with perhaps two 'dry' guitars, a bottle for percussion and two vocalists. Indeed two-part singing became a characteristic of Kenyan guitar bands. This generation of guitarists also utilised a number of influences including the guitar style of George Sibanda, a Zimbabwean guitarist who was extremely popular in East Central Africa throughout this period. Kenyan guitarists were also influenced by the 'Nyasa Sound', introduced by Malawian guitarists who were themselves influenced by South African Kwela music. The traditional music of Kenya also played a part in the development of the Kenyan sound. Kikuyu vocals, Luhya instrumentation (particularly the Luhya lyre) and local rhythms all contributed to the emerging sound. Mention should be made of the 'Sukuti' style which was invented by George Mukabi and later popularised by John Mwale, George Agade, Jim Lasco and Daudi Kabaki. The 'Sukuti' style still survives today in some rural areas. Another major influence during the 1950s was the finger-picking style of Katanga in Zaire. Led by Jean Bosco Mwenda and popularised by other Zaireans like Losta Abelo and Edouard Massengo, the Katanga style sold widely throughout East and Central Africa. The musicians sang in Kiswahili and with their superior technique, witty lyrics and strong dance rhythms dominated the Kenyan market. Eventually Kenyan guitarists caught up and developed a distinctively Kenyan variant which was lighter and more fluid than the original Katanga sound. Finally, there was the influence of Latin and Cuban music which arrived in East Africa through the famous imported GV series of discs. American and European pop also played a very minor role. The late 1950s can be considered the heyday of Kenyan guitar bands. Professional musicians received sponsorship and although many were viewed unfavourably by the authorities, they did act as agents of social change in the years leading up to Independence.

3. The 1960s. By the 1960s there were dozens of guitar bands singing in Swahili and building on the various vamping, finger-picking and electric styles of the previous decade. Amplification and the introduction of electric instruments marked a major step forward by permitting a better balanced sound. Kenyan music was still a hybrid sound, in a constant state of flux, and a number of new external influences continued to alter the Kenyan sound. Chief amongst them was the influence of Zairean guitar bands and many Zaireans arrived in Kenya to work in the clubs and dance-halls. Class differences also began to emerge in the enjoyment of music. The nascent urban working class tended to prefer Swahili bands while the new urban elite preferred to listen to imported western or Zairean music. Another strong influence was a new wave of Kwela music from South Africa. It was known in Kenya as 'Twist' and appears to have been imported through records. Finally, there was the western pop influence which was favoured by

the urban elite and reflected in the repertoire of the guitar bands. Gradually however, out of this melting pot of styles and sounds a distinct Kenyan sound was emerging. Lacking the intensity and power of the Zairean orchestras, the Kenyan sound had a lighter, more 'country' feel. The lyrics reflected the achievements and implications of Independence although the usual themes – love and money problems – could also be heard. In general terms, the 1960s was a boom period for the Kenyan guitar bands. The musicians, by singing in Swahili helped create a national consciousness and a detribalised life-style. Instrumental in this development was the small record company known as Equator Records. None the less, the foreign influences remained and the 1960s witnessed the re-release of an extraordinary number of Zairean hits.

4. The 1970s. By the 1970s, mainstream Swahili music had more or less vanished to be replaced by songs sung in local languages – Kamba, Luo or Luhya. The reasons underlying this weakening of Swahili music remain controversial but Low has isolated a number of tendencies which helped undermine the position of Swahili. First there was the collapse of Equator Records. Secondly there was the continuing dominance of foreign music, buttressed by the arrival of soul, disco and reggae. Finally, and perhaps more difficult to assess with any degree of certainty, was the revival of tribalism in Kenya as capitalist competition created divisions and tensions between the various ethnic groups. This development stood in marked contrast to the Tanzanian experience, where conscious efforts had been made to develop a national culture around the Swahili language.

5. The 1980s. By the 1980s a new style known as 'benga' had emerged in Kenya. The term was used loosely to describe quite a variety of styles. For example Kikuyu benga differed from Luo or Kamba benga. The style was extremely popular in Kenya but many observers believed that the guitar playing was well below what Kenyan guitarists were capable of. Leading Kikuyu stars included Joseph Kamaru and Daniel Kamu. The Luo style, a balanced and bright sound, was led by the Victoria Kings and Daniel Owino while the Luhya variant, a bright and bouncy sound retained elements of the older 'Sukuti' style.

The Zairean Musical Invasion

The arrival of dozens of Zairean musicians in East Africa during the 1960s and 1970s continued on into the 1980s. Originally, these musicians left Zaire to escape civil unrest and to establish solo careers away from the domestic dominance of Franco and Rochereau. In Kenya they found appreciative audiences and a number of record companies, both large and small, willing to release their material. In time, many of these bands adopted specifically Kenyan idioms but their popularity certainly helped to undermine the development of a Kenyan national sound. Listed below are the major exponents of Zairean music in Kenya. What must be remembered is that Kenya is basically a singles market: LPs are relatively few and far between.

Gaston, Baba and L'Orchestre Baba National. Born in Lubumbashi, Ilunga Wa Ilunga (Baba Gaston) started his career in Zaire and by 1970 had established a national reputation with several hit singles. In 1970 he moved to Kenya to continue his career.

1980s	POLP 900	20th Anniversary
	POLP 901	Greatest Hits Vol. 1
	POLP 933	Greatest Hits Vol. 2
1983	ASLP 1004	Revival
1985	ASLP 1006	Safari

Virunga, Orchestra. Led by Samba Mapangala and singing in Lingala, Virunga arrived in Kenya during the late 1970s and soon established a devoted following with their light and spacey guitar playing and solid dance rhythms. In 1984 they became one of the few 'Kenyan' bands to score an international success with their first British release on the Earthworks label.

1984	AR 0986	Malako Disco (also ERT 2006)
	ASLP 927	Disco Time
	JLP 0069	Greatest Hits

Mangalepa, Les. Another top Lingala band, they eventually outstayed their welcome in Kenya when they were forced to leave the country in 1985 following a government crackdown on foreign musicians.

	ASLP 913	1st Anniversary
	ASLP 919	Action All The Way
	ASLP 921	Live on Tour
	ASLP 928	Lisapo
	ASLP 988	Safari Ya Mangalepa
	JJLP 005	Greatest Hits
1985	ASLP 413	Madina

Mazembe, Super. Comprised entirely of Zairean nationals, the name of the band means 'Earth Movers'. In 1984 they had an international hit with their reworking of the Kenyan classic 'Shauri Yako', written by Nguashi Timbo.

1980	EMA 0520	Mazembe
1981	EMA 0530	10th Anniversary

1982	EMA 0540	Double Gold
1983	V 2263	Kaivaoka
	LOVY	L'Orchestre Super Lovy
1982	LVLP 01	1st Album
	LVLP 02	2nd Album
	LVLP 03	3rd Album
	LOVY 04	Ye Ye Ye
	LOVY 07	Keba Yo

Swahili Bands

Maroon Commandos. A military pop group from the 7th Battalion, Kenyan Army, led by Habel Kifoto (b. Taita Province). Habel started his career in the early 1960s as a bass player. In 1967 he switched to lead guitar and formed the Maroon Commandos in 1970. He made several singles for Phonogram before establishing a national reputation with the hit 'Emily' in 1971. During the next year the band toured widely in Kenya until early in 1972 when the band's bus crashed, killing several musicians. Habel and the rest of the band then dropped out of the music business for several years before being persuaded to return in 1977 with the hit 'Charenyi Ni Waso'. Today, they are one of the top attractions in the country.

| 1981 | POLP 518 | Riziki Haivatu |
| 1982 | POLP 532 | Dawa Nimuone Hani |

Wanyika, Les. Formed in 1978 as an offshoot of Simba Wanyika, who came from Tanzania, Les Wanyika are perhaps the most popular Swahili band in Kenya. Their 1979 record 'Sina Mokosa' was a massive hit, earning them a gold disc. Indeed they proved so successful that the band underwent a number of splits with new outfits establishing separate reputations as Super Wanyika Stars and Issa Juma and Wanyika. The most prolific of all the Wanyika bands remains Simba Wanyika led by Wilson Peter Kinyanga.

1979	POLP	Sina Mokosa
1980s	JJLP 002	Pamela
	POLP 506	Jiburudisheni
	POLP 510	Jiburudisheni Vol. 2
	POLP 513	New Dance
	POLP 540	Shilling Mauwa Tena Yaua
1985	POLP 552	Halleluya

Super Wanyika Stars

1984   NYIKA 01   Mpita Njia

Issa Juma and Wanyika

1984   NYIKA 02   Pole Pole

Mwinshehe, Mbaraka. Mwinshehe was known as the Franco of East Africa. He died in a car crash in 1979 on the Mombassa-Malindi highway. By then he had enjoyed a 15-year career as guitarist, composer and bandleader of the Orchestra Volcano. Producing a sound very close to that of the big Congo bands, Mwinshehe's death was a major blow to the musical development of East Africa.

1970s	POLP 001	Shida
	POLP 002	Mtaa Wasaba
1979	POLP 512	The Very Last Recording
1982	POLP 517	Baniani Mwinshehe Minaruka
1983	POLP 527	Ukumbusho Vol. 1
1984	POLP 537	Ukumbushu Vol. 2
	POLP 542	Ukumbushu Vol. 3
	POLP 544	Pesa No. 1
1985	POLP 550	Ukumbushu Vol. 4

Morogoro Jazz Band. Morogoro are one of the most popular of all the Swahili bands, releasing dozens of singles and several LPs.

1984	POLP 500	Morogoro
	POLP 502	Mfululizowa Wa Muziki

Them Mushrooms. A six-piece Swahili reggae and benga band.

1985   POLP 548   New Horizon

Mlimani Park

1985   POLP 523   Taxi Driver

Shirati Jazz. One of the top Luo benga bands, led by Owino Misiani, the 'king of benga'. Their melodic, danceable style mixes traditional luo beats with the 'Katanga' style of guitar playing popularised by Bosco and a form of women's group singing known as bodi. The lyrics include praise songs and discussions of important social issues. In 1987 they embarked on their first

European tour and recorded an album for Arts Worldwide of London.

MEA708	Shirati Jazz
JCLP 001	Shirati Jazz
WCB 003	Shirati Jazz; Benga Beat

There are dozens of other dance bands in Kenya, the majority of whom never have the opportunity to release long-playing records. These include Mombassa Roots, Safari Sound Band, Orc. Super Matimila, the Forest People Band, Orc. Les Volcano, Orc. Jobiso, Orc. K.Z. Africa, Orc. Butere Sharp Shooters, Les Kilimimbogo Brothers, Soweto Boys and Phontex Success. Leading Kikuyu bands include Banana Hill Band and Kamaru Celina Band. Other leading purveyors of Kenyan sounds include Mara Jazz, Vijana Jazz and Fadhili and the Blacks, Salum Abdalla, the Kalambaya Sisters, Peter Muambi, Mbiri Stars and the Kiko Kids. Many of the best singles are often presented on compilation albums put out by the big two record companies - AIT and Polygram.

Compilations

POLP 403	Save the Rhino
POLP 551	Kweya
POLP 549	Dunia Kigeu-geu
POLP 316	Tribal Songs of Kenya
AGLP 001	African Gold Vol. 1
AGLP 002	African Gold Vol. 2

27
Tanzania

Tanzania is a large country which straddles East-Central Africa, linking the island of Zanzibar in the Indian Ocean with Lake Tanganyika in the centre of the continent. The capital is the port city of Dar Es Salaam with its centuries of tradition as a meeting place for African, Arabic and Eastern cultures. The official language is Swahili, a vital unifying force in a country with some 120 ethnic groups, the main ones of which are the Sukuma, Maasai, Chagga, Nyamwezi and Nguni. Not surprisingly, there is a rich vein of musical tradition, much of which remains intact, due in part to the Ujaama policy of cooperative rural development which discourages the frantic urbanisation so prevalent throughout the Third World. One of the main strongholds of music tradition in East Africa is the Bagamoyo College of Arts to the north of the capital, where a group of musicians under the leadership of Hukwe Zawose preserve, teach and perform the sounds of Tanzania. The group visited Britain in 1985 and recorded a superb quality album, *Tanzania Yetu*, which features a spectrum of traditional music instruments like mbira (which here means both xylophone and thumb piano), the iseze, a stringed instrument, drums and percussion of various kinds.

1985   TERRA101   Tanzania Yetu.

Popular Music

The pop music scene began in the 1960s when Zairean musicians began to migrate east, bringing western guitars and wind instruments and their infectious rumba. Tanzanian groups immediately picked up on this congolese style. During the 1970s the growing availability of electric instruments and exposure to western pop music saw some groups start singing in English, while the congolese imitators began to record in Swahili, so developing the beginnings of a Tanzanian style. Throughout the 1970s they blended the traditional ngoma with Zairean, Swahili jazz and western soul music. The early recordings were made in Kenya but by the mid-1970s Radio Tanzania had started to broadcast this local 'jazz'. By the end of the

TANZANIA

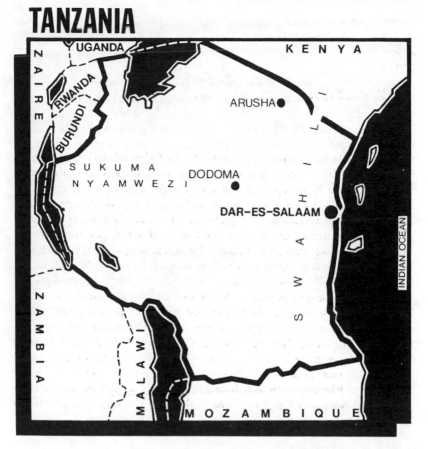

decade Wallis and Malm (*Big Sounds from Small People*) estimate there were 120 bands active, with jazz music finding acceptance even among the educated elite.

The Afro 70 band represented the country at FESTAC 77 in Lagos, with the support of the National Music Council. By then the national radio station was playing Tanzanian music exclusively, yet plans to open a pressing plant at the Tanzanian Film Company did not materialise as quickly as expected. Many artistes continued to travel to Nairobi to record and even though piracy became a serious threat to their commercial well being, the scene remained buoyant. Very little Tanzanian pop has been heard outside East Africa but in Kenya, Tanzanian bands are very influential. The Arusha Jazz Band found fame in Kenya as Simba Wanyika in the late 1970s (see Kenya for entry). In 1982 they received Tanzanian government support to tour the major towns before visiting Mozambique and Zimbabwe. Another Tanzanian musician who has succeeded in Kenya is Issa Juma, whose single 'Sigalame' was the big hit of 1983. Others include Mlimani Park, Maquis Original, Vijana Jazz and Orchestra Safari Sound International.

Makassy, Orchestre. Led by Mezee Makassy, the band has made the biggest impression outside Africa, simply because their album *Agwaya* was licensed by Virgin for European release in 1983. The line-up is predominantly Zairean. There was a 12-inch single which became a minor club hit in London. The record did give British listeners a foretaste of Mose Se Fan Fan, whose signature song 'Mosese' had been a favourite in Tanzania. For several years a resident of Dar Es Salaam, Fan Fan had been chef d'orchestre following the disbandment of the original Somo Somo. After reviving his career with a British band, he returned to Dar Es Salaam in 1985 for a brief reunion with Makassy.

V2236   Orchestre Makassy: Agwaya

This East-Central African republic has had a turbulent history, involving invasion and internal strife lasting for centuries up to the present day. Although the site of the oldest discovered human remains is in Uganda, most of the peoples now living there are descendants of those who came from the Sudan and Congo regions. The Ganda, who traditionally inhabited the north shore of Lake Victoria, are the ethnic group which came to dominance in the late nineteenth century, assisted by the British. Other peoples include the Nyankole, the traditional rulers of the south-west region and the Chwezi whom they deposed. In modern Uganda many of the old ways and customs are disappearing, but the Nyankole retain some of their old skills in poetic praise songs. Also from western Uganda come the Nyoro and Toro who were part of the Bunyoro-Kitara empire. Bunyoro is famous for its traditional music and crafts. The Sogo of the eastern region, who were the court musicians of the traditional king, also have a rich variety of traditional music, as do the Acholi people of the north, whose dancers and musicians are popular throughout the country.

Instruments heard in Ugandan music which are rarely heard elsewhere include double-note horns, found only here and in northern Zaire, and a single-stringed lute. There are also mbiras (sanzas), xylophones, harps, stick zithers and, of course, a range of drums. The Ganda use an eight-stringed lyre called the endongo and they are also renowned for their massed drum ensembles. For all its wealth of traditional music Uganda, like several other African countries, suffers from a paucity of recorded material, with the notable exception of the Kaleidophone and Hugh Tracey discs.

| GALP 1319 | Music of Uganda |
| KMA 10 | Uganda 1 |

Popular Music

As in all the countries in central Africa, the congolese influence on popular music has been dominant, to the extent that most of the groups playing at dances and social events are either Zairean nationals or imitators of that

UGANDA

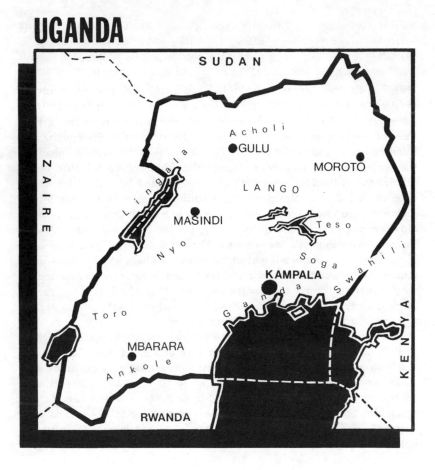

style. In the north east the Luo benga influence is also heard. There is virtually no record industry; discs, and more often cassettes, are most often smuggled in across the Kenyan and Zaire borders. Sandwiched between two relatively vibrant sectors of commercial pop music, it is not surprising that Uganda trails behind them.

Of the few names to have had exposure in the west are Sammy Kasule, Maria Wandaka and Jimmy Katumba. Wandaka, who played in London in 1979, now lives in Sweden. Katumba is a popular variety singer, who records with his group, the Ebonies, at their own studio in Kampala. In 1982 they visited Britain with a stage show that gave a musical tour of the country. The dramatic content was provided by students at Makarere University. Katumba's voice has echoes of church-choir training, but the Ebonies have much in common with other central African groups, particularly the ubiquitous soukous guitar. On record they are subservient to the ballad style of Katumba, but on stage they can fly. They have had several national hits, the most popular being 'Twalina Omwukano'. As most of the market for recorded music is in cassettes and singles, there are few albums available.

> Jimmy Katumba & The Ebonies: Queen of
> Love Drum Beat
> Maria Wandaka: Greatest Hits

29
Sudan

Historically, the Sudan is a vast region stretching across Africa south of the Sahara. The modern Republic of Sudan is the largest country on the continent, covering some 2.5 million sq km, slightly larger than Zaire, its southern neighbour. The capital Khartoum has been an important commercial centre for centuries. It has a university and international airport, but no recording industry. As one of the poorest countries in Africa it also suffers from lack of contact with the developed world, and little is heard of the music outside the country. Culturally it has many elements in common with the Sahel countries as well as with the seven states that border it – Chad, CAR, Zaire, Uganda, Kenya, Ethiopia and Egypt. Of these Egypt, and Arabia in general, has had the greatest influence on the northern part of the country, as this was the scene of the earliest expansion of Islam into Africa. In contrast to many strict Islamic cultures, music is an acceptable and necessary attribute to daily life. The elements of traditional Sudanese music are similar to those of the Swahili culture which dominates East Africa. They use the tambour, a lyre of great antiquity, as is the oud, a fretless Arabic lute. These are supported by pottery tabla drums, and such western instruments as accordion and violin. Such is the line-up used by Abdul Aziz il Mubarak, a popular star who has toured in many of the neighbouring countries and in Europe. At home in Khartoum, the music is spiced for local consumption with the addition of electric bass and drums, although outside the capital the people's tastes are generally more conservative. Mubarak and his co-singer Abdel Gadir Salim are both graduates of the Institute for Music and Drama, founded in 1969 by Mahi Ismael, a curator of Sudanese music traditions. Radio and TV regularly broadcast music, and there is a thriving market in cassette tapes, whether bootlegs or legitimate releases. Mubarak has released 'official' cassettes on the EMI Greece label. There is no copyright control agency, so popular musicians must gauge their success by the number of people they can attract to their shows. An international release of Abdel Gadir Salim, recorded in London in 1986, titled *Sudanese Music Vol 1*, is available from World Circuit, with others due to follow. The Berlin Music Collection have also released a double album, *Music of the Nubians*, with explanatory sleeve notes in German and English. For more electric pop the Sudanese

SUDAN/ETHIOPIA/SOMALIA

apparently tune their radios to stations broadcasting from their nearest neighbouring country. From the southern part of Sudan, the non-Islamic tribal music of the cattle-farming Dinka people is well represented on disc.

MC9	Music of the Nubians/ North Sudan
ETH 4301	Dinka War Songs and Hymns
ETH 4302	Dinka Women's Dance
ETH 4303	Dinka Burial Hymns and War Songs
STLP 500	Music and Songs of Abdul Karim
WCB 003	Abdel Gadir Salim; Sudanese Music Vol. 1

30
Ethiopia

Ethiopia borders the Red Sea facing Arabia to the north east, with Sudan to the west, and Kenya and Somalia to the south and east. The enclave of Djibouti is virtually enclosed by Ethiopia. It has one of the oldest documented histories in Africa, and apart from a brief occupation by the Italians in the Second World War, it has never been colonised. Originally settled by Arabians who founded the Axum dynasty, Ethiopia converted to Christianity in AD 200. Various imperial lines succeeded, including the Zagwe, Lasta, Amhara, Gojjan and Shewa, right up until 1930 when Hailie Sellassie became Emperor. Sellassie was most active in African affairs, being instrumental in setting up the Organisation of African Unity (OAU) in the 1960s and leading peace initiatives in Nigeria and Sudan. His title Ras Tafari was taken up by the Rastafarian movement which originated in Jamaica, but efforts to make Ethiopia a cultural homeland for people of the black diaspora have had little success. Sellassie was deposed in 1974 and died in prison. The Ethiopian Church, on which the Rasta religion is based, is one of the oldest Christian churches, to which most Ethiopians belong.

The Church has a powerful vocal tradition using the Ge'ez language. Amharic, the national language to which it is related, is rich in oral literature including praise poems, traditional stories and animal fables. Gallegna is spoken in the south. The main ethnic groups are the Amharic Tigre and Agau, and the Eritreans, a Moslem people whose territory was annexed in 1962. Since Sellassie was deposed in 1974, civil war has raged. The famine which came to light in 1984 brought intense media interest in the country, although very little of its contemporary culture is known in the west. The Ocora collection includes some fine singing, accompanied by lyres, sanzas, flute and accordion.

| M6 | Musik der Hamar, Sudathiopian |
| OCR 75 | Musique Ethiopiennes |

Popular Music

There is a vibrant music scene in Ethiopia with bands who can fill stadiums and sell hundreds of thousands of cassettes – and it is a cassette-dominated market with very few recordings on vinyl. The first disc to be made internationally available came in 1986, courtesy of Crammed Discs. The Ethiopian sound is different from anything else to be heard coming out of Africa, with a mix of bluesy pianos, riffing saxes, Middle Eastern rhythms and above all haunting melodies based on almost Indonesian scales.

Roha Band. Formed just after the 1974 revolution, the Roha Band collaborate with most Ethiopian stars in the studio and on tour. They perform regularly in hotels and clubs, and at major concerts which can attract crowds of over 20,000. Among the singers they have supported are Mahmoud Ahmed, one of the great singers of the past 20 years, and Neway Debebe, a rising star who writes modern songs which attract the younger generation, in a country where more than half the population is under 20.

CRAM 047   Mahmoud Ahmed & the Roha Band; Ere
                Mela Mela

31
Somalia

The Somali Republic is situated in the 'Horn of Africa' in the far north east corner, bordering Ethiopia and Kenya, into which many of the Somali people have dispersed over the centuries. A traditionally nomadic people, they were among the earliest converts to Islam. Their land has been colonised by the British, French and Italians and large areas have been annexed by Ethiopia. The country became independent in 1960, with the French-dominated enclave of Djibouti remaining separate. The Somali language has a great tradition of oral poetry, often accompanied by music. Complex verse forms deal with the gamut of topics from love to politics and war. Dramatic performance is popular in the towns and villages.

The music is most closely related to Arabic forms, although it is more rhythmic. The oud is the most prominent instrument in which, it is said, all other instruments can be heard. Somali groups also use flute, violin and bongo drums or tablas for 'quai' music, which is accompanied by the chewing of 'quat', a stimulant leaf. Traditionally the musicians who play at these sessions do not receive payment. Although only men play instruments there are both male and female singers who are appreciated for the quality of their verse and the classic language in which it is delivered. Historically the main subjects were praises to camel and cattle stock, but now love is the main topic, along with fate. Elements of pre-Islamic philosophy have been absorbed from Sudanese music which is popular in Somalia.

One of the most influential of modern oud players was Muhamed Mooge who died in 1983, killed by his own government while fighting with Ethiopian-based rebels. Abdul Quadir Junicomar and H.M. Timayere recorded singles for Columbia in the 1950s, but probably the best known and most popular oud player today is Ismael Hudaide. The top female singer is Margol. There is no record market in Somalia, although cassettes are plentiful. As there is no copyright protection, most available music is recorded at live shows. The commercially made copies are distributed from Djibouti. A more 'poppy' form of the music, called 'metallic' by traditionalists, uses horns, drum kits, electric guitars and even synthesisers. The BBC's Somali service has a huge archive of recorded music on tape but only one LP featuring Somali music, and that is from Djibouti.

ACCT 38212   Musique de Djibouti (4 songs in Somali, also Afar and Arabic.)

Part VI
Southern Africa

NAMIBIA / BOTSWANA / S.AFRICA
(A)SWAZILAND (B)LESOTHO

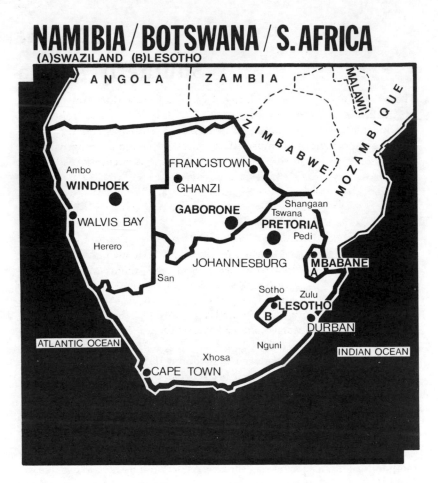

ANGOLA ZAMBIA MALAWI

ZIMBABWE

MOZAMBIQUE

Ambo
WINDHOEK
FRANCISTOWN
GHANZI
GABORONE
Shangaan
Tswana
PRETORIA
Pedi
WALVIS BAY
Herero
JOHANNESBURG
MBABANE
A
San
Sotho
Zulu
LESOTHO
B
DURBAN
ATLANTIC OCEAN
Nguni
INDIAN OCEAN
Xhosa
CAPE TOWN

256

32
South Africa

The vast expanse of South Africa has produced a diversity of music unequalled in any other African country. With its extremes of colonialism and turbulent history, South Africa has been a unique melting pot for European and indigenous musical influences. Although a strong harmonic and rhythmic unity can be heard throughout South African recorded music, there is a bewildering range of musical expression and style of music available – from superb gospel recordings and pure country (concertina music) through American-inspired jazz to R & B influenced jive music (mbaqanga). Yet in each style the derivation is secondary to a powerful synthesis. Arguably nowhere else in Africa can boast as fine a tradition of internationally acclaimed artistes in vocal, performance and jazz fields; indeed nowhere else in Africa has a local jazz sound grown to such proportions. Black jazz in the UK during the 1960s and 1970s was almost entirely synonymous with a handful of exiled South Africans (like Chris MacGregor, Dudu Pukwana, Johnny Dyani, Dollar Brand, Hugh Masekela, Ernest Mothle, Louis Moholo, Lucky Ranku, Mongezi Feza, to mention only a few).

South Africans have produced and toured the world with many fine dance musicals, bringing the rich black urban culture to a wider public. Although the theatre and dance are beyond the scope of this introduction, they are often inseparable from the music itself.

In South Africa, as in the rest of Africa, the music is completely linked to social and community life. The roots of modern mbaqanga (or township jive – a blend of traditional and urban music) and South African jazz lay in thousands of black people being forced off their land by brutal laws like the Land Act of 1913, restricting blacks (who comprise 75 per cent of the population) to owning land in only 13 per cent of the country and expropriating all their properties outside these designated 'tribal homeland' areas. The earlier discovery of gold also played a significant role in forcing black people to seek employment in the mines or on white farms. All this to serve white economic interests, then as now. European instruments such as accordion (or concertina) guitar, banjo and saxophone had been introduced long before 1900. By the 1950s, the guitar and saxophone were prominent in township jive. Missionaries had introduced church music and this was mixed with traditional singing (call and response, accapella, mbube) to produce the famous choral sounds distinctive to South Africa (as in the South African anthem 'Nkosi Sikilel'i Africa' written by Enoch Sontonga in 1912).

The early introduction of records, mainly American jazz and blues, was another important influence in the development of local music. Johannesburg (Egoli – city of gold) became the centre of modern South African music. Shebeens sprang up to cater for migrant workers, who were usually cut off from their families and communities. Musicians in the shebeens played a mixture of the music they had heard on records with a strong influence of indigenous sounds; choral groups were also popular. The early jazz records by Ellington, Basie and Louis 'Satchmo' Armstrong had a huge impact.

By the early 1930s jazz bands like the Jazz Maniacs and the Merry Blackbirds were playing to wide acclaim. The Jazz Maniacs were probably the most popular band and developed an exciting synthesis of jazz, swing and local melody known as Marabi music, the inspiration for future generations of musicians like Dollar Brand, Hugh Masekela, Jonas Gwangwa, Kippie Moeketsi, etc. The Jazz Maniacs were formed in 1933 by pianist 'Zulu Boy' Cele who had learnt piano from listening to shebeen entertainers in the slums of Johannesburg. Wilson 'King Force' Siligee took over the leadership of the band 10 years later when Cele was murdered. Also prominent in the group around 1960 was the brilliant 'Zakes' Nkosi, supreme on sax, who later formed his own band, City Jazz Nine. Zakes was a major influence on sax-jive mbaqanga and backed mbaqanga bands until his death in 1982. The Jazz Maniacs, although very popular at dances, split up in the 1950s, due to a combination of musical differences, gang pressure and the introduction of forced removals under the 1950 Group Areas Act.

At first the record companies recorded a few indigeneous acts. Later some recordings became internationally popular. In the 1950s, composer Solomon Linda's 'Mbube', which became 'Wimoweh' (The lion sleeps tonight), was heard all over the world; an excellent version of the song was recorded by Miriam Makeba. The big band jazz scene, meanwhile, virtually ended in the 1950s with the introduction of forced removals to the new townships for black people (e.g. Soweto), the segregation of venues and increasing gang activities as society was threatened by the new policy of apartheid: extreme legal separation of the races and the establishment of complete white domination of every aspect of life.

Between the 1940s and the late 1960s, kwela or pennywhistle music was popularised mainly by township children. Loosely comparable to skiffle, one or more pennywhistlers were usually featured with acoustic guitar and tea-chest bass. Kwela groups would often busk on street corners where appreciative crowds would gather. There were some big hits on record, the best known being 'Tom Hark', the original 1956 version of which (by Elias

Lerole and his Zigzag Flutes) charted high in Europe and has done so again recently as a cover version. Sax would occasionally replace pennywhistle. The music's major stars were Spokes Mashiyane and Lemmy 'Special' Mabaso, the latter still prominent today as sax player with the Soul Brothers. The record companies paid a pittance to stars of the time; royalty payments were virtually unheard of until the 1960s. During the 1950s many kwela artistes were backed by jazz musicians like Bra 'Zakes' Nkosi, who needed to supplement earnings from (mainly 78 rpm) records with live and session work backing other people. Some jazz musicians preferred not to record and in this way avoided the studio exploitation of music to obtain a quick, anonymous and above all cheap product, which would be disposed of immediately it stopped selling. The records from this era of South African music are rare today and in the hands of a few collectors. No archive material was ever kept by record companies it seems, let alone release dates or session details. Many fine kwela performances on 78s are by musicians better remembered for their jazz recordings (the fine guitarist, Alan Kwela, appeared on many releases both featured and as a session player).

From the 1940s onwards one of the major focal points of South African music has been Dorkay House. It functions as a meeting place and a base for a musicians' association which has a long history of helping artistes who used to hang out at Dorkay; Hugh Masekela, Dollar Brand, Makay Davashe, Jonas Gwangwa, Kippie Moeketsi, Ntemi Piliso among them. Excellent plays and musicals were created at Dorkay, including the pivotal smash musical *King Kong* which launched dozens of international careers. Dorkay is managed by a remarkable woman, Queeneth Ndaba, who still organises benefits for the musicians, and together with Ntemi Piliso, who leads the band, has helped re-form the African Jazz Pioneers. Piliso later co-wrote some of the Mahotella Queens' songs on 'Umculo Kawupheli' (1974) released in 1986 as 'Duck Food'.

In the 1950s alto saxophonist Kippie Moeketsi led the Harlem Swingsters and later the Shantytown Sextet, which backed the extremely popular vocal group, the Manhattan Brothers. Miriam Makeba, a featured vocalist with the Cuban Brothers, was induced to join the group. Later she joined the Skylarks with Letta Mbulu. Whilst on tour in Cape Town, Dollar Brand replaced Tod Matshikiza as pianist with the Shantytown Sextet. Later in Port Elizabeth the group started playing a more local flavoured music, as their audiences became less responsive to their 'English' sound (Moeketsi, in a recent interview, uses this phrase to contrast derivative with more indigenous music). Later Dollar, who was from District 6, and Kippie, formed the Jazz Epistles, who in 1962 recorded the first ever 33 rpm jazz LP in South Africa (until then they had all been 78s).

By the late 1950s many of the most prominent musicians were involved in township jazz musicals and reviews, like *King Kong*, based on the rise and fall of boxer Ezekiel Dlamini, which gave an opportunity to many musicians to tour abroad. The white-sponsored show, with music by Tod Matshikiza, was a huge success. Featured were Makeba, Masekela, Lemmy, Mackay Davashe, Kippie, Dambuza Mdledle and the Manhattans. Despite all this talent and the undoubted commercial success, according to the musicians, the big money did not filter down to the cast. A number of less successful musicals followed, usually featuring black life from a white point of view.

Films starring black artists were produced. The best was probably Lionel Rogosin's 1957 production, *Come Back Africa*, the powerful and moving story of life as a migrant worker in Sophiatown, the cultural heart of Johannesburg, which was later bulldozed after being declared 'white'. There were cameo roles for Makeba and Lemmy (as a street urchin playing pennywhistle). With the worsening political climate and tighter segregation in the 1960s it became much more difficult for jazz bands to survive (there was less live work) or for young developing musicians to learn to read music. Record companies also took a firmer control of the new commercial mbaqanga bands. Many of the best musicians of the time travelled abroad to a more conducive climate. In this way the talent of Hugh Masekela, Dollar Brand, Miriam Makeba, Letta Mbulu and many others was brought to the attention of the outside world.

1960s	DGL GALLO 85	Music of Africa: African Dances of the 1970s Witwatersrand Gold Mines
	HQ2020	Jazz and Hot Dance in S. Africa 1946-59
	LK 4392	King Kong: Original Cast
	LON 5672	King Kong: London Cast
	MMTL1282	Music Sounds of Africa

Makeba, Miriam (b. Miriam Zenzi Makeba, 1932, Johannesburg). Now known as the Empress of African song, Miriam Makeba received her early education at the Methodist Training School in Pretoria. On leaving school she began to sing locally before joining the Black Manhattan Brothers from 1954 to 1957. She then moved on to perform with the African Jazz and Variety Troupes – musical reviews which at one time or another included all the leading black South African musicians. However, by the end of the 1950s the political situation had deteriorated such that, after a brief spell with the Skylarks, Miriam left South Africa for good. By this time she had attracted international attention for her roles in the film *Come Back Africa* (1957) and the stage show *King Kong* (1959). Following her BBC debut in 1959 she moved on to the USA as a protégé of Harry Belafonte. During the 1960s Miriam established her reputation with a succession of widely-acclaimed albums, demonstrating the Makeba magic on such songs as 'The Click Song', 'Westwinds' and 'Pata Pata'. In the mid-1960s she married trumpeter Hugh Masekela, and continued to tour widely. In 1969 she moved to Guinea with her second husband, the black activist Stokely Carmichael, and from her base in Conakry she continued to tour Africa, performing before heads of state, receiving countless awards and becoming the living symbol of African liberation.

1960s	KL 754	The World of Miriam Makeba
	ESP 1555	The World of Miriam Makeba
	RR3001	Makeba
	ESP155564	The Click Song
1972	443 046	Pata Pata
	GSL 32	Miriam Makeba

Mashiyane, Spokes

GL1049	Spokes of Africa
SGALP 1652	Mashiyane and Lemmy Mbaso: Penny Whistlers of Africa
33NK1001	All Sax Greats (Ntemi's Sextet, the Five Boys, etc.)
BLO 40	The Members (Shadrack and Ntemi Piliso)
BUMP 1231	Marabi Jive Brothers: Looking Back

Masekela, Hugh (b. 1939, Witbank near Johannesburg). He lived with his grandmother until the age of seven, then returned to his parents, who eventually moved to Alexandra township, Johannesburg, in 1948. In 1952 he attended St Peters Secondary School run by father Trevor Huddleston. Whilst playing truant, he and his best friend, Ernest 'Stompie' Manana saw the film *Man with a Horn* about the American trumpeter, Bix Beiderbicke, which had a big impact on Hugh. Huddleston later gave him a trumpet and, after practising for some time, Hugh started a band. Huddleston meanwhile persuaded an American businessman to sponsor equipment for the group which became the Huddleston Jazz Band. They played American swing and marabi music. In 1955 the government closed down the school and Huddleston, who played a prominent role in opposing the destruction of Sophiatown, was forced to leave South Africa. On his way back to Britain via the USA he met Louis 'Satchmo' Armstrong and told him about the band. Satchmo was moved to send Hugh one of his trumpets and this led to plenty of much-needed publicity in the national press. Hugh started playing in musicals and jazz reviews, with people like Kippie Moeketsi and Todd Matshikiza. He played in the Manhattan Brothers backing the Shantytown Sextet in the 1950s, which eventually included Dollar Brand. In 1959 Hugh played trumpet for 18 months with *King Kong*; later he joined the Jazz Epistles. Then came the Sharpeville massacre and restrictions on crowds, making it difficult for bands to survive. Hugh left for England, where he stayed for five months before moving to New York with Miriam Makeba and Harry Belafonte to study music at the Manhattan School of Music. He formed Chisa Records with his friend Stewart Levine. His colleagues in the States were Caiphus Semenya and Letta Mbulu; he also recorded with H. Alpert.

In 1968 his giant hit 'Grazin' in the Grass' (number one in the USA) was released, followed by a steady stream of records. Chisa also released albums with Fela, Letta Mbulu and the Crusaders. He toured extensively in Africa, played with Fela Kuti in Nigeria, recorded with Hedzolleh Sounds from Ghana, Kenya and Zaire and in 1971, *Union of South Africa* was released, featuring Hugh, Caiphus Semenya and Jonas Gwangwa. During 1980 he appeared in Maseru, playing in southern Africa for the first time in 20 years. 1982 saw the release of *Home*; outstanding tracks are 'Soweto' (a Dollar Brand composition) and 'Johannesburg'. *Working for a Dollar Bill* paved the way for important changes. His record company, Zomba Productions, sent a mobile studio to Gaberone, Botswana. Now Hugh could get back close to his roots, helped by some of South Africa's finest artists like the Soul Brothers. Two highly acclaimed LPs followed: *Techno Bush* and *Waiting for the Rain*. His records have always sold well in South Africa and now he is internationally famous.

	TML5195	Hugh Masekela and the Union of South Africa (with Jonas Gwangwa, Caiphus Semenya)
1973	BTS 62	Introducing Hedzoleh Soundz
1971	CHISA 73041	Masekela
1978	TMH 5909	Woza and other Hits
	SP 728	H. Alpert with Hugh Masekela
	SP 3158	H. Alpert with Hugh Masekela 1982: Main Event Live
	SHINE5574	Home 1983
1983	VUC 1001	Working for a Dollar Bill
1984	HIP 11	Techno Bush
1985	HIP 25	Waiting for the Rain
	GSL 43	I am not Afraid (fine collection of early material)
	GSL 123	Child of the Earth
	GSL 124	Thula
	GSL 166	The African Connection
	DEL 729	Home is Where the Music is
	NAL 27013	The Boy's Doin It (with Stewart Levine in Lagos)
1987	WEA	Tomorrow (Bring Him Back Home)

Mbulu, Letta. From the same school, often uses the same musicians and facilities as Masekela.

MUNC2003	In The Music
MUNC 2004	Streams Today Rivers Tomorrow

Brand, Dollar (Abdullah Ibrahim). Born in District Six, Cape Town (which was razed to the ground in the 1970s), Brand came from a musical family and benefited from piano lessons during his schooldays. He soon became an accomplished musician. Playing with older and experienced musicians was also a boost to his development. Dollar joined the Shantytown Sextet and later the Jazz Epistles, who won the Jazz Band category at the first Castle Lager Festival in Johannesburg, 1961. They also recorded the first South African jazz LP. After a long period of experimenting, to varying degrees of audience acceptance, he decided to try his luck overseas in the mid-1960s. Luckily he was seen by Duke Ellington who was on tour in Europe and Ellington arranged for him to record. Dollar also played at the Newport Jazz Festival a number of times. He jammed with many famous musicians and toured to wide acclaim in the USA and Europe. Dollar returned to South Africa in the late 1960s after an absence of six or seven years; now famous, he was greeted with wildly enthusiastic applause at concerts all over South Africa. In 1974 all his experience and experimenting culminated in his seminal work, the *Mannenberg* album – a brew of Marabi, Jazz and Eastern influences. This was recorded by Rashid Vally, an independent producer, and released on his label, Sun. Later he left South Africa to release many fine LPs, some dedicated to the freedom struggle.

	SRK786137	Peace
1973	KRS 113	Dollar Brand Plus 3, with K. Moeketsi
	JAPO60002	African Piano
1974	JAPO60005	Ancient Africa
	SRK786134	Mannenberg
1975	SRK786135	African Herbs
1976	SRK786136	Blues for a Hip King
	SRK786138	Black Lightning
	BID155502	Black Lightning
1977	SRK786139	Natural Rhythm
1978	BID155501	Soweto
	RTLE 703	The Journey
1979	SRK 786145	Bra Joe from Kilimanjaro
1980	ELK 52217	African Marketplace
1983	ENJA 4056	Zimbabwe
1984	HUL 507	Ekaya

1986	BKH 50207	Water from an Ancient Well

Collaborations, compilations and re-releases.

	AL 1003	(with Gato Barbieri) – Confluence
	2383099	Anatomy of a South African Village
	MVC 3595	African Space Program
	ENJA 2032	African Space Program
	ENJA 2026	African Sketchbook
	ENJA 2070	The Children of Africa
	ENJA 2043	Good News from Africa
	ENJA 3039	Africa Tears and Laughter
	ENJA 3047	Dollar Brand and Johnny Dyani: Echoes from Africa
	ENJA 3079	Dollar Brand and Johnny Dyani: Dollar Brand at Montreux
	ENJA 4030	Dollar Brand and Johnny Dyani: African Dawn
	88231	Matsidiso
	88293	South African Sunshine
	A1001	(with others: Liberation: South African Freedom Songs)

Various. Jazz records from musicians with creative connections with Brand.

1975	GL1796	Pat Matshikiza and Kippie Moeketsi: Tshona
1976	Gl1857	Pat Matshikiza: Sikiza Matshikiza
1977	GL 1912	Kippie Moeketsi/Hal Singer: Blue Stompin'
	STAR 206	Dennis Mpale with Kippie Moeketsi: Our Boys are Doing it
	N9031	Jazzministers: Nomvula's Jazz Dance
	ML 4258	Basil Coetzee, Tete Mbambisa, Zulu Pindi and Monty Weber: Did you tell your Mother?

Ngozi, Winston 'Mankunku'. A famous jazz artist from Guguletu in Cape Town. As a tenor saxophonist, inspired by John Coltrane, his music is a blend of jazz, fusion and marabi. He appeared as guest artist with many groups (with Mike Makhalemele, for example on *Lion and the Lamb*). Winston was famous for his LP *Yakhal Inkomo*, well known throughout the country. He recently played a series of gigs with bass-player/arranger Victor Ntoni's band including Duke Makasi and Tete Mbambisa. He also plays and composes with pianist Mike Perry. A new LP is due in 1987, which will only be the second record released under his own name in 20 years.

1968	GSL 266	Mankuku Quartet: Yakhal' Inkomo (his only solo LP)
1970s	PVA 6	Super Jazz Vol.1: (Various: Mankunku, Allen Kwela, Makhalemele etc.)
	TJL 13007	Super Jazz Vol.2: (Various: Mankunku, Allen Kwela, Makhalemele etc.)
	SRK 786151	Mike Makhalamele: The Peacemaker
	SRK 786152	Blue Mike
	GL 1830	Tete Mbanbisa: Tete's Big Sound
	TJL 13001	Soul of the City (Makhalemele, Kippie Moeketsi and others): Diagonal Street Blues

Pukwana, Dudu. Left South Africa in 1964 to play in a freer environment. Originally from Walmer, Port Elizabeth, he started on the piano at the age of six. He was semi-professional during secondary school. Dudu was influenced by Kippie Moeketsi, Mackay Davashe and Nick Moyake. He worked with various bands in the late 1950s, including his own Jazz Giants with Dollar Brand. Dudu was saxophonist of the year in 1962. He played with Chris MacGregor's Blue Notes: Chris (piano), Dudu (alto), Mongezi Feza (trumpet), Johnny Dyani (bass), Louis Moholo (drums), Nick Moyake (tenor). MacGregor's integrated band won the Jazz Band prize at the Castle Lager Festival in 1963. They recorded an LP but conditions were by now too difficult for a multiracial band to survive. They moved to Europe, where Ronnie Scott helped them to get started in London. The Blue Notes became the Brotherhood of Breath. Later, in 1969, Dudu formed Spear. Chris MacGregor is now based in France. Dudu's current band is Zila, with Lucky Ranku on guitar and Pinise Saul on vocals.

1971	VIRGIN	Spear: In the Townships
	SZB 8162	Macombo Jazz Makers: Vol. 2
		Zila Live
	ZL3	Zila 86 ZL3
		Brotherhood of Breath
1978	JBL 2003	Jabula in Amsterdam
1979	JBL 2002	Jabula: Jabula
1982	TSA 001	Julian Bahula's Jazz Afrika: Son of the Soil

Mbanqanga

Mbaqanga is a the unique blend of South African traditional music with urban influences, which took off on record in the 1960s. Workers wanted music that was new and exciting but still retained cultural roots. There have been many problems besetting the music, including unsympathetic record companies, lack of gigs, bad contracts and a general lack of investment by companies in proper promotion and marketing of many bands, especially at the traditional/mbaqanga end of the market. There were also problems with censorship in a difficult political climate. Until the last few years, when multiracial gigs have become more widespread in certain major cities, very few whites got to see the best groups of the 1960s and 1970s unless they played the liberal 'English' university campuses.

Sax Jive

Sax Jive outlasted the pennywhistle-based kwela (1940s to 1960s) into the 1970s. It has a more powerful sound and harder driving beat than kwela. The top stars were people like 'Zakes' Nkosi, West Nkosi (now top producer at Gallo), Thomas Phale, Wilson 'King Force' Silgee, David Thekwane and Lulu Masilela. The music utilised a simple, repetitive and muscular rhythm section with distinctive South African saxes, paralleled by violin and accordion jive styles – both more rustic sounding varieties of the same three-minute hit format favoured by Sax Jive. The mid-1970s Mavuthela (Gallo's black music division, headed by West Nkosi) compilations have a good mixture of sax, accordion and concertina jives with hilarious spoken instructions and even novelty voices. Current jive stars include Johnson Mkhalali, who appears with the Boyoyo Boys on 'Gumboots', from Paul Simon's *Graceland* LP. This recent line-up has Lulu Masilela with Johnson on accordion; honking sax jive horns are by Barney Rachabane, Mike Makhalemele and Teaspoon Ndlela. The title 'Gumboots' refers to a mine dance which was also the title of an early pair of 1970s Boyoyo Boys' LPs. Teaspoon and 'T' Boys were on *Seven Mabone*, a 1974 release with the oddly named track 'Mr. Big Face'. Bands like the Boyoyo Boys. Zwino Zwino Boys, Marks Mankwane and his Shaluza Boys were session bands with a producer having the sole rights to the name. Thus did David Thekwane churn out material with the name Boyoyo Boys.

Nkosi, Zacks (Zakes) Nkosi

RG1026	Our Kind of Jazz
STR 30038	Our Kind of Jazz Vol.1
STR 30061	Our Kind of Jazz Vol 2

1973	GGL 4006	Radio Lesotho Hits Vol.1
	GGL 4007	Radio Lesotho Hits Vol.2
	SML 7000	Six Mabone (various – Phale, Masilela, Thekwane)
	LBPS 21	17 Mabone (various – West Nkosi etc.)
1974	LBPS 19	Seven Mabone (various)
	PKL 8010	Special Special (various - Boyoyo Boys, Johnson Mkhalali etc.)
1975	PKL 8013	Thomas Phale and his Mad Sax
1977	BL 45	The Members: Whole Day Bump
	TL 511	Sax Jive: Top Hits Vol.2 (various)
1979	LZG 21	The Best of Accordion Jives (various)
1980s	TL505	Sax and Accordion Jive: Top Hits
	BL 128	The Boyoyo Boys: Back in Town
	BL 461	Makgona Tshole Band: Mathaka
	SUNL 623	Patrick Biyana: Amagwala
	BL404	Bra Sello: Boogie Centre
	IAL 3080	Johnson Mkhalali: Mantinti No.3
	BL 513	Johnson Mkhalali: Sunshine Boots
	CNH 1029	Malume Kid: Ingwavuma Blues
	BL4	Thala Thala (Inkonkoni) (various)
	LZG 2GRC	Phoyisa (various artistes)
	RCL 1206	The Hockers (Lulu Masilela, Thomas Phale, David Thekwane): Fly Home
	PKL 8014	Eloff Street 500 (various - Johannes Lenkoe Acc, Boyoyo Boys etc.) The Best

Tabane, Philip. Born in Riverside near Pretoria, he started playing the pennywhistle while at school and also learnt to play his brothers' guitars. His mother bought him an electric guitar in 1958. Philip played at weddings and social events and won some talent contests at the beginning of the 1960s. He eventually formed Malombo (Spirits), a band that took a unique new direction in music. At first sidemen were Abe Cindi (flute) and Julian Bahula (traditional Malombo drums). The repertoire drew deeply on Venda and Pedi roots with a strong jazz/blues influence, showcasing Philip's guitar. He has always been keen to remain true to his heart in his music and not commercialise. Philip won the 1964 Castle Lager Jazz Festival. Cindi and Bahula took the opportunity to go to London; Bahula later formed Jabula and now plays in London and promotes shows. Philip formed a duo with Gabriel Thobejane on African drums. He played many gigs in townships, clubs and English-speaking university campuses. In the 1970s and 1980s Philip went through different line-ups. He released a few excellent records over the years. In 1986, he was back together with Gabriel Thobejane (who had been in the fusion band, Sakhile, in the intervening years).

1964	N9033	Castle Lager Jazz Festival 1964 featuring the Malombo Jazz Men and the Early Mabuza Quartet
1969	AYC1004	The Indigenous Afro-Jazz Sounds of Philip Tabane and his Malombo Jazzmen (also GSL 267)
1972	ATH 4024	Sangoma
1974	ATC 8003	Malombo: Pele Pele
1984	KAYA 300	Malombo
1986	PAM 04	Man Phily

Bopape, Rupert. One of the most famous talent scouts of the 1960s and early 1970s, Rupert was in the forefront of the record company policy of tightly controlling new mbaqanga bands. He exerted a strong influence on groups under his wing and hired and fired bands. Rupert helped form a style combining indigenous sounds and American harmonies. Joyce Mogatusi's Dark City Sisters were the first group to popularise this style, coached by Aaron Lerole. Many incredible talents were discovered by Bopape – including the brilliant vocalist/composer Simon 'Mahlathini' Nkabinde.

Mahlathini, Simon Nkabinde. Mahlathini developed and brought to prominence 'groaning' – a style of deep-voiced singing with traditional roots. This was heavily influenced by Aaron Lerole's Black Mambazo, that also featured his cousin Zeph Nkabinde. The style is at the crossroads of kwela, marabi and a tougher blend of mbaqanga. He recorded as Indoda Mahlathini (Mahlathini the man) and also with the Mahotella Queens. He had a riveting stage show, whipping audiences into a frenzy with his brand of call and response music, usually with the Queens doing dance routines and singing close harmonies. This was backed by the legendary Makgona Tshole Band playing the traditional equivalent of a synthesis of Howlin' Wolf/Chuck Berry/Bo Diddley. It is difficult to describe, as it is music for city people who still retained strong traditional roots. After some lean years in the late 1970s, Mahlathini resurfaced on Gallo in 1983 as Mahlathini Nezintombi Zomgqashiyo. His LPs are mostly in Zulu but he has also recorded one classic mbaqanga LP in Sotho. In 1983 he released some of the best mbaqanga records featuring the original Mahotella Queens and the Makgona Tshole Band. In the same year he said of his music, 'I won't commercialise, because that would be tantamount to parting with your roots and culture.' In 1985 Mahlathini guested on two LPs with Amaswazi Emvelo and then released an excellent traditional/gospel LP in 1986. In 1987 Mahlathini was expected to tour Europe, with a record deal imminent.

| 1975 | KGA 100 | Umkhovu |

1976	KGA 101	Guga Mzimba
1976	KGA 102	Mahlathini and the Queens
1977	ZSW 14007	Ngibuzindlela
	ZSW 14034	Ubodlomane
	YGA 300	Wavutha Umlilo
	DJR 1051	Indoda Mahlathini
	MFPFF80200	Kudala Besibiza
1979	GOL 307	Na Madodana
1983	BL 396	Uhambo Lwami (with the Queens)
1984	BL 448	Amaqhawe Omgqashiyo
1984	BL 457	Pheletsong ya Lerato
1984	BL 474	Umahlathini Nabo: Ulungile
	BL 478	Mahlathini Nezintombi Zomgqashiyo: Ditoriso Tsa Morena
1986	BL562	Mahlathini Namatshezulu: Ejerusalem Siyakhona; Also see: Amaswazi Emvelo
1962	JSX 60	Flute Kwela Africa (Black Mambazo,Elias and his Zig Zag Flutes etc.)
1967	JCLP 46	Dark City Sisters: Star Time, Vol.1
	JCLP 69	Dark City Sisters, Vol.2
	33JP1002	Dark City Sisters, Vol.3
1985	EMW 5502	The Indestructible Beat of Soweto (Mahlathini Nezintombi Zomgqashiyo, Amaswazi Emvelo etc.)

Mahotella Queens. Formed in 1964 by Rupert Bopape. The Queens were the premier mbaqanga harmony group, especially through the 1970s. They were backed by the Makgona Tshole Band which included ace guitarist/composer/producer Marks Mankwane, and they have released many brilliant records over the years. At various times the featured groaners were Mahlathini, Robert Mbazo Mkhize, Potatoes Mazambane and Joseph Mthimkhulu. The latter three formed Abafana Baseqhudeni. The Queens' music has tight, punchy, sweet vocals, call and response with groaners, thrilling dance steps and rock steady backing. The Mahotella Queens and Mahlathini call their style of mbaqanga music mgqashiyo – the 'Indestructible Beat'. This is a tough mix of traditional and urban sounds with only a slight western influence. They toured extensively in Southern Africa. Over the years there have been personnel changes. They recorded mainly in Zulu in the early 1970s but later released LPs in Sotho, Pedi and Tswana.

1972	LPBS 9	Marks Umthakathi
1974	LPBS 20	Umculo Kawupheli
1975	BL 39	Phezulu Eqhudeni

1977	BL 111	Izibani Zomgqashiyo
	BL123	Best of the Mahotella Queens
1982	BL 366	Hamba Minyaka
	IAL 3034	Ezesimanje
1983	IAL 3096	Tsa Lebowa
	IAL 4005	Khwatha o Mone
	BL 456	Tse Hlwahlwa
	HIL 2006	Peggy and the Mahotella Queens: Mosese o Mosweu

Compilations

| 1980 | RL 315 | Mahotella Queens/Abafana Baseqhudeni and others: Ezipholile |
| 1986 | EMW 5505 | Duck Food (originally: Umculo Kawupheli) |

Abafana Baseqhudeni

1975	BL 49	Umshado Ugcwele Amasaka
1978	BL 146	Bakhuphuka Izwe Lonke
1980	RL 301	Edzidla Ubhedu
	BL 88	Imbumbulu
	BL 89	Umdumo
	BL 107	Madoda Sitsheleni
1982	LR44009	The Cockerel Boys (Abafana Baseqhudeni): from Soweto, Mbube Jive And Soul

Ladysmith Black Mambazo. South Africa's greatest mbube (accapella) group consists of two families, the Shabalalas and the Mazibukos. Leader and composer Joseph Shabalala was born in Ladysmith, Natal. He took a close interest in his father's choir from an early age. He first joined a group called the Highlanders in Durban, later forming a new group with his cousins Albert and Milton Mazibuko. They were soon joined by their brothers. Ladysmith Black Mambazo was named after Aaron Lerole's Black Mambazo (black axe). At concerts they all wear the same clothes and dance in unison; their dance is called 'Cothoza Mfana' (walk proud boy). Their first original composition was 'Nomathemba', named after a girl Joseph was keen on at the time. Since then they have released more than two dozen LPs. Most songs are in Zulu but they have also recorded some songs in Sotho, English and German. The group has toured in Europe and the USA. They have recently been brought to worldwide acclaim on Paul Simon's *Graceland*, where he lets Ladysmith Black Mambazo's music shine through undiluted, giving mbaqanga music international recognition. Hopefully this may have some influence on the strange antics of local record companies who try to americanise their acts without realising the potential popularity of indigenous music. (Note also the success of Malcolm McClaren's reworked mbaqanga *Duck Rock* and the mbaqanga-based hit of Bow Wow Wow.) The group has signed to WEA with a 1987 release produced by Paul Simon.

1973	BL 14	Amabutho
	BL18	Imbongi
1974	BL23	Umama Lo
	BL27	Isitimela
	BL35	Ukukhanya Kwelanga
1976	BL 81	Amaqhawe
	BL 86	Ukusindiswa
	BL 91	Shintsa Sithothobala
	BL 92	Phezulu Emafini
1977	BL 129	Ushaka
	BL 153	Indlela Yasezulwini
	BL 186	Ezinkulu
	BL 205	Intokozo
	BL 253	Ngonqotha Mfana
	BL 300	Ulwandle Olungcwele
1981	BL 321	Phansi Emgodini
1982	BL 353	Umthombo Wamanzi
1983	BL 393	Induku Zethu
1984	BL 472	Ibhayibheli Liyindlela
1985	BL 504	Inkazimulo
1986	BL 531	Inala
	BL 548	Ezulwini Siyakhona
1987		Shaka Zulu

More Mbube/Choral Music:

BL22	Empangeni Home Tigers: Umfakazi Yibeshuu
MAL 7006	Royal Star
SML7002	The Black Axe (AKA The Transvaal Black Axe)
RPM 7064	Mthunzini Brothers: Intandane

Izikhova, Ezimnqini

BL 524	Ivangeli Kakudala
BL 554	Khaya Elihle

Holy Spirits

	TEL 2113	Kabelo Ya Ka Entle
	TEL 2124	Okholwa Kujesu
	CT5	Baragwanath Choir

Soweto Teachers Choir

	TEL 2021	Your Songs
	TEL 2022	Shaka
	TEL 2023	Qeu Qeu Majaona
	HT 313	Iscathamiya, Zulu Workers Choirs in South Africa

Various

	BL 401	Mafembile Naba Hlobo Bakhe:Inamba
	SML 7004	Yezulu Ohinina (Xhosa Traditional Choir)
1976	BL 83	Hambani Magoduka

The Soul Brothers. One of the best-selling mbaqanga bands, the Soul Brothers started in the 1970s playing soul-influenced music and moved into mbaqanga with great success. The group leaders today are David Masondo (lead vocalist) and Moses Ngwenya (keyboards). They often feature Lemmy 'Special' Mabazo and Thomas Phale on saxes. The Soul Brothers backing bands have always set standards in proficiency with their smooth vocal harmonies over strong mbaqanga rhythms and usually featuring distinctive South African sax riffs. Recently Masondo and Ngwenya set up their own company, Soul Brothers Records, with Stanley Nkosi. This very popular live band has released many LPs over the years. 'Zakes' Mchunu, bassist and a founder member died tragically in a car crash in 1984. In 1987 the band was due to tour Europe.

	LMS 526	Mshoza Wami
	LMS 528	Dumela
	LMS 530	I Feel So Lonely Without You
1977	LMS 532	Ayke Niyeke Botsotsi
1978	LMS 534	Mantombazane
	LMS 550	Kulukhuni
	LMS 555	Nilindeli
	LMS 585	Ke Kopa Tshwarelo
1982	LMS 597	Oganda Ganda
	SLMS 700	Isiphino
1983	MUNG 4000	Isicelo

1984	MUNG 4001	Isithembiso
1985	PRYB 4002	Isilingo
1986	PRYB 4006	Uthando

Amaswazi Emvelo was formed by Albert 'Jerry' Motha and composer Meshack Mkhwanazi in 1978. Albert had been a singer with California Kids. Together with Meshack he set up his own group to play traditionally inspired music. They were signed to Gallo and produced by West Nkosi, who also wrote many of their songs. Vocalists Albert Motha, Wilson Buthelezi and Sipho Madondo fronted the band for most of the time. They had a pulsating rhythm section, melodic guitars, sharp chords on the organ and superbly tight harmonies and vocals. Their biggest hit was *Thul'ulalele*. Most of their LPs went gold. In 1985-6 Mahlathini was guest artist on two albums. In 1986 the group split up. With luck two good bands will rise from the ashes.

1979	BL167	Siphuma Eswazini
	BL212	Mama Ka Nomvula
	BL243	Jabulani
1980	BL292	Thul'ulalele
1981	BL322	Umkovo Wendawo
1982	BL365	E Soweto
	BL392	Ezintabeni
1984	BL480	Izulu Elimnyama
1985	BL509	Amaswazi Emvelo and Mahlathini: Utshwala Begazati
1986	BL540	Ngiyamthandu Jesu

Harari (originally The Beaters). One of the most influential of the fusion/Mbaqanga bands in the 1970s. Groups active at this time include Spirits Rejoice, the Drive and Dick Khoza's band. Harari was started by the more assertive musicians Sipho 'Hotstix' Mabuse and Alec Khaoli and the late Selby Ntuli, who took much more control over their music and hired their own producers. With a string of hits and LPs containing a rich blend of music that still retained some ties to their roots, Harari was one of the most successful bands; it eventually split, with members forming their own groups. Alec Khaoli has in recent years been mainly recording funk-inspired music.

Mabuse, Sipho. 'Hotstix' Mabuse has recently released two excellent albums: *Burnout* with the giant hit 'Jive Soweto' and his new LP *Afrodizzia*. During 1986 he toured extensively with one of the best live shows. The band features Khaya Mahlangu on sax and a new incarnation of Harari. The music is balanced between excellent mbaqanga music and funk. In 1987

Sipho Mabuse signed to Virgin Records, bringing his powerful and accessible music to a worldwide audience.

1984	HUL 509	Burn Out
1986	HUL 40120	Afrodizzia
1987	VIRGIN	Sipho Mabuse

Many South African bands are now playing funk/disco styles, the best known probably being Brenda and the Big Dudes.

Various

1975	GL 1814	The Beaters: Harari
1976	GL 1874	Harari: Rufaro
	GL 1930	Genesis
	GSL 170	Manana
	ML 4186	Harari Memorial
	ML 4636	Home Brew
	HUL 501	Street Life
		Kalahari Rock
	HUL 4092	Heartbeat
1984	HUL 516	Set Me Free
		Alec 'Om' Khoali: Say You Love Me
	HUL 40095	Umoja: Party
	RCL 1202	The Drive: Can Your Feel It
	BL271	The Drive: Lets Cool It
	RTL 4100	Batsumi (with Sipho Mabuse): Moving Along
	GL 1873	Dick Khoza: Chapita
	SNL 101	The Actions (with Strike Vilikazi): Soweto
	HIP7	Sakhile: Sakhile
	HIP 13	Sakhile: New Life
	CCP4051081	Condry Ziqubu: Gorilla Man
	FLY 10	Brenda and the Big Dudes: Touch Somebody

Hotline (a white band popular with both whites and blacks)

1983	FML 1001	Music for Africa
1984	FML 1003	Jabulani
1985	FML 1007	Wozani
1986	FML 1010	Current

Stimela. Led by the talented guitarist/producer, Ray Chipika Phiri, Stimela is one of the most popular bands in South Africa, and was brought to wider attention by being featured on Paul Simon's *Graceland*. The band toured in the USA with Ladysmith Black Mambazo at Paul Simon's request. Ray started playing in the 1960s and became a dancer with the Dark City Sisters. Then, after a few lean years, he formed a group called the Cannibals which lasted for twelve years. Ray became a session musician when the group disbanded. Later he formed Stimela to back various artists like Sipho 'Hotstix' Mabuse and Steve Kekana. Stimela has become one of the most important bands in South Africa, playing mainly funk-influenced music.

1984	HUL 513	Fire Passion Ecstasy
1985	HUL40089	Shadows Fear and Pain
1986	HUL40103	Rewind
	HUL40109	Look Listen and Decide

Juluka (Zulu: sweat). Started out as a duo in the 1970s with Sipho Mchunu, a migrant worker, and Johnny Clegg, a social anthropologist at Wits University, who has a deep interest in Zulu music and culture. Together they rose above racial barriers and harassment, gradually gaining acceptance at large venues and festivals. Initially, after playing small black gigs, Juluka became a band noted for their devastating live performances, especially the stamping Zulu 'Indlamu' dancing by Johnny and Sipho. Juluka released a highly successful string of albums and toured abroad. In 1985 Sipho decided to return to his family in the countryside and Juluka came to an end. The band had been extremely popular with blacks and whites. The music, a mix of strong mbaqanga with catchy tunes, had broken down many barriers.

Clegg, Johnny. Released some interesting solo records before starting his formidable group: Johnny Clegg and Savuka, a six-piece multiracial band, whose first single, 'Asimbonanga', was a tribute to heroes of the struggle. Their new single and album point to future successes in South Africa and acceptance abroad with their exciting blend of progressive mbaqanga/rock and non-racial identity. The impressive Indlamu dancing has been further refined, and shows during the band's 1987 tour of Europe were packed out.

		Universal Men
	MINC 1020	African Litany
1982	MINC 1030	Ubhule Bemvelo
	SHAKA1	Scatterlings
1983	MINC 1070	Work For All
1984	MINC 1100	Musa Ukungilandela
1986	MINC 4051481	The Good Hope Concerts

MINC 1140   Johnny Clegg: Third World Child

Zulu Traditional Music

Presently Zulu artists account for 75 per cent of recorded mbaqanga music, despite being only one of the three main groupings in the country, with roughly the same size population (6 million) as the Xhosa and Sotho peoples. Interestingly, many bands contain members from different backgrounds which helps to forge a nationwide sound. The official system of forcing tribal groups to live separately has had some negative effects, however, as people would normally mix together. Some bands record in more than one language, usually Zulu, Sotho or English. Zulu, Xhosa, Swazi and Ndebele have related languages. Hence some Xhosas, for instance, will buy Zulu music and so on. Zulu traditional music usually features a stomping fast beat, guitars and often violins and concertinas, bluesy soulful vocals or tight choral harmonies. Top artists include Moses Mchunu, Nganeziyamfisa No Khambalomvaleliso, Mzikayifani Buthelezi.

Mchunu, Moses

1975	BL57	Inkunzi Emnyama
	BL69	Senzeni Madoda
	BL155	Ngixoleleni Bazali Bami
	BL232	Baningi Abangithandayo
1980	RL311	Ezidla Ubhedu
	BL252	Sigiya Ngengoma
1981	BL320	Babulala Umuzi Ka Baba
1982	BL355	Qhwayilahle
1983	BL 441	Awukho Umuzi Wempohlo
1984	BL 487	Umshado
1985	TEL 2056	Sibezwile Bekhuluma
1986	TEL 2092	Wena Ntombi Ungalile
1986	TEL 2047	(Jozi) Isangoma

Phuzushukela

1981	LZG 39	Umhlaba
	NZL 88	Sehlule Umkhomazi

Various

1980	BL 197	Zuma Nezasemsinga: Eyami Iyogana
1982	SUNL605	Kati Eliclean: Amalabi (also on ELP 2003)

UKL1002	Izingwenya: Wakhal' Uthekwane

Mbambo, Aaron

1983	TSL 7522	Nizizwile Webalaleli
	TSL 7524	Amashushu
	TSL 7522	I Jika Jika Nojomo

Mzikayifani Buthelezi

1982	BOL106	Isitimela
	BOL 121	Sanibonani
1983	BOL 123	Kulukhuni Ukuba Indoda
1984	BOL 304	Hamba Kahle Mfowethu
1985	BOL 321	Umlilo
	BOL 327	Amadayisi
1986	BOL 332	Sathane

Segebengu Nomagilogilo

1982	ERH 2001	Ngihleli Ngikulinde
1985	ERH2041	Kwachitheka Ubendle
1986	ERH 2055	Segebengu Nabafan Besitina

Nganeziyamfisa No Khambalomvaleliso

1982	IAL 3015	Yiyo Lentombi
	IAL 3052	Sizoyivala Imilomo
1983	IAL 3070	Intandane Enhle
	IAL 3090	Walimbamba Lomfana
1984	IAL 4032	Laduma
1985	BL 532	Liya Bhubha
1986	BL 563	Kwankunge Nje

Various

1982	CT 48	Philemon Zulu: Sesaba Izulu
	BL 394	Abalandeli: Umfokazana
	BL 395	Udokotela Shange Namajaha: Awungilobolele
	UNL 608	Shoba Ndimande: Sinoti Xaba
1984	BOL 305	Dilika: Ngayishela
	BL 486	Amashosa Kaduza: Smith Street
	NZL 126	Izipehle Ezinothuli: Asihambe Sobula

	NZL 149	Masente Sikhakhawe: Wentombi
	BOL 330	Ziyashiyana
1985	CGH 5022	Uthwalofu Namankentshane: Impendulo
	SIH 2	Ihashe Elimhlophe: Intandane
	VUH 40	Ihashe Elimhlophe: Wololo
	VUL 6004	Fihlamahlazo Nabochwepheshe: Ziphansi Izinsizwa
	TEL 2052	Raymond Mbele: He Madoda

Shangaan Music

Shangaan is another very popular form of music, with a big beat, special guitar tunings, gruff male vocals and often high, wild, female back-up harmonies. Top artistes include Thomas Chauke, J.J. Chauke, Makhubela and Obed Ngobeni. At its best Shangaan music is very powerful.

Makhubela and the Nkhohlwani Girls

1981	BL 312	Ku Na Nqambhi
1982	BL 362	Mhana Sibongile
1983	BL 403	Vabombisa Kutshelela
1985	BL 545	Gazankulu

Thomas Chauke with the Shinyori Sisters

1981	LZG 36	Nyoresh
	QBH 1030	Shimatsatsa No.2 Don't Be Surprised
1984	QBH 1053	Shimatsatsa No.5
1984	QBH 1084	Shimatsatsa No.6

Various

1981	RPM 7056	Elias Maluleke and Mavambe Girls: Jive Xibeiana
1982	MMC 951	Baloyi and the Twanano Sisters: Avikatini
1983	EAD 1010	J.J. Chauke and Tiyimeleni Young Sisters: Madyisa Mbitsi
	BL 417	Mabasa's Singing Birds: Engenirari Va Hiakirili
	BL 397	Khosa and the Giyani Disco Sisters: Nghenani Mi Cina
1984	BL 463	Khosa and the Giyani Disco Sisters: Mhani Wa Solani
	BL 422	Matanato Brothers and Gaza Queens:

		Hivona Sivara
	EAD 1017	Obed Ngobeni and the Kurhula Sisters: Ku Mluvukile Eka 'Zete'
	TWL 512	Norman Mathebula: Xibhamubhamu
1985	RAIN 1150	General M.D. Shiranda and Gaza Sisters: Music is the Food of Love
1986	BL 551	Banda Six: Pfukani Rixile

Sotho Traditional Music

Sotho music is very rustic, with piano accordion, shouted vocals or chanting and mid-paced stomping beat. It occasionally has choral music but rougher harmonising than Zulu music. The best artists include Tau Ea Linare and Ta Ea Matsekha.

CGL 4032	Johannes Lenkoe and Oupa Khetha
NOL355	Isaac Sibiya: Kidebone
RAIN 1028	Tau Ea Linare: Thabang
RAIN 1042	Tsamaea Ntate Motaung
RAIN 1151	Sekipa Se Setala
BL 314	Dihoba Tsa Belina: Nyaka Nyaka
BL 358	Basotho Mamelang
BL 413	Kesa Imametse
NZL 108	Tau Ea Lioli: Ha Re Rapele Balimo
IAL 3075	Moshoeshoe 7: Majuteng
IAL 3076	Moshoeshoe 8: Batho Ke Bana
TWL 511	Dioli Tsaeja Matsheka: Mamate Bona
BL 356	Lioli Tsa Eja Matsekha: Malaeta No.1
CJS 1008	Sebata Sebata: Bontate Ba Kopane
KWALP 7019	Tau Ea Matsekha: Manyetse Ke Lekholwa
KWALP 4051381	Khutsana Ea Lesotho
BL 541	Moshoeshoe No10: Batho Bamaseru
ORB 003	Puseletso Seema & Tau Ea Linare: He O Oe Oe

Liberation Music

Much of the anger and commitment of the liberation struggle is represented on certain political records; the liberation movements abroad have released several records/tapes of music, polemics, poetry and chants. All of these would be automatically banned in South Africa, since they are sold and produced under the auspices of banned organisations like the ANC and SWAPO. Several people have to date been imprisoned (two years in one case) for possession of such banned recordings. However this does not prevent the spread of Freedom Songs; both Pink Floyd's 'The Wall' and the Specials' 'Free Nelson Mandela' were banned but were immortalised by the kids in the streets. The recent War on Want Freedom Music tape has stunning field recordings of the marching and chanting. During the current wave of unrest and massive state repression in South Africa (since at least 1984), support for democratic change has come from many areas and increasingly from musicians. The Sun City Project (USA) involved many famous musicians (Miles Davis, Bruce Springsteen, Gill Scott Heron, Bobby Womack, Little Steven) for the first time in a powerful statement of solidarity. Although artists are urged not to visit South Africa, it has become a favourite topic in musical diatribe, particularly in view of the increasing politicisation occurring in musical circles. This interest has also intensified the debate about the cultural boycott of South Africa (selective versus blanket). There is a strong feeling that progressive South African culture (i.e. literature, theatre and music) should not be boycotted, simply because of the irony involved in isolating the oppressed and not the oppressor. In the UK Robert Wyatt and Jerry Dammers produced *Wind of Change* (with SWAPO singers and Onyeka) and Dammers has gone on to form Artists Against Apartheid to campaign in the UK. His earlier 'Nelson Mandela' single in 1982 was a top-ten hit in the UK and was even a favourite with crowds in South Africa despite being banned there.

1980	BS 800718	Amandla: ANC Cultural Workers (Swedish prod)
1982	C6018207	Amandla: ANC Cultural Group (USSR)
1983	AGIS 002	Amandla: First Tour Live (Sweden)
1986	REV 1010	Radio Freedom (Voice of the ANC)
	WOW 003	Freedom Music (Kintone, Sankomota, Somo Somo,Taxi Pata Pata, Jabula & chants from South Africa)
	RTT 168	Robert Wyatt/SWAPO Singers: Wind of Change
1984	IDAF 001	SWAPO Cultural Group: Onyeka, The Torch

Until the recent Warner deal with Ladysmith Black Mambazo, only small foreign labels have taken an active interest in South African music. Although many of these releases appear in the relevant discographies above, they are listed here separately. In London, Earthworks has been most influential in releasing some real gems from South Africa – starting with the *Zulu Jive* compilation in 1983, Shifty's first release *Sankomota* and then three classic jive releases featuring the Mahotella Queens with songs from the 1970s. The ultimate compilation yet to appear from the modern

Joburg/Soweto sound is Earthwork's *The Indestructible Beat of Soweto* (1985) featuring Mahlathini and his Queens, Amaswazi, Nganezi Yamfisa, Nelcy Sedibe, Johnson Mkhalali and Ladysmith Black Mambazo. *Soweto Street Music*, a double LP release (1984), with sides by Super Tens, Special 5, Amentkentshane and a track from Kid Malume, has also proved popular. Globestyle (an Ace label) has thus far released one Sotho traditional album by Tau Ea Linare in their 'Accordions that Shook the World' series. Their two Madagascar releases provide interesting regional comparisons. Stern's Africa label have released an album by London-based Cape Town band, Kintone, *Going Home* featuring ex-Spirits Rejoice personnel. They have also released Ivorian skankers Alpha Blondy's *Apartheid is Nazism*. Another South African group, Brian Abraham's District 6 bring out their own records. During 1986, Kintone produced and paid for a 12" release, *State of Emergency*, to comment on conditions in South Africa. The biggest commercial successes pertaining to South African music so far have been McClaren's *Duck Rock* (1983); three of the mbaqanga tracks charted high in the UK charts. And, of course, Simon's *Graceland* (1986). Earthworks have released the original versions of the McClaren covers *Duck Food* (1986) and Ladysmith's 1983 *Induku Zethu*. In 1987 Earthworks signed a contract with Virgin Records which should see many more international releases of South African music.

EMW 5502	The Indestructible Beat of Soweto (Mahlathini, Amaswazi, Emvelo, Ladysmith Black Mambazo etc.)
EMW 5505	Duck Food (Mahotella Queens, Dark City Sisters)
ERT 1002	Phezulu Eqhudeni (Mahotella Queens, Mahlathini)
ELP 2002	Zulu Jive (Various Artists)
ELP 5504	Mahotella Queens: Izibani Zomgqashiyo
ELP 2006	Ladysmith Black Mambazo: Induku Zethu
ELP 2003	Kati Eliclean Namanono: Amalabi
ATXLD04	Soweto Street Music (various artists)
ORB 003	Puseletso Seema & Tau Ea Linare: He O Oe Oe
ELP 2007	Sankomota: Sankomota
DC001	District 6: Akuzwakale (Let It Be Heard)
STERNS1013	Kintone: Going Home
KMC 01	Kintone: State of Emergency (12")
HNBL6301	Poppie Nongena (stage musical; various artists)
ZENSOR 05	Soweto (various artists)

ZAMBIA

33
Zambia

The music of Zambia is seldom available outside the country and is thus hardly known to non-Zambians. Yet this apparent neglect of the variety of Zambian music, both traditional and modern, is certainly undeserved. For like the majority of African countries, Zambia retains an extraordinary variety of musical styles varying from the xylophone playing of the Western Province, to the drum chimes of the north and the yodelling of the Chikunda people. Indeed, the music of Zambia is one of the most diverse on the continent, featuring instruments and techniques found in many other African countries but seldom all in one. Thus we have the rapid text utterances and yodelling similar to the pygmy vocal tradition, drum ensembles and dance orchestras reminiscent of Ghana as well as the warrior tradition of stamping and concussion found in Southern Africa. Then there is the sanza tradition found in neighbouring Zimbabwe, the orchestrated dance pieces and highly personal and emotional depth of the Tonga people.

In terms of instrumentation alone Zambia offers a variety of idiophones – rattles, bells, hand pianos (kalimba), xylophones (silimba); membraphones – drums of various types and sizes including double headed drums, friction drums and water drums; chordophones – including mouth-bows, zithers, harps and fiddles; aerophones – the tonga flute, pan-pipes and various antelope horns.

In Zambia it is rare for musical instruments to be used outside the context of dancing. Zambian dances come in a variety of forms from solo virtouso to group dances. Dance is both functional and aesthetic, marking puberty, marriage and death as well as acting therapeutically and accompanying social and religious observances.

Yet the variety and vitality of Zambian culture should not surprise us. For several millenia, Zambia has been at the crossroads of Africa. Trade routes from north to south and east to west passed through the territory. It was along these trade routes that musical ideas travelled as various ethnic groups migrated and settled. Linking the Congo basin with Mozambique and the Swahili-speaking east coast with Angola, Zambia today enjoys a heterogeneity of culture and language almost unmatched in sub-Saharan Africa. A single village can thus produce Cewa, Yao, Swahili, Lamba and

Tonga musical styles side by side, practised with a conscious sense of history and purpose. To this extent then, Zambia can be considered an area of centripetal influence; a country where external musical sources have been important in musical development.

By the twentieth century, Zambian music presented a blurred picture of musical form and identity. Musical influences continued to flow in from all directions. The eastern region adapted styles found in Malawi and Mozambique. 'Kateke', a modern pop idiom, derived from Angola and is popular in the west of the country. A variety of styles from southern Africa took hold in the south of the country including simanje-simanje and kwela while perhaps the greatest influence came from the north – the urban Zairean pop music of the 1960s and 1970s. Styles like kiri-kiri and Zairean rumba were widely appreciated by the Zambian public. Yet it has not been an entirely one-way process and such is the speed of social change in Zambia that these various external influences have quickly been coopted by Zambian musicians and in some cases indigenised. Zambian musicians are today popular in Kenya and Tanzania, contributing a distinctively Zambian flavour to the modern urban pop scene. Early Zambian pop bands featuring electric instruments included the Lusaka Radio Band, the Mapoma Brothers and the Crusaders. Many of the early bands featured the accordion which tended to impose western harmonies on the traditional base.

Yet the danger still remains that despite the richness of the traditional musical heritage, Zambian urban music reflects influences which are at best a hybrid of neighbouring and western styles. Observers feel that this dominance of external influences (particularly Zairean) may in the long run limit the creativity of Zambian musicians and thus deprive the country of a vital medium of self expression. Because of these worries the government has been particularly active in the preservation and dissemination of uniquely Zambian musical traditions. It has established institutions to promote Zambian culture while many local groups promote indigenous musical traditions.

Today the Zambian pop market is dominated by 45 rpms of local bands imitating Zairean or South African styles. Few LPs are released and like Kenya, the LP market is dominated by imported music – either from Zaire or the west. The country's largest record company is still an affiliate of the South African Gallo label. Yet despite all this, Zambia has produced several truly national stars. Given the vitality of traditional music and the professionalism of Zambian musicians it remains to be seen whether the country can now produce an authentic Zambian style to reflect the political unification succesfully created by President Kaunda.

Traditional Music

ER 12013	Inyimbo: Songs of the Bemba People of Zambia (An Ethnodisc compilation recorded in 1969-70 featuring various types of Bemba music – from funeral dirges and hunters' songs to the songs of the Ngomba, the royal musicians.)
FE 4201	Music from Petauke of Northern Rhodesia Vol. 1
FE 4202	Music from Petauke of Northern Rhodesia Vol. 2 (A Folkwave double set featuring music from the Eastern Province of Zambia. The Petauke are the fifth largest ethnic group after the Tonga, Bemba, Cewa and Lunda.)

Modern Music

Pichen. Nazil Pichen Kazembe. Pichen started his career in 1960 and has proved to be a significant influence on the development of a distinctly Zambian sound. At the peak of his career he could sell upwards of 50,000 singles. He utilised both East African and Zairean rhythms in his music and tended to follow the Zairean tradition of releasing songs in two parts.

1983	NKP 001	Nahili Malenda
1984	UAMLP 1010	Hot Hits

Mulemena, Emmanuel. Founder of Mulemena and the Sound Inspectors, Mulemena died tragically in 1982. Singing in Kaonda, Bemba, Lamba and Nyanja, Mulemena established a short career as one of Zambia's most popular musicians with several hit singles to his credit. On his death, the band continued as Mulemena Boys.

1984	ZMLP 70	A Tribute to the Late Emmanuel Mulemena

ZIMBABWE

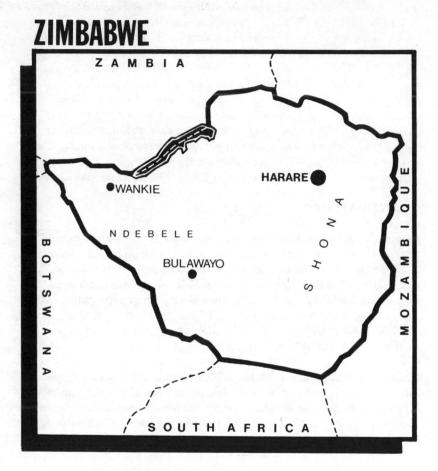

The musical culture of Zimbabwe presents the culmination of one of the most unusual musical evolutions in all of Black Africa. Colonised by the British towards the end of the nineteenth century, bitter wars of resistance followed by the steady imposition of white minority rule, neo-apartheid and the proclamation of UDI in 1964, finally led Zimbabwe to a protracted war of national liberation. In 1980, after five years of civil war, Robert Mugabe was able to announce the independence of Zimbabwe. It would be impossible to ignore this century of division, exploitation and civil war in any analysis of the contemporary musical scene in Zimbabwe.

Thankfully, the music of Zimbabwe is now finally receiving the popular attention it merits. Not only is the music being regularly aired around Africa and Europe, with regular and increasing popularity, but several writers and academics have turned their hand to helping explain the growth and development of contemporary Zimbabwean pop. Fred Zindi, in his best-selling account *Roots Rocking in Zimbabwe*, picks his way through the last 20 years of Zimbabwean urban pop. Pongweni, in *Songs that won the Liberation War*, provides a thorough analysis (including a transcription of the lyrics) of the 'chimurenga' music which accompanied the recent war of liberation. Subtitled 'An Assessment of the Role of Music in the History of a People', the book leaves no one in any doubt that not only was music an important element in the struggle for independence but that the collaboration of ZANU and ZAPU led to the creation of a stronger sense of national identity.

Today, the urban pop music of Zimbabwe reflects mainly, but not exclusively, the influence of Shona culture, encompassing over 70 per cent of the population. The Ndebele, the other major ethnic group in Zimbabwe, emerged from the Zulu tradition and, historically, made use of very few musical instruments. As Kauffman noted, this further enhanced Shona dominance in the music scene of the major urban centres.

Amongst the Shona, the most widely used instruments include the mbira, drums, rattles and musical bows. And as in all African countries, the use of these instruments in pre-colonial society accompanied all major social, work, recreational and ritual occasions. Unaccompanied choral singing was also prominent. But perhaps the key instrument remains the mbira; one of the most ancient and popular forms of music in Africa (sanza, likembe, marimba). Shona people have always held mbira players in high esteem. Comprising metal keys mounted on a wooden frame, with an accompanying resonator, mbira music has established several major musical traditions. Featuring anywhere from eight to 50 keys, Paul Berliner has argued that the mbira represents the soul of the Shona people.

In 1971, Robert Garfias played glowing tribute to the master mbira players. 'The Shona musician uses repetition as a means of establishing a line of predictability between himself and the listener... Changes and variations grow out of the overall mood or style of the piece; each of these is then given time to "grow into" the piece before another is added. It is never the composer-musician who consciously creates new variations.'

The mbira is most usually accompanied by the hosho, a rattle made out of a gourd either with seeds inside or beads attached to a net outside. The two instruments, and the vocal melodies accompanying them, interact in a stimulating and complex way.

By the 1960s and 1970s this music had arrived in the cities in two principal ways. On the one hand there were the drum and dance traditions of the beer halls where people met to dance. Several major dances emerged from this tradition including the ngororomba, jerusarema and mbakumba. On the other hand there also existed the Friday-night mbira parties in the townships where several players would gather to sing, play mbira and hosho in what was often a semi-religious observance. Prior to UDI in 1965 this type of music-making flourished in the cities but really only recovered its full vigour after Independence. Despite the apparent secularisation of the mbira music in the urban environment it has still retained something of its traditional and ritual meaning.

Like the majority of African countries, the introduction of western electric instruments in Zimbabwe during the 1960s partially replaced traditional instruments. For example, Ngwara Mpundu would play mbira pieces on the guitar. However, two distinct styles did develop featuring either acoustic playing to accompany solo singing or electric guitar bands to play in nightclubs.

Since the 1950s Zimbabwe has been subject to a number of external influences which have all left their mark on the contemporary music scene. The Beatles and Elvis gave way to James Brown and Bob Marley just as kwela and South African jazz gave way to disco, rumba and chimurenga. Fred Zindi has produced an authoritative account of the various bands and styles of the 1960s and 1970s and anyone interested in the post-war growth of Zimbabwean pop music should consult his excellent book.

Leading exponents of the more traditional mbira style of music included Greenford Jangano and his Harare Mambos and Ephat Mujuru and the Spirit of the People. The leading electric guitar bands include Devera Ngwena, Elijah Madzikatire, the Bhundu Boys, Oliver and the Black Spirits but above all Thomas Mapfumo, who has suceeded in combining traditional and modern elements to the satisfaction of both domestic and international audiences.

Traditional Music

In terms of the traditional music of Zimbabwe, very little is currently available, with most of it originating during the 1950s and early 1960s. Hugh Tracey, a pioneer in African sound recording, made many trips to Zimbabwe recording a variety of traditional styles including those of the Karanga, the Ndebele, the Zezuru, the Sena, the Tonga, the Mayika, the Ndau and the Shona. Recorded during the 1930s-1950s, very few of these recordings are available commercially.

However, as Kauffman has persuasively argued, as the spirit of nationalism develops there will surely be a cultural renaissance of major proportions which will perhaps lead to the recording and marketing of traditional Zimbabwean musical styles.

KMA 8	The Music of Africa: Rhodesia
H 72054	The Soul of Mbira: Traditions of the Shona People
H 72043	The African Mbira: Music of the Shona People

Modern Music

The modern music scene in Zimbabwe is dominated by three major styles of music. Zairean rumba continues to influence the development of local rhythms while the Shona mbira tradition is increasingly modernised to suit current tastes. Amongst the leading mbira pop bands should be included Ephat Mujuru and the Spirit of the People, Elijah Madzikatire and the Ocean City Band, the Fallen Heroes, Sungura Boys, the Four Brothers and Nyami Nyami Sounds.

Leading urban pop bands combining local idioms with western pop influences include Oliver Mtukudzi, John Chibadura, Rozalla Miller, The Marxist Brothers, Children of Nundi, The Bhundu Boys (including the off-shoot Biggie and David), Safiro Madzikatire, the Jairos Jiri Band and the Okavango Boys, Job Mashanda and the Muddy Face, New Black Montana, Zexie Manatsa and the Green Arrows. Clearly, the liberation struggle has influenced both the content and nomenclature of modern day Zimbabwean bands. The ideology of the ruling ZANU-PF party has also helped shape the ambiance of modern music in Zimbabwe. Yet, despite the proliferation of music in Zimbabwe since Independence, very few LPs can be found outside the country. One can only hope that in the future, the modern pop music of

Zimbabwe will receive the kind of commercial interest expressed in the modern music of Senegal, Zaire, Nigeria and South Africa.

Mapfumo, Thomas (b. Marondera, Zimbabwe, 1945). An outstanding singer and composer, Thomas Mapfumo is largely responsible for putting the music of Zimbabwe on the map. A Shona speaker who grew up during the heyday of white minority rule, Thomas first came to music in the form of traditional drumming and mbira playing. However he soon turned to western pop music playing cover versions of songs by the Beatles, Otis Redding and Wilson Picket. During the 1960s he achieved a limited success with this kind of music, occasionally being featured on the radio. In 1965 he composed his first song in Shona, but by the time UDI had been declared and while Thomas continued to compose in Shona, little indigenous music was actually played on the radio. In 1973 he formed the Hallelujah Chicken Run Band, which despite playing copyright music in public, continued to experiment with Shona compositions. In 1974 Thomas was approached by a representative of Teal Records who had heard of his Shona fusions and was keen to record a few of them. He subsequently released many of them as 45 rpms and so chimurenga music was established. Meaning 'the music of struggle', chimurenga quickly established itself as the distinctive and authentic sound of Zimbabwe. Making full use of innuendo and traditional proverbs, Thomas's singles became immediate hits, recording eight gold discs. However, his national popularity also held some dangers and Thomas came under government investigation. In 1976 Thomas formed a new group known as the Acid Band while continuing to perform with the Pied Pipers, another top Zimbabwean band. In 1977 the Acid Band released their first LP, *Hokoya* (Watch Out), which was immediately banned with Thomas himself being detained for 90 days. During the late 1970s the authorities did their best to discredit Thomas in the eyes of the people, even blackmailing him into performing at a fundraiser for the puppet Muzorewa. Yet despite these efforts to undermine his popularity and credibility, Thomas continued to churn out his chimurenga songs. In 1978 he formed another new group, the Blacks Unlimited, releasing another hit album, *Gwindingwi Rine Shumba*. However, despite his popularity inside Zimbabwe, Thomas really only established an international reputation when Jumbo Van Renen, the far-sighted proprietor of the London-based Earthworks label, decided to risk releasing some chimurenga songs in the UK. By this time Independence had come to Zimbabwe and with a great deal of international attention on the country, Thomas Mapfumo emerged as the standard bearer of the new music of Zimbabwe. In 1983 Earthworks released the classic compilation of chimurenga music, *The Chimurenga Singles*, and brought Thomas to Europe for live shows. Several more stirring LPs followed and by the mid-1980s Thomas was firmly established as an international star. He and the band toured widely in Europe and Africa, introducing new audiences to the richness and vitality of Zimbabwean culture.

1978		Hokoya
1980		Gwindingwe (re-released on Earthworks, 1986)
1983	ELP 2004	Chimurenga Singles (1976-1980)
198	ELP 2005	Ndangariro
1985		Mabaso (Work)
	ERT 1008	Mr Music
1986		Chimurenga For Justice

Real Sounds. An 11-piece band, composed mainly of Zaireans, the Real Sounds were formed in Zambia in 1975 and moved to Zimbabwe in 1978. Led by guitarist Ghaby Mumba, the core of the band comprises Joseph Kabange (drums), Charles Kalenga and Mbuyi Sangana (trumpets), Jojo Kavuna and Ghaby Mutombo (vocals), Jeff Kumwamba and Illunga Sam (sax), Jack Moloss (bass), Mpopani Modeste (rhythm guitar) and Mwandue Modeste on keyboards. Once settled in Zimbabwe, the band soon became one of the country's hottest acts, touring the country and facing harassment from Smith's forces. As a result, they decided to quit for a while and let things cool down while several members attended the Zimbabwe School of Music. In 1981 their work permits were not renewed and the band was forced to return to Zambia. However, they were invited to perform at the SADCC Conference and after meeting several Zimbabwean ministers were invited back to Zimbabwe. They picked up where they had left off and were soon filling dance halls throughout the country. In 1984 they released their first album. However the band continued to churn out singles at an astonishing rate, including several number one hits like 'Non-Aligned Movement' and a reworking of the Franco classic 'Azda'. Playing sweet and fast soukous, the band were perfectly poised for a wider international success and in 1986 Fred Zindi, musician, author and now promoter, brought the band to Europe for several shows. They were widely appreciated and, along with Thomas Mapfumo and the Bhundu Boys, now provide the cutting edge of the new Zimbabwean sound.

1984	ZML 1015	Harare (also available from the Africa Centre in London)
1987	COOK 004	Wende Zako

Mutuzudzi, Oliver (b.1952, Zimbabwe). Singer, composer, leader of the Black Spirits. The only artiste to approach Mapfumo in stature within Zimbabwe, Mutuzudzi is a husky voiced singer of traditional lyrics who blends them with a style similar in feeling to mbaqanga. He began playing in the late 1970s, since when he has had many hits. In 1979, when the wartime curfew was lifted, he took his band on the road and established himself throughout the region, including Zambia, Botswana and Malawi. He had released 10 albums between 1978 and 1985. Almost all his lyrics deal in a melancholy way with social issues like starvation, poverty and suffering. Most of his songs are in Shona, although he does sing in English and has recently begun to compose in Ndebele.

1978	Ndipeiwo Zano
1985	Hwena Handirase

Bhundu Boys. A five-piece band playing 'jit' music, the Bhundu Boys were one of the great African acts of 1986. Comprising Biggie Tembo on guitar and vocals, Rise Kagona on guitar, Shakie Kangwena on keyboards, David Mankaba on bass and Kenny Chitsvatsva on drums, the band took the UK by storm, being described by John Peel as playing the most perfect music he had ever heard. Playing a Zimbabwean style of soukous at breakneck speed, the band was brought to the UK by a new and imaginative company called Discafrique. From a base in Scotland, the band toured the width and breadth of Britain, thrilling audiences with their direct, no-nonsense approach to dance music. They released a mini-LP featuring the hit song 'Hatistose' and in 1986 followed up their initial success with the album entitled *Shabini*. Critics wonder why the Bhundu Boys have been chosen to succeed when Zimbabwe contains so many first-class bands but one only has to hear the LP to realise why they are one of the most exciting bands to have come from Africa in the last decade. In 1987 they were signed up by WEA.

1983	RUG 100	Chekudya Chose
1986	AFRI LP02	Shabini
1987	AFRI LP03	Tsimbodzemoto

Pied Pipers. Formed in Harare in 1971, the Pied Pipers quickly became one of Zimbabwe's top bands. A five-piece band, fronted by the singer Doreen Ncube, the band released many hit singles, playing a Shona style highly reminiscent of reggae. While this resemblance might have accounted for the band's popularity, it should be borne in mind that not only is reggae African inspired in the first place, the reggae rhythm is also to be found in traditional culture throughout Africa.

WIZ 5000	People of the World Unite

Mujuru, Ephat and the Spirit of the People. Six musicians who specialise in the mbira tradition. Featuring three mbira players, two hosha players and a drummer, the band remain one of the most popular mbira-pop bands in Zimbabwe. They toured the USA in the early 1980s.

	ZML 1013	Mbavaira
	ZML 1003	Mbira Music of Zimbabwe

Devera Ngwena. Led by Babra, Devera Ngwena play a new style known as Shona-rumba. Influenced by Congo music, their music resonates with reggae influences although this derives more from indigenous traditions than Bob Marley – who made a spectacular appearance at the 1980 Independence celebrations.

	ZML 1001	Devera Ngwena
	ZML 1004	Vol. 2
1982	ZML 1006	Vol. 3 (also SUH 1005)
	ZML 1009	Vol. 4 SUH 1013
	ZML 1011	Vol. 5 SUH 1021
1985	ZML 1024	Vol. 8
1986	ZML 1026	Masvingo Ne Carpet

35
Malawi

Malawi, which runs the length of the huge Lake Malawi in south-eastern Africa, is situated between Zambia, Mozambique and Tanzania. Many of the population are descended from the Malawi or Maravi people who came from the Congo region some hundreds of years ago, and later became known as the Chewa and Chipeta. In the south are the Nyanga and Manganja peoples; in the north the Timbuku. Later the Yao established themselves in the south, as did the Angoni, Nguni-speaking peoples from the south. Most of the population speak the Chichewa (Chinyanja) language. The population includes many adult males who work as migrant labourers in Zimbabwe or South Africa. Much of the popular music is brought home from these countries and at the same time the shortage of able-bodied young men presumably accounts for the relative scarcity of recording artistes from Malawi. The country is undoubtedly rich in musical tradition, with a catalogue of indigenous instruments to hand, including bows, xylophones and sanzas (both known as kalimbas), the bangwe, a multi-string zither and, of course, drums.

1017 GALP   African Music Society's Awards 11
                             (Contains humorous group singing and a
                             women's praise song from Malawi, together
                             with other music from the region.)

Popular Music

The pop or jazz culture has been strongly influenced by South African kwela, with flute and banjo players still very active. The Malawian ingredient is known as makwanya. The first generation of recording stars were mostly banjo or guitar pickers playing folk and country styles. In the 1950s names like Wilson Makawa and HMV recording artiste Thailo Kapiye rose to prominence. Apparently the Nyasa style of guitar playing, with its South African inflexion, influenced Tanzanian popular music back in the 1960s. Among the few popular musicians whose names have been heard in the west are the Kachamba Brothers Kwela Band, whose recordings exemplify this style. According to Dr. J. Lwanda, writing in *Africa Beat* No. 3, others who have made national reputations include the Ndingo Brothers, who record for the independent Nzeru record label. The other indigenous label is Ngoma, a subsidiary of the Malawi Broadcasting Corporation, which releases folk music such as that by Stonart Lungu, Katenga Humming Bees, Barton Harry and Nyrere. There is also an MBC house band who made their recording debut in 1975. Other recording artistes include Mulanje Mountain Jazz Band, the Mitoche Brothers Band, Kalambe Band and the Kamwendo Brothers.

AEL1	The Kachamba Brothers Kwela Band
0120031	The Kachamba Brothers
0120240	Donald Kachamba
AIT	Donald Kachamba
HMV	Thailo Kapiye
NGOMA	Kokoliko Ku Malawi

36

Mozambique

One of the last African countries to become independent, Mozambique suffers from its close proximity to South Africa, which dominates it economically and, therefore, influences popular culture to a great extent. Historically the Mozambique coast was a trading base where Bantu Africans met and dealt with Arab traders from the Indian Ocean. Portuguese settlers arrived in the sixteenth century to set up plantations and profit from the slave trade. It was not until 1951 that Portugal declared the country an overseas province and in 1972 it became a 'state' of Portugal. Independence was achieved in 1975 under the late Samora Michel. As the country is such an elongated shape it contains many different ethnic groups, from the Shangan in the south to the Makonde in the north. Each region displays the expected variety of traditional music forms, but the most impressive national music is probably that of the 'timbila' orchestras with their massed xylophones. These were first recorded in the Xopi (Chopi) and Tswa regions during the 1940s by Hugh Tracey.

LPL0133   Rhythms and Dances of Mozambique
Traditional Music and Songs of
Mozambique (Anthology of first folk music
festival.)

Contemporary Music

As a result of continuing political difficulties which overshadow daily life in Mozambique, there has been no real synthesis of rural music with contemporary styles. Most of the pop music available is from South Africa and, although the Mozambiquean variant has subtle differences, to the uninitiated it closely resembles mbaqanga. Popular urban music forms are the marabenta, majika and shigubu, first brought to light in the 1950s by such stars as Orchestre Djambu, Ontonio Williams and Rosa Tembe. Others who are still current include Alexandre Langa, Daniel Langa and Pedro Langa, Fani Pfumo, saxophonist Chico da Conceiçao, Wazimbo, Jose Barata and Ghorwani, one of the top groups.

    Ben Mandelson, who visited the country in January 1987 collecting material for Globestyle, reports that before the revolution there were two record labels, a studio and a pressing plant in operation, but nowadays records are put out under the auspices of the national radio station. Apparently the industry is waiting to be revived by the delivery of pressing equipment held in South Africa. The Zairean singer Sam Mangwana recorded a short but impressive album there in 1982 which conveys much of the marabenta flavour. The radio house band, Orchestre Marabenta Star da Mozambique, one of the most popular units in the country, was due to tour Germany in 1987. While there is a plentiful supply of recording artistes and a national hit parade, almost all the discs are singles, with the few albums available in the country being compilations of recent hits. Mandelson reported the record shops to be empty with no record players in sight. But there is a ready market and he talks of plans to manufacture local Tiger record players to run on 6 volt car batteries. It seems things can only get better for the Mozambique music industry. In 1986 Elsa Mangue Felipe was voted Best Young Singer in Radio France International's 'Discovery' awards.

LPL 0131 Parado de Sucessos: Eyuphuro (A selection of pop and traditional recordings.)

MADAGASCAR

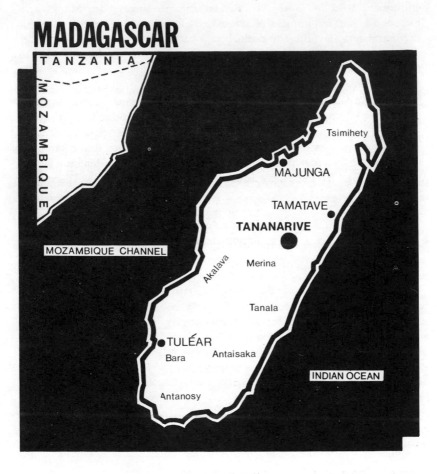

TANZANIA

MOZAMBIQUE

Tsimihety

MAJUNGA

TAMATAVE

TANANARIVE

MOZAMBIQUE CHANNEL

Akalava

Merina

Tanala

TULÉAR

Bara

Antaisaka

INDIAN OCEAN

Antanosy

Lying in the Indian Ocean, some 400km off Mozambique, Madagascar is the fourth largest island in the world. The earliest inhabitants were descended from the Bantu-speaking peoples of central Africa and from Indonesian settlers who established the Merina kingdom in the eleventh century. Other kingdom/states were Betsimisaraka, Betsillo and Sakalava which were not united until the early nineteenth century. There is also a strong Islamic presence from Arab traders who have been in contact with the island for centuries. It became a protectorate and then a colony of France until its independence in 1960. Malagasy, the main language, is related to Malay of Indonesia. The culture is, therefore, a mixture of African, Indonesian, Islamic and Creole. Among the functional, traditional music there is a strong element of ancestor worship notable in the 'tromba' dance. There are also hereditary court musicians.

The national instrument is the valiha, a 22-stringed zither, built on a wide bamboo tube in the high country, or else on a square box body. Rakotozafy is an influential valiha master still playing today. In the 1950s accordions became popular and these are now almost as ubiquitous, played in a range of styles, often with Creole inflections. The blind accordionist Rakotarimanana, one of the most popular on the island, is a hereditary musician attached to the royal palace. The tamatave bands use military type drums and trumpets, although the music is strictly Malagasy. The best known of these is Tsimbialona Volambita, who have toured in Europe, USSR and Canada. Malagasy music in general has the light, skippy feel of 'island' music with its blend of cultures and external influences.

1986   ORBD012   Madagasikari Vol. 1

Popular Music

The strong musical tradition on the island has blossomed into a healthy pop industry. In 1985 the guitarist Ben Mandelson visited the island to record material for Globestyle records and for further information on the contemporary music scene one should refer to his sleeve notes. Mandelson points out that distinctions between traditional, pop and popular music are blurred but on Vol. 2, *Current Popular Music*, he identifies several contemporary styles: the basese dance rhythm from the north east; the salegy of the Sakalava people; the watsa watsa, influenced by Mozambique and Congo/Zaire; the tsapika from the south, and the sigaoma with its mbaqanga influence. Indian Ocean music has also had an influence, although mainland Africa provides the biggest input. The local record company Discomad has introduced mbaqanga, benga and Congo rumba records to the market, suitably disguised as local product. Well-known groups on the island include Mahaelo, Rossy, Tarika Sammy and Les Smockers. These and several others can be heard on Globestyle's introductory collection.

1986   ORBD013   Madagasikara Vol. 2

Select Bibliography

African Urban Studies, Articles on Nima/Zaire/Zimbabwe/Jo'burg/ Ethiopia/Malawi, No. 6, 1979-1980

Aig-Imoukhuede, 'Contemporary Culture (Music)', in *Lagos, The Development of an African City*, A.B. Aderibigbe (ed.), Longman, Nigeria, 1975.

Ajibero, M. *Discography of Ebenezer Obey*.

Ajibola J.O. *Yoruba Songs*, University of Ife Press, Nigeria, 1974.

Akpabot, Samuel 'Standard Drum Patterns In Nigeria', in *African Music*, Vol. 5, No. 1, p. 37-39, 1971.

——'The Talking Drums of Nigeria', in *African Music*, Vol. 5, No. 4, 1975/76.

Alaja-Browne, Afolabi, *Juju Music: a Study of its Social History and Style*, University of Pittsburgh, 1985.

Alexandre, P. *An Introduction to Languages and Language in Africa*, Heinemann, London, 1972.

Ames, D.W. Urban Hausa Music, *African Urban Notes*, 5. 4, 1970.

Ames, D.W. & King, A.V. *Glossary of Hausa Music and its Social Context*, Northwestern University Press, Evanstown, 1971.

Anderson, A.M. *Music in the Mix; The Story of South African Popular Music*, Ravan Press.

Asante-Darko, N. 'Male Chauvinism: Men and Women in Ghanaian Highlife', in C. Oppong (ed.), *Female and Male in West Africa*, London, Allen & Unwin.

Bebey, F. *African Music; A People's Art*, Lawrence Hill, New York.

Bemba, S. *50 Ans de Musique du Zaire-Congo*, Presence Africaine, Paris, 1984.

Bender, W. *Sweet Mother: Africanische Musik*, Trickster Verlag, Munich, 1986.

Bergman, Billy, *African-Pop; Goodtime Kings*, Blandford Press, Dorset, 1985.

Berliner, P.E. *The Soul of Mbira*, University of California Press, London.

Berger, Renate, 'African & European Dance', in *Nigeria Magazine* No. 92, 1964.

Blades, James, *Percussion Instruments and their History*, Faber, London, 1974.

Bowers, Carol, 'Nupe Singers', in *Nigeria Magazine* No. 84, 1965.

Brandel, R. *The Music of Central Africa*, Nijhoff, The Hague, 1961.

Broedeke, Tineke van, 'Zwarte Magie in Chaotisch Lagos', in *Slagwerkkrant*,

No. 13, p. 4-7, October 1985.

—— 'Fuji-hallucinatie', in *Slagwerkkrant*, No. 14, p. 13-15, December 1985.

Bwantsa-Kafunga, S.P. *Congo en Musique*, Lovanium, Inshasa, 1965.

Carrington, J.F. *Talking Drums of Africa*, Carey Kingsgate Press, London, 1949.

Charters, Samuel, *The Roots of the Blues, an African Search*, Quartet, London, 1981.

Chernoff, John Miller, *African Rhythm and African Sensibility; Aesthetics and Social Action in African Musical Idioms*, University of Chicago Press,Chicago, London, 1979.

—— 'Africa Come Back, the Popular Music of West Africa', in *Repercussions, a Celebration of African-American Music*, Geoffrey Haydon and Dennis Marks (eds.), Century Publishing London, 1985.

Clark, Ebun, 'The Rise of Contemporary Professional Theatre in Nigeria', Part 1, in *Nigeria Magazine*, 114, 1974.

Clayton, A. *Communication for New Loyalties; African Soldiers Songs*, Africa Series, No. 34, University of Ohio, Athens, Ohio, 1978.

Clyde Mitchell, J. *The Kalela Dance*, Manchester University Press, 1956.

Collins, E. John, 'Ghanaian Highlife' in *African Arts*, October 1976, Vol. X, No. 1, p. 62-68, Los Angeles.

—— 'Post-War Popular Band Music in West-Africa', in *African Arts*, April 1977, Vol. X, No. p. 53-60, Los Angeles.

—— *African Pop Roots, The Inside Rhythms of Africa*, Foulsham, London, New York, 1985.

—— *Musicmakers of West Africa*, Three Continents Press, Washington, 1985.

—— *E.T. Mensah, King of Highlife*, Off the Record Press, London, 1986.

—— 'Kwaa Mensah; Palm-Wine Rootsman', in *African Music* No. 12.

Collins, E. John & Richards, Paul, 'Popular Music in West- Africa: Suggestions for an Interpretative Framework', in *Popular Music Perspectives, Papers from The First Conference On Popular Music Research*, Amsterdam, June 1981, David Horn and Philip Tagg (eds.), Goteborg & Exeter, 1982.

Coplan, David 'The African Performer and the Jo'burg Entertainment Industry; the Struggle for African Culture on the Witwatersrand', *Labour, Townships and Protest*, Ravan Press, 1979.

——, 'Go to my Town, Cape Coast! The Social History of Ghanaian Highlife', in *Eight Urban Musical Cultures*, Bruno Nettl (ed.), p. 96-114, University of Illinois Press, Chicago, 1978.

—— *In Township Tonight*, Longman, London, 1986.

Dandatti, A. *The Role of an Oral singer in Hausa/Fulani Society; A Case Study of Mamman Shata*, PhD, Folklore Institute, University of Indiana, 1975.

Dikobe, Modikwe, *The Marabi Dance*, Heinemann, London, 1973.

Durbar, R. 'La Musique Africaine et Son Influence Dans le Monde', Presence Africain, Paris, 1959.

Durosinlorun, Mal, 'The North-Eastern State Arts Festival: Mendugin 1970', in *Nigeria Magazine* No. 104, 1970.

Echezona, W. C. 'Ibo Music', in *Nigeria Magazine* No. 84, 1965.

Euba, Akin, 'The Interrelationship of Music and Poetry in Yoruba Tradition', in *Yoruba Oral Tradition*, Wanda Abimbola (ed.) p. 471-487, Ibadan University Press, 1975.

—— 'Yoruba Music', in *The new Grove dictionary of music and musicians*, Vol. 20, p. 575-576, Macmillan, London, 1980.

—— 'Islamic Musical Culture Among The Yoruba; A preliminary Survey', in *Essays on Music and History in Africa*, (ed.) K.P. Wachsmann.

Ewens, G. *Luambo Franco and 30 Years of OK Jazz*, Off the Record Press, London, 1986.

Harper, Peggy, 'Dance and Drama in the North', in *Nigeria Magazine*, No 94, 1967.

Haydon, Geoffrey & Marks, Dennis, *Repercussions, a Celebration of African-American Music*, Century Publishing, London, 1985.

Hennion, A. & Vignotte, J.P. *L'Economie du Disque en France*, Paris, 1978.

Hooker, N.W. 'Popular Musicians in Freetown', *African Urban Notes*, Vol. 5, No. 4, 1970.

Ita, Chief Bassey, *Jazz in Nigeria, an Outline Cultural History*, Radical House, Calabar, 1984.

Johnson, A. 'Songs by Ebenezer Calender in Krio and English', *Song Texts of African Popular Music No. 2*, Iwalewa, Bayreuth, 1984.

Kala-Lobe, H. 'Music in Cameroon', *West Africa*, November 1982.

Kaufman F. & Guckin J.P. *The African Roots of Jazz*, Alfred Publishing, 1979.

Kavanagh, R. M. *Theatre and Cultural Struggle in South Africa*, Zed Press, London, 1984.

Kazadi, W. M. 'The Origins of Zairean Modern Music: A Socio-economic Aspect', *African Urban Studies*, Vol. 6, 1979–80.

Kebede, A. *Roots of Black Music*, Spectrum.

Keil, C. *Tiv Song*, University of Chicago Press.

King, Anthony, *Yoruba Sacred Drums*, Caxton Press, Ibadan, 1976.

King, B. 'Introducing the Highlife', *Jazz Monthly*, July 1966.

Laade, W. *Neue Musik in Afrika*, Asien Ozeanien, Heidelberg, 1971.

Laotan A.B. 'Brazilian Influence on Lagos', in *Nigeria Magazine* (Lagos), No. 69, August 1961.

Ledesma, C. de, 'Hugh Masekela', in *The Wire*, No. 10, 1984.

Mackay, Mercedes, 'The Traditional Instruments of Nigeria', in *Nigerian Field*, Vol. 15, No. 3, July 1950, p. 112-115, London.

Mandelson, Ben, 'African Guitar', in *One Two Testing*, April 1985.

Marre, Jeremy & Hannah, Charlton, *Beats of the Heart; Popular Music of the World*, Pluto Press, London, 1985.

Matondo, K. *La Musique Zairoise Moderne; Situation Actuelle et Perspectives D'Avenir*, Kinshasa, 1972.

May, E. *Music of Many Cultures*, University of California Press.

Merriam, Allan P. *The Anthropology of Music*, Northwestern University Press, 1964.

——, *African Music on L.P.: An Annotated Discography*, Northwestern, 1970.

Moore, Carlos, *Fela, Fela, This Bitch of a Life*, Allison & Busby, London, 1982.

Mustapha, Oyebamji, 'A Literary Appraisal of Sakara: A Yoruba Traditional Form of Music', in *Yoruba Oral Tradition*, Wande Abimbola (ed.), p. 517-549, Ibadan, 1975.

Nettl, Bruno, *Eight Urban Musical Cultures*, University of Illinois Press, 1978.

—— *The Study of Ethnomusicology; Twenty-Nine Issues Concepts*, Chicago, London, 1983.

Ngumu, C. 'Les Mendzan: Des Chanteurs de Yaounde', *Acta Ethnologica et Linguistica*, No. 34, Vienna, 1976.

Nketia, Kwabena J.H. *The Music of Africa*, Norton, 1974 (edition Victor Gollancz, London, 1979)

—— *The Music of Africa*, Gollancz, London, 1982.

Ogunba, Oyin, 'The Performance of Yoruba Oral Poetry', in *Yoruba Oral Tradition*, Wande Abimbola (ed.), p. 807-876, Ibadan, 1975.

Okagbare, Benson C. 'I.K. Dairo M.B.E.' in *Musical Traditions*, mid 1983, No. 1, Summers, Essex.

Okwong, Eteyen, 'The Way Out for African Musicians', in *Africa Music*, No. 24, 1984.

Olema, D. 'Societe Zairoise dans le miroir de la chanson populaire', *Canadian Journal of African Studies*, Vol. 18, No. 1, 1984.

Oliver, P. *Savannah Syncopators*, November Books, London.

Omibiyi, Mosunmola A. 'Bobby Benson: the Entertainer-Musician', in *Nigeria Magazine*, No. 147, p. 18-27, 1983.

—— 'Nigerian Musical Instruments', in *Nigeria Magazine*, No. 122-123, 1977.

Oyelaran, Olasope O. 'On Rhythm in Yoruba Poetry', in *Yoruba Oral Tradition*, Wande Abimbola (ed.), p. 701-775, Ibadan, 1975.

Pongweni, A.J.C. *Songs That Won The Liberation War*, College Press, Harare.

Ranger, T.O. *Dance and Society in Eastern Africa*.

Roberts, J.S. *Black Music of Two Worlds*, Original Music, New York.

Rycroft, D. 'African Music in Jo'Burg: African and Non-African Features', *Journal of the International Folk Music Council*, No. 11, 1959.

Smith, E.M. 'Popular Music in West Africa, *African Music Society Journal*.

Sowande, Fela 'The African Musician in Nigeria', in *The World of Africa*, No. 3, 1967, p. 27-36.

Tchicou, C. *Le Crepuscule de la Rumba Congo-Zairoise 1970-1980*, L'Université Congolais.

Tracey, H. *The Sound of Africa Series Catalogue*, Roodeport, 1973.

Van Oven, C. *An introduction to the Music of Sierra Leone* (2 vols), Evans, London, 1981.

Wallis, R. & Malm, K. *Big Sounds from Small Peoples*, Constable, London, 1984.

Ware, Naomi, 'Popular Music and African Identity in Freetown, Sierra Leone', in *Eight Urban Musical Cultures*, Bruno Nettl (ed.), Illinois, 1978.

Washsmann, K.P. *Essays on Music and History in Africa*, Northwestern University Press, 1971.

Waterman, Chris, 'I'm a leader, not a boss': Social Identity and Popular Music in Ibadan, Nigeria, in *Ethnomusicology*, Vol. 26, p. 59-71, 1982.

—— *Juju Roots, 1930s-1950s* (text on record sleeve), Rounder Records, Cambridge Massachusetts, 1985.

Zindi, F. *Roots Rocking in Zimbabwe*, Mambo Press, Harare, 1985.

Index